Galaxy
MAGAZINE
THE DARK AND THE LIGHT YEARS

Galaxy

SCIENCE FICTION

OCTOBER 1950

25¢

TIME QUARRY—A Suspense Novel By Clifford D. Simak
CONTEST—STARTLING PRIZES—Introduced By WILLIE LEY

Galaxy
MAGAZINE

THE DARK AND THE LIGHT YEARS

by David L. Rosheim

Advent:Publishers, Inc.

Chicago: 1986

For **H. L. Gold**—
The Genius and Originator
of *Galaxy Science Fiction Magazine*,
Its First Editor and Its Heart and Conscience Throughout

Illustrations reproduced by permission of the proprietors of Galaxy Magazine.

Covers photographed for reproduction by Gary Carson, Maquoketa, Iowa.

International Standard Book Number: 0-911682-28-7

FIRST EDITION: July 1986

CONTENTS

FOREWORD

by Frederik Pohl

SOMEWHERE IN THIS VOLUME DAVID ROSHEIM quotes me as saying, of my time as editor of *Galaxy*, that although the work was never-ending and the pay lousy, it was the best job I ever had in my life.

That's an accurate statement. It is exactly the way I felt at the time, and in retrospect I haven't changed my mind. I'll go further: editing *Galaxy* was for me the fulfillment of a heart's desire. I was like any little boy who played with electric trains, and grew up to run Amtrak.

See, from about the age of puberty on, what I wanted to be when I grew up was an editor. And what I wanted to edit was a first-rate science-fiction magazine.

At fourteen the real thing was far outside the range of possibilities, but there were cheap and easy substitutes available to practice on. We called them "fan mags." (You youngsters under the age of sixty might call them "fanzines," but that term hadn't been invented yet.) I began writing for fan mags, and sometimes editing them and even publishing them, while I was still in high school. Some of them were collective efforts, sponsored by a science-fiction fan club: *The Brooklyn Reporter* and *The International Observer* were two of those. Most were individual enterprises.

It wasn't hard to launch a fanzine. All you needed was a typewriter, the price of some stencils and paper and a friend who owned a mimeograph. My own personal 'zine was called *Mind of Man*, and it was small. I mean, *small*; in fact, it was about as small as a magazine can be without microscopy. I realized that if you took a single sheet of mimeograph paper, cut it in half and folded the two sheets together you would come out with eight pages each measuring 4¼ by 5½ inches. It developed that you also came out with eyestrain and nervous tics from the strain of cutting stencils in the right orientation and imposition, plus a wardrobe that smelled of correction fluid and fingers permanently stained with mimeograph ink. But who minded that? I was an *editor*. It was *my magazine*, lock, stock and barrel. I think its all-time high in circulation was maybe 35 copies, but that meant 35 people reading my words, in the presentation I decreed for them, just as I wanted them to appear. Oh, Godlike power!

To become an editor of real-live professional science-fiction magazines a few years later, when I was nineteen, was still outside the realm of reasonable possibility. But the lightning struck. Through a combination of industry, brashness and dumb luck I happened to be standing in the right place at the right time, and an actual paying job editing two actual paying magazines fell in my lap. They were called *Astonishing Stories* and *Super Science Stories*. I cannot pretend they were very good magazines. Part of the reason was that I had a tiny budget; I couldn't compete with the couple of dozen other editors in the field for stories. An even more important reason was that I had no idea of what a good editor was supposed to do. I slavishly copied what I saw other editors doing. I tried a few innovations of my own. The magazines did somehow survive until the paper shortages of World War Two blew them away, but, honestly, there wasn't much to them.

From time to time after that I was employed as editor on a variety of other projects—book editor for *Popular Science* and *Outdoor Life* in the late 1940s, editor of various anthologies and series for various publishers in the 1950s, but they were only jobs, not Heaven. But then, in 1960, when Horace Gold could no longer handle *Galaxy* and I fell heir—oh, wow! It was the real thing at last!

When *Galaxy* started I wasn't its editor. In fact, I wasn't an editor of any kind at all just then. Temporarily, I wasn't even a writer. I had taken a sabbatical from all that in order to work at being that natural predator on both editors and writers, a literary agent.

How a nice guy like me got into a career like that is a whole other story. I didn't plan it. It just happened. It didn't work out very well in the long run, either, and by 1953 I was extricating myself from the agency business as fast as I could. But in 1950, when Horace Gold got backing from World Editions for a new science-fiction magazine, I happened to be the major purveyor of the raw materials he needed to fill it, namely stories by people such as Isaac Asimov, Fritz Leiber, Frank Robinson, Clifford D. Simak, Cyril Kornbluth, Jack Williamson, William Tenn, Damon Knight, James Blish, Algis Budrys, Robert Sheckley, H. Beam Piper and about a dozen others.

Horace knew this well, and so he got on my case well before the first issue of the magazine appeared. He consulted the experts. You may well believe that Horace Gold had strong ideas of his own about what his magazine should be—oh, boy, did he!—but he wanted no bases untouched. So to get all the ideas he could from all the people he could he held a series of parties/conferences/brain-picking sessions in his apartment in Stuyvesant Town, New York. He involved any number of people— Theodore Sturgeon, Willy Ley, Groff Conklin, W. I. Van Der Poel and Martin Gardner are the names that come to mind, but there were plenty of others, myself among them. And we talked and talked, and Horace listened and listened.

I don't know how much of the final shape *Galaxy* took was the result of these marathon meetings. I must confess that I didn't take the meetings very seriously. Horace seemed both bright and determined, but so what? The science-fiction magazine field was exploding into its biggest boom just then. New magazines were appearing, or at least being announced, by the dozen—I mean, literally by the dozen; if I remember correctly, there were actually some thirty-eight of them that did in fact hit the stands in that period. Horace Gold was just one more hopeful editor among many.

There was another thing. Although Horace was persuasive and able, what I could find out about the corporate backing for the magazine was not promising. Horace didn't even have an office. He was proposing to edit *Galaxy* from his three-room apartment at 505 East 14th Street. His publisher was some foreign outfit (the boss didn't even speak English), whose only success had been an Italian-language adult comic. His immediate supervisor, a woman named Vera Cerutti, was colorful and energetic, but whether she knew anything at all about the publishing business, much less about science fiction, was hard to determine.

After the first meeting at Horace's apartment I considered it about a fifty-fifty shot that the magazine would ever appear, and the odds far worse that it would still be around a year later.

In this I was wholly wrong. I had made the mistake of greatly underestimating Horace Gold.

Fortunately, Horace didn't allow anybody to underestimate him for very long. He kept after me. He kept after everybody else too; Horace used the telephone as a cattleprod, more efficiently than any other editor I've ever known. I let him prod me into sending over a few manuscripts from my vast store. He read them fast, reported fast, paid fast for the ones he bought.

I began to believe the magazine was real.

Then, when a messenger turned up at my office with a hot-off-the-press copy of the first issue, I even began to believe it was going to be good.

Some of the consequences of those early meetings contributed to that. Willy Ley began to write articles for *Galaxy* from the beginning. Soon he began his regular monthly column, *For Your Information*, and continued it under several editors until he died; it was the most popular single feature *Galaxy* ever had. W. I. Van Der Poel became *Galaxy*'s first art director, and did it brilliantly. As long as Van was in charge it was the best-looking sf magazine on the stands. Sturgeon wrote some of his best work for *Galaxy*. Groff Conklin contributed book reviews. I don't think Martin Gardner's ideas for a sort of every-issue semi-fact feature ever got past the talk stage, but I don't think they were wasted, either; I think ultimately they turned into the feature he now does for *Isaac Asimov's Science Fiction Magazine*.

The rest is history—in fact, it is what this book is a history of.

It's a good one, too, although there are a few statements of fact that aren't exactly right. None of them is important. (For instance, Horace didn't commission Lester del Rey and me to write *Preferred Risk*. The guilt is ours. We thought it up on our own and began writing it on our own, and Horace didn't know it existed until I flopped the first 25,000 words of it on his desk one day.)

There are also a few opinions I don't share, but that is the natural result of David Rosheim being David Rosheim and me being me.

(There is one opinion that I do share relevant to things said in the book, but the person I share it with isn't Rosheim but the late James Blish. The subject is my novella "The Midas Plague." Jim thought the idea of the story was truly dumb. So did I. So *do* I. Horace coaxed me to write it. "I want," he said, "a story about a future society in which the problem of economics is not the allocation of scarce resources but the impossible task of somehow getting rid of too much of everything." I told him how hopelessly stupid the idea was and flounced off. He then tried Asimov, Sheckley, Kornbluth and I know not how many other writers, all of whom gave him the same answer. Finally he came back to me. One could not escape Horace Gold once he had you in his sights, and after a while he wore me down. I wrote the story. He published it. And it is in the SFWA *Science Fiction Hall of Fame* and is by all odds the most frequently reprinted novella I ever wrote. I still think both Jim Blish and I are correct in our assessment of its basic preposterousness . . . but it is possible we were wrong.)

The reason Horace Gold worked out of his apartment was that he never went anywhere else.

The reason for that is a little hard to explain. Horace had suffered some sort of disability when he served in the war in the Pacific in 1945. It kept him housebound. The term for the disability was "agoraphobia" —basically, fear of open spaces—but that's a description, not an explanation. Whatever it was, it got him a disability allowance from the Veterans Administration, and it was real. (Years later, when Horace seemed to be mending, he ventured out into the world once in a while. Much of the time I would take him out in my car for brief excursions, and there was no doubt of his distress.)

However, Horace was not disabled in any other sense at all. He was, in fact, formidable. He and I often disagreed. We sometimes battled. But he produced a magazine that set the pace for the most interesting parts of the science-fiction field. Horace Gold never wholly dominated science fiction as John Campbell had a decade or two earlier, but that was only because the field had grown so much larger. John Campbell rarely had more than a handful of other magazines as competition, and effectively no book publication of science fiction at all. Horace had any number of competitors, including John himself.

Over the years of the 1950s Horace became one of my closest friends, as well as a major force in my own work. While I was still an agent I supplied him with more than half of what he published. (Actually that was also true of *Astounding* and of the most important of the new book lines as well.) When I finally extricated myself from the literary agency and went straight as a writer, *Galaxy* was the magazine I usually wrote for. In fact, during Horace's term as editor I had more stories in *Galaxy* than any other writer—in spite of the fact that I gave all the others a three-year head start, because I didn't write while I was an agent. I used half a dozen pen names as well as my own, because I sometimes had more than one story in an issue.

And now and then I helped him out with the actual editing of the magazine.

Horace's condition had not seemed to matter much to his work for the first five years and more. Then it began to be troublesome.

He had an upswing around 1958 and seemed to be getting better, even going out of the house quite frequently; but on one of those trips he was involved in a taxi accident. Then things got worse. He lost weight. He was in constant pain.

A magazine doesn't stop because its editor is ill, and the clock kept ticking. Horace was up against the constant pressure of deadlines, and he no longer could respond to all the challenges as swiftly and decisively as before. From time to time he would ask me to help out by reading manuscripts for him, then sometimes putting whole issues together, even writing the editorials and filler materials, copy-editing the manuscripts, proofreading and fitting them together.

Around the end of 1959 Horace was hospitalized, and when it became clear he would not be coming back I took over the reins.

I stayed on as editor of *Galaxy* (and its companion magazines) for just under a decade. I finally had my set of real trains to run and I ran them with joy.

Editors are not paid really well in comparison with some of the people they work with. No editor ever earns as much as a best-selling author, seldom even as much as a major agent. My own experience, over the many years when I did both, has been that most of my working time went into editing, but most of my income came from writing.

Of course, that did not matter in the least. I don't do either of those things just for the money. One of the great good things in my life is that I rarely have to do anything just for money. I do things that I would be willing to do for nothing, and people give me money for them.

Editors have more fun than most people, because editors get to play God. The editor reaches down from his golden, gossamer cloud into the slush pile; he picks out this writer or that, and gives him an audience. Sometimes, if the writer has what it takes, he can even make the person a household name. He can help a writer over road blocks of many kinds, personal and professional; he can steer the writer into areas he might otherwise have missed; he can find ways of packaging a "difficult" story so that readers will be helped to perceive its worth.

And, of course, he can sometimes exert all the skill and diligence he possesses at all of these things, and still have it all fail, but that's what makes it challenging. Even trains sometimes crash.

I stayed with *Galaxy* longer than I ever have at any other job. Then I began to feel staleness coming on. When, in 1969, I came back from a trip to Rio de Janeiro and discovered that Bob Guinn, the publisher, had sold the magazines to a man named Arnie Abramson while I was away, it was time to move on. I remained on the masthead as "Editor Emeritus" for a year or so, but took no further part in the operation of the magazine.

I did continue to write for it, now and then, right up to the end. But I didn't read it. That was a calculated decison on my part. I knew that people would ask me how I thought the magazine was doing under its succession of later editors. I didn't want to have to answer, and the best way to do that was to be able to say honestly that I didn't know.

For that reason, a good deal of what is in this book about the declining days of *Galaxy* is as new to me as to any reader.

Galaxy didn't die. It was put to death by Arnie Abramson. As long as Bob Guinn owned the magazine it paid its authors, got its copies out to its subscribers, met its obligations. Arnie Abramson simply did not perform these basic functions of a publisher. Even now there are many writers, myself included, who are still owed for stories published a decade ago. Editors quit because they couldn't stand it. Replacements were reluctant to sign on. Issues were skipped . . . and the magazine I loved faded away in misery.

There are still effects of *Galaxy* around, and they include some of the brightest spots of the field. Any number of writers had their careers reshaped and brightened by *Galaxy*. And its later editors, when they couldn't stand Arnie any more, sometimes went on to triumphs. Jim Baen now has his own imprint as "Baen Books." So does Judy-Lynn del Rey; in fact Del Rey Books has contributed an astonishing number of titles to the best-seller lists over the past few years. (Although as I write this Judy-Lynn herself is gravely ill and the prognosis discouraging.)

At one point Hugh Hefner, a closet science-fiction fan, wanted to buy *Galaxy* to add to his *Playboy* empire. His financial advisors talked him out of it; but if he had followed his impulses. . . . Or if Bob Guinn hadn't made that deal. . . . Or if Arnie Abramson had been a different sort of man. . . .

If any of those things had happened *Galaxy* would very likely still be with us. But it isn't; and I miss its presence very much.

—Frederik Pohl

December, 1985

PART ONE:
THE GOLD YEARS

INTRODUCTION

I WAS INTRODUCED TO *GALAXY SCIENCE FIC-tion* in the following way: In the early spring of 1957 the curious seventh grader that I was, all of 12 years of age, picked up a copy of *GSF* from the magazine rack of Nerby's Rexall Drug in Lake Mills, Iowa. I had an extra thirty-five cents for some reason and I decided to risk it on a magazine I'd never read before. I took it back to the ice cream and soda counter, ordered a nickel coke, and began to read.

To go back in time a little from 1957, I remember the first science fiction I read, which was in 1953. It was the book *The Last Space Ship*, by Murray Leinster. This was more or less a pulp juvenile, but it was a lollapalooza of a curtain raiser. It dealt with killer beams, paralyzer fields, matter transmitters (intergalactic, no less), and the fall of dozens of wicked empires and monarchies. Little wonder that I barely raised an eyebrow when I saw *Star Wars* and its sequels. The general public may have been wowed, but the general public seems still to be in the 1930's or 1940's as far as sf goes. That is to say, those members of the general public whose cosmology dates from later than the Babylonian-Egyptian or the Medieval periods.

However, after that I went into the usual adventure books for kids, a diet varied with some adult history books and the Sherlock Holmes stories. It was only in early 1957, when I was home prostrate with one of the innumerable varieties of flu then going around, that I remembered there was a kind of literature which could revive my spirits. As soon as I was well enough I took some more sf novels out of the Lake Mills Public Library and resumed the quest.

I was fortunate enough to find a copy of Groff Conklin's anthology *Omnibus of Science Fiction*, an excellent selection with a lot of old *Astounding SF* stories and others. I also read Malcolm Jameson's *Bullard of the Space Patrol* stories. These were also very good. I soon had gone through the library's sf stock, so I turned to buying paperbacks and magazines, and these became a steady source of learning and entertainment for the next four years or so, until the great Hiatus of the Sixties, which functioned in my life as some kind of intergalactic gulf in which only a few fantastic stars shown amidst the ideologies. But that's jumping ahead; we are still in the Eisenhower Age. I was fascinated with this April, 1957 *Galaxy*, and I began looking for it on the magazine rack every month. In fact, I began pestering the store clerks whenever a magazine parcel arrived to see if the *Galaxy* was in yet.

Through 1957 and the first half of 1958 I went from month to month, but after that I began contacting *Galaxy*'s publishers and old book dealers to locate the back issues. Slowly they started to come in by mail. By the fall of 1958 I had all but the first seven issues. In the summer of 1959, after some wheeling and dealing with an antiquarian sf and fantasy dealer in Philadelphia, I finally got the remaining issues.

The first issue of *Galaxy* was October, 1950. Now, I will do again what I did then: go right back to the beginning of this unique and lamented magazine, and to the decades immediately preceding *Galaxy*'s advent.

1. ANTECEDENTS

THERE ARE DIFFERENCES OF OPINION AMONG students of science fiction and science fiction authors as to the actual date of origin of the genre. To shorten the debate in these pages, I will simply go along with James Gunn, who traces the roots back to the Gilgamesh Epic of 2000 B.C. The reader may want to refer to his recent *The Road to Science Fiction* for a splendid job of editing and selecting science fiction stories and prototypes of sf.

For my own purposes, however, I will confine the discussion to American magazine fiction of the Twentieth Century. There was *Munsey's* and *Argosy*, which carried various sf-fantasy tales by such authors as Jack London and Edgar Rice Burroughs in the first two decades of this century. Then came Hugo Gernsback and his *Electrical Experimenter*, which gradually carried more and more speculative fiction. Gernsback, who had been born in Luxembourg, and had come to this country very low on funds, became enamoured of what he called "scientifiction." He also wrote an sf novel called *Ralph 124C 41+*, which he serialized in his magazine.

It was in 1926 that he made a daring innovation. In April the newsstands began carrying Gernsback's *Amazing Stories*, a magazine devoted entirely to sf. The early issues were devoted to reprinting the works of Jules Verne, H. G. Wells, and other forerunners, but soon original fiction by new sf writers started to appear. Bizarre fantasy, a genre closely linked to sf, had already found its own magazine, *Weird Tales*, which had started publication in 1923.

Some of the authors appearing in the 1920's *Amazing* were: E. E. "Doc" Smith, Stanton A. Coblentz, Jack Williamson, and P. Schuyler Miller. E. E. Smith became famous for his "Skylark of Space" stories. They were genuine mindblowers because space travel all of a sudden became intergalactic and not merely interplanetary, and his heroes and heroines "scared themselves green and purple with their audacity."

Hugo Gernsback lost *Amazing* in the later Twenties but got back into the field with *Science Wonder Stories* and *Air Wonder Stories*. It was in the former magazine that the term "science fiction" first was used. These two publications appeared in the summer of 1929. Several months later, the American economy collapsed.

The Great Depression did not, however, wipe out the sf magazines. In fact, a new one appeared in December of 1929—the most famous and cherished of all the old pulps (with the possible exception of *Weird Tales* and a few other fantasy periodicals). This was *Astounding Stories of Super-Science*. This very revered magazine was first published by the Clayton chain; the editor was Harry Bates. The early *Astounding* was chock-full of classic space opera, alien invasions, derring-do in outer space, amazing inventions and so on. It was not awfully intellectual, but for action and sense-of-wonder it was hard to beat.

Hard times wore down the Clayton chain and it vanished. *Astounding* went down with it in the spring of 1933. But by the fall of that year it was back again. This time it was published by Street and Smith and had a new editor, F. Orlin Tremaine. The magazine grew in reputation, and little wonder, for "Doc" Smith, Murray Leinster, John Taine, Jack Williamson, and the great Stanley Weinbaum (dead tragically soon) wrote for it.

As the 1930's rolled along, as the Depression receded and the Nazi menace grew, *Wonder Stories* became *Thrilling Wonder Stories* and it was soon joined by *Startling Stories*. Both were publications of Standard Magazines. Sf magazines were beginning their pre-war proliferation.

There are also some differences among sf fans as to what years actually constituted the Golden Age of *Astounding*. Some would say it began in 1937 with the advent of John W. Campbell, Jr., as editor. They certainly have a strong case, because under Campbell's guidance, Isaac Asimov, Robert Heinlein, Clifford Simak, Lester del Rey, A. E. van Vogt, Alfred Bester, and Theodore Sturgeon all had classic short stories, novelettes, and novels published in its pages, even before the U.S. entered World War II. It was a genuine quantum jump and it took place in under four years, which is perhaps the chief marvel. It was almost like a night sky that is suddenly lit by powerful new stars—something like the conclusion of Asimov's "Nightfall," though with much more favorable results.

One new Campbell author who also appeared in that glorious time was a fellow by the name of Horace Leonard Gold. His story "A Matter of Form" was published in the December, 1938 issue. He had earlier written two stories for the Tremaine *Astounding* in 1934, using the name of Clyde Crane Campbell. The 1938 story was a true classic and has been much anthologized. Briefly, it dealt with a sinister doctor who placed a man's personality into the body of a collie, and vice versa. The doctor's plan failed because the dog with the human mind was able to use code to tell some newsmen what was going on.

A number of magazines disappeared during the war, and many of the major writers were off on military tours of duty. Then the Bomb came out of the pages of sf and into reality. This caused several years of grim stories about the effects of nuclear warfare, among them a good one called "Thunder and Roses," by Theodore Sturgeon.

Postwar sf magazines began to abandon their old large pulp size, and most soon became their present digest size. This made them much handier to carry around, but also they lost some of their old grandeur when the big gaudy covers vanished. Another development in this period was the appearance of the hardbound sf anthology, starting with *The Best of Science Fiction*, edited by Groff Conklin. Various small presses sprang up—Arkham House, Fantasy Press, Gnome, and others—to publish the tales of sf and fantasy which had hitherto had only brief magazine circulation. Most of these presses did not last for long (though Arkham continues), but they lasted long enough to prove that sf had a considerable reservoir of good material by that time, and also to show that the anthology idea was commercially feasible. In proving the latter point, the path was made clear for paperback story collections. The germ of the idea for one-writer theme story collections also came from the hard-bound collections, and thus we later had Bradbury's *Martian Chronicles* and Robert Heinlein's *The Past Through Tomorrow*.

This was approximately the state of the art when some new magazines, including *Galaxy Science Fiction*, came on the scene half a decade after the end of the Second World War.

2. FIRST LIGHT FROM *GALAXY*: 1950

IN THE EARLY FALL OF 1950—ACTUALLY DUR-
ing the first phase of the Korean War—a new
magazine appeared on the newsstands of the
U.S. This was *Galaxy Science Fiction*. It was
digest size, and would retain that size all of its existence, with the notable
exception of the ill-fated last issue. Its editor was the former writer of
short stories for *Astounding*, H. L. Gold.

It was published by World Editions, Inc., a European firm that would
continue to publish *Galaxy* until the October, 1951 issue. H. L. Gold
wrote a retrospective article about those early days in the October, 1975
Galaxy:

> . . . a girl who had worked for me called me in to present a publishing
> program to a French-Italian publishing firm . . . World Editions.
>
> It seems they had a big slick magazine in France and Italy that was
> selling two or three million copies a week. A cross between beautifully

8   GALAXY

executed comics and confession stories, less beautifully executed, it was
dubbed *Fascination* and set loose on the American public . . . . There
were five issues—the last sold 5% of its print order of several hundred
thousand . . . Anyhow, they were too stubborn to get out of the American market . . . and so I was asked to submit a publishing program.

I surveyed the entire magazine market. It was early 1950, and everywhere I looked, magazines were in deep trouble. As soon as paper
rationing had ended in 1946, everyone who could read—or could hire
someone to read—was putting out everything from comics to fashion
magazines. The one exception was science fiction.

On the basis of experience, I should have submitted anything but an sf
magazine, a fantasy magazine projected for later, once the sf one was
established, and a series of paperback sf novels. But I saw that *Astounding* was going off into one cult after another—John Campbell was rush-
ing up dead ends, the latest being Dianetics, in his search for a meaningful universe—and *Fantasy & Science Fiction* was brand new, and flying
in the face of the single immutable law of those fields: that readers don't
like fantasy in their sf, or sf in their fantasy. A very high-grade sf magazine could fit right between them. And thus I offered my publishing
program to the Italian representative of World Editions, a great guy
named (Marco) Lombi. He offered it to the publisher who lived on the
Riviera, who must have flipped a coin, because neither he nor Lombi
knew anything at all about sf or fantasy, and it came up yes.

The first editor of *Galaxy* was born in 1914 and held dual Canadian/
American citizenships. Besides his stories for *Astounding*, Gold had also
assisted with the magazines *Captain Future, Startling Stories* (the sf magazine with the memorably lurid covers) and *Thrilling Wonder Stories*, a
former Gernsback holding. Thus, he had gotten considerable experience
with the field. Horace Gold began his magazine some months after
Anthony Boucher and Francis McComas began the *Magazine of Fantasy,* later to be known as *Fantasy and Science Fiction*, which managed to
defy the "immutable laws" after all. It is still in publication!

Gold was fortunate in having generous publishers. He got a leg up on
the other sf magazines by being able to offer authors three cents a word as
a minimum, four cents for regular contributors, and $100 for short-short
stories. The standard rate at that time was two cents per word. This began
to draw superior talent to the magazine.

Galaxy's editor was also highly pleased with the magazine's appearance. The initial editorial, in the October, 1950 issue, is largely devoted to
the magazine's cover and most especially to Champion Kromekote:

... an ideal high finish paper, one that would duplicate the intense luster of the glossy photograph . . . Kromekote has a 20 per cent higher index of refraction than the costliest grade of enameled stock! It can also be soaked in water and still retain full color with practically no loss . . .

There was also a policy of high-quality cover content, as well as good materials. To quote again from the first editorial:

We never were convinced, in any case, of the actual commercial appeal of naked maidens, prognathous youths in winter underwear of gold lamé, and monsters that can exist only on the nutrients found in India ink and Bristol board . . . No reader will be ashamed to carry *Galaxy*.

H. L. Gold was quite right about the amazing Kromekote. My copy of the first issue still has a very bright appearance, unlike so many of its contemporaries. One feature that stands out is the inversion of the magazine's name and date on the spine. The second issue got these right side up. The cover is very decorous, illustrating the serial by Clifford Simak, "Time Quarry"; it depicts a scene on one of Jupiter's satellites, with figures approaching a reddish-yellow peak and a hunting lodge of sorts, perched near its top. The planet Jupiter appears rather mistily overhead.

The back cover of the first issue became particularly well known, for on it was one of the basic tenets of the Gold editorial policy. Its heading was:

YOU'LL NEVER SEE IT IN GALAXY

Then the following example was printed:

Jets blasting, Bat Durston came screeching down through the atmosphere of Bblizznaj, a tiny planet seven billion light years from Sol. He cut out his super-hyper-drive for the landing . . . and at that point, a tall, lean spaceman stepped out of the tail assembly, proton gun-blaster in a space-tanned hand.

"Get back from those controls, Bat Durston," the tall stranger lipped thinly. "You don't know it, but this is your last space trip."

Then, in "contrast":

Hoofs drumming, Bat Durston came galloping down through the narrow pass at Eagle Gulch, a tiny gold colony 400 miles north of Tombstone. He spurred hard for a low overhang of rimrock . . . and at that point a tall, lean wrangler stepped out from behind a high boulder, six-shooter in a sun-tanned hand.

"Rear back and dismount, Bat Durston," the tall stranger lipped thinly. "You don't know it, but this is your last saddle-jaunt through these here parts."

Finally, this conclusion is made:

> Sound alike? They should—one is merely a western transplanted to some alien and impossible planet. If this is your idea of science fiction, you're welcome to it! YOU'LL NEVER FIND IT IN GALAXY!

Gold wanted to publish stories which would be entertaining. He said somewhere, "There is nothing so grim as an entertainment man in search of entertainment."

But, he had something different in mind than the old pulp kind of interplanetary shoot-em-up, obviously. The author Cleve Cartmill, who once wrote such a convincing atom bomb story (well before Hiroshima) that national security forces came around the *Astounding* offices, had a rather different idea of entertainment than what Gold sought. In a fanzine (*Bixel* No. 1, September, 1962) Cartmill stated:

> ". . . What is man, why is man, where is he going?" That sort of thing.
>
> This is all very fine, and has been the subject in one respect or others of some rewarding "mainstream" fiction. But when you try to fit it into the traditional format of science fiction it sometimes becomes dull reading, talky, pedestrian, probing without action.
>
> The late Hank Kuttner once told me, "First you get your hero up a tree. Then you throw rocks at him." This was science fiction: action and reader identification. And if the story started to sag, you had somebody walk through a door (or a wall) with a blaster in his hand.
>
> It wasn't sophisticated, maybe; it wasn't slick. But it was entertaining and if the writer wove in a philosophical theme it seemed to have stature.
>
> The primary purpose of fiction is to entertain. So says Somerset Maugham, who ought to know . . .

James Gunn writes clearly how H. L. Gold differed from Cartmill in his approach to entertainment:

> In *Galaxy* social science fiction found its true home. Gold wanted stories not about scientists and engineers but about the ordinary people who were most affected by scientific and technological change. The emphasis of science fiction shifted from the scientific culture to society itself. . . .
>
> In the early 1950's *Galaxy Science Fiction* provided a home for a different attitude toward science, technology, and the future, whipping up a kind of early "New Wave." Many of the stories implied that the future may not turn out well—in fact, that it is *likely* not to turn out well, and that it won't turn out well because humans are flawed, and if not fallen creatures in some theological sense, at least spoiled by the evolutionary process.

To indicate more of Gold's individuality (and ability), Barry Malzberg says in his *Down Here in the Dream Quarter*, an elegy of sorts to sf, "Horace Gold, the first editor of *Galaxy*, perhaps the greatest editor in the history of all fields for the first half of his tenure: ah, Horace, who saw history as spite."

Galaxy's approach, then, was bound to be different. In an article in Reginald Bretnor's *The Craft of Science Fiction*, James Gunn further says:

> *Galaxy* concentrated on social science fiction; Gold asked for heroes who were losers as well as winners, jerks as well as jocks. In order to make this kind of story hold reader interest, the writers must convince the reader of the reality of the characters. *Galaxy* also featured satire; satire requires characters who are types.

The October, 1950 issue contains the first installment (of three) of "Time Quarry" by Clifford Simak, an author who at that time was already an old pro. His serialized novel has a rather mind-bending plot in which the character Asher Sutton shuttles back and forth in time in the general interests of a group of androids and robots who want to become co-equal with biologically-created humans. He has come back from a very mysterious world whose hyper-civilized inhabitants have told him much the same thing. The pro-biological human party tries to stop him from writing a book that will be crucially influential. Their attempts to tamper with time and Asher's countermoves against them result in a certain amount of confusion. Still, it is a lively story.

There is a fine story by the late Theodore Sturgeon, "The Stars Are the Styx," in this issue. It deals with a plan far in the future to send ships all over the universe to join sooner or later in a vast linkage of matter transmitters which will, in effect, give mankind access to all parts of the universe (not just the galaxy, but the universe!). The ships and volunteers are being sent out over a six thousand year period and only 54% are expected to see Old Earth again.

The volunteers are called Outbounders and leave from a space station in orbit around Earth. The story is told by the manager of the space station, who refers to himself as Charon, after the ancient mythical figure who ferries the souls of the dead into the afterlife across the River Styx. The plot, which consists of a love triangle, a murder, and a fitting act of justice, is somehow less important than the galaxy-spanning concept upon which the characters' actions are superimposed.

"Contagion," by Katherine MacLean, is a story based on biology, a science oddly unrepresented in science fiction in relation to its importance. On the planet Minos an exploration team runs into a family of red-headed supermen and women called Mead. They are ruggedly handsome and the explorers from Earth envy them their looks and physique. After an interval, the male explorers all are infected by a mysterious plague which attacks the blood. The men are saved by transfusions of blood from the Meads, but this produces startling results!

The short stories are also of high quality. "Third From the Sun," by Richard Matheson, deals with an escape by a young couple and their children from a repressive society which sounds like it could be one of those on our planet, but not so. The freedom-seekers are bound to Earth, "the green planet with the single moon."

In "Later Than You Think," by Fritz Leiber, a seminar is going on in which an Explorer and an Archaeologist talk about the exciting news: Relics of intelligent life have been found on Earth, mammalian intelligent life! This civilization was apparently destroyed by uncontrolled atomic energy. The Archaeologist has found out what the members of this lost culture termed themselves and we presume the discovery was as startling to them as to the reader.

Isaac Asimov's "Darwinian Pool Room" is another seminar. It consists of speculations on the disappearance of the dinosaurs and whether humans will escape the same fate and not die out all at once. It also makes short work of the idea of a super new human or animal species replacing us, and one speaker wonders why we have developed hydrogen bombs and thinking *machines* both at the same time. The simultaneous development apparently struck him as being somewhat sinister.

The short story "The Last Martian" is a Fredric Brown mind-bender (he was good at those). A character in a bar thinks he is the Last Martian who has somehow teleported to Earth after seeing the rest of his race all lying dead. He is talked out of his delusion and all is well until we realize that the person who does this counseling is himself a Martian inhabiting a human body. How all this came about is fascinating and quite logical.

Other sections of the first issue consist of a book review feature by noted sf anthologist Groff Conklin called "Galaxy's Five Star Shelf," and the first of Willy Ley's science articles. The latter deals with the phenomenon of flying saucers, a subject of interest for years to come.

The content of *Galaxy* was obviously to be at a mature level. The

November, 1950 issue continues along this course. It contains the Fritz Leiber classic "Coming Attraction." This story takes place in a post-World War III New York. The city was spared from direct destruction but was heavily irradiated, and many of the residents have radiation scarring or mutated children. The scene is observed by a man from Britain who is horrified by the physical, moral, and social degeneration of the New Yorkers since the inconclusive war. America and the U.S.S.R. are still struggling for world domination, and thus the world backdrop to Leiber's tale is not terribly promising.

Another of the short stories in the November issue is the ironic "To Serve Man," by Damon Knight, an author who would appear regularly in *Galaxy*. This story tells of some supposedly benevolent aliens who come to us and pacify the Planet Earth by rendering all the big-bang weapons totally ineffective, all under the guise of altruism. Little did they know . . .

I liked best the short stories in this one. There is an Asimov short in this issue also, "Misbegotten Missionary," again on a biological topic. A small animal mimics a section of electrical cable in order to stow away on an Earth ship returning from exploration. This animal is actually part of a world mind on its own planet, and it seeks to bring the same kind of unity to Earth, though Earth won't like it at all since it can only be accomplished after some dreadful mutations such as the loss of eyes. Luckily, the alien fails to understand the function of an electrical cable.

December, the last issue for 1950, carries the conclusion of "Time Quarry." It also has a story called "Second Night of Summer." This tale by James H. Schmitz is a kind of gypsy-picaresque interlude among the sociological grimness of some of the other stories in the magazine. An alien invasion on a far-off planet is prevented by a young boy, an old woman named Grandma Wannattel, and a grimp, a sort of saurian draft animal. It is fun, and tense, too, because of the absolutely deadly qualities of the inhuman Halpa, who have to be stopped on their very first appearance on a planet, or else it's too late.

In his last editorial for the year, Gold announced that he was pleased with reader response and the excellent sales at the newsstands, good omens for the upcoming year.

The interior art in these early issues is variable. A variety of people were doing the work. The Paul Calle illustrations and the ones by David Stone to illustrate "Time Quarry" seem the most effective. Stone also did the first cover for *Galaxy*. Gold apparently was trying different artists until he got some feedback from the readership. In the November, 1950 editorial he says, "How are we doing on inside illustration?"

In a conversation with me, Gold explained that he himself did not buy the art work, but left that up to the art editor and others in a kind of co-operative venture. Gold also had no way of knowing exactly how a cover would turn out, due to the printing processes of the era, and so, now and then, a few mistakes and misspellings would occur, but so rarely that they are statistically insignificant.

The original *Galaxy* logo and inverted "L" design, Gold said, was discussed and agreed on by many people.

Though Gold did not have a letter column, on the advice of various of his contributors he still urged and responded to reader feedback. After one appeal for reader ideas he got 6,000 letters, which was representative of a broad section of the American public and not just the 250 or so hard-core fans who always wrote to *GSF* and *Astounding* in those days.

In that November, 1950 editorial, Gold also asks the readers to spread the word about *Galaxy*, to talk magazine dealers into giving the magazine good display space, and so on. He also continues in a missionary vein, "New readers are necessary not only for us, but also to enlarge the entire market . . . This means spreading the word that science fiction is adult fiction."

Another nugget Gold gave me was the fact that he would not "anthologize"; that is, he would not let his personal taste dictate the kind of stories he would print. He operated on a less personal level and would choose a story on the basis of how well it *worked*, if it clicked along and got the reader somewhere. Questions of preference in style and characterization were secondary to the ability of the story, whether short or long, to function properly. This is, of course, what made H. L. Gold an editor's editor whose devotion to the field of sf has not since been surpassed.

3. IN FULL CHORUS: 1951

ISAAC ASIMOV'S THREE-PART SERIAL "Tyrann" started the year off for *Galaxy*. The January cover was by Don Bunch and illustrates a scene from Asimov's novel. The story (which appeared in book form as *The Stars, Like Dust*) deals with intrigues in the Nebular Kingdoms of the Galaxy which are dominated by the imperialistic Tyranni. People called Tyranni almost have to be domineering, one would think; one can't imagine people called the Docili or the Ignomini being very overlordly.

There is a search for a mysterious document which has been missing from the Earth's archives for twenty years. Biron Farrill, a young member of the leading family of the planet Widemos seeks the document and also the slayer of his father. He is captured by the Tyranni, who release him on the planet Rhodia. The Tyranni are looking for a rumored "Rebellion World" which may overthrow their empire, and they use Biron. The weak ruler of Rhodia, a tool of the Tyranni, has a cousin who opposes them. This man, Gillbret, and his niece, Artemisia Hinriad, escape with Biron to the Horsehead Nebula to seek the Rebellion World. Unknown to them, the Tyranni are following them with the help of a spaceship-detecting "massometer." There is some unpleasantness with the Autarch of Lingane, who is trying to work both sides of the street and ends up the worse for it. Finally, the Tyranni close in. No one has found a planet full of insurgents, so the Tyranni are pleased that all the fuss has come to nothing, and they go home. But, there *is* a Rebellion World. It is Rhodia, and the "weak" ruler has only been putting on an act while his subjects plot and plan. He has his own solution.

Also in the January issue is "Rule of Three," a fine story by Theodore Sturgeon which deals with an attempt by extraterrestrial triadic beings to pacify humankind, which they see as dangerously infested with pa'ak, a fearful war-producing virus. They have some success and the story ends on an optimistic note. What is most successful about the story, however, is Sturgeon's ease with the inner psychological workings of his characters. This was to become a major strong point in his work.

Sturgeon's was a rather progressive pacifistic story. Some of the other stories are also forward-looking, but one of them, "Dark Interlude," by Mack Reynolds and Fredric Brown, ends grimly. A man from an advanced future Earth civilization returns to the Twentieth Century to do some historical research right on the spot. He mixes well with the rural local people he meets, and, in fact, gets married to a nice young woman named Susan Allenby. One night Jan, the man from the future, sits around with his wife and her brother and casually mentions that there are no races as such in his time, all races having intermingled. Susan's brother asks him if he has "nigger blood" in him, and when Jan says he has, there is an unpleasant denouement. Lou Allenby tells this to the sheriff later on, and they agree to hush up the incident. The area Jan visited so briefly was in the old unimproved South. This story was particularly effective because of its brevity.

The cover of the February issue was by the noted artist of other-planetary scenes, Chesley Bonestell, who also did paintings for books by Willy Ley. Ley's science column, incidentally, was missing from both the January and February issues, as Gold experimented with the format.

In *Science Fiction: The Great Years*, an anthology edited by Carol and Frederik Pohl, the editors remember those early years of *Galaxy*:

When we collaborators on this volume were struggling young married with a small baby and limited mobility, there was one night a week when we could Get Out of the House together with very little strain. Friday night was poker night at Horace Gold's apartment, and a merciful providence had so arranged things that it was an easy walk, even pushing a baby carriage, from our apartment to his. So it happened that little Karen Pohl spent hours every week playing with poker chips and being patted and dandled by people like John Cage, the avant-gardest composer alive, a few psychologists whose names are forgotten, an occasional editor and an awful lot of science fiction writers . . . But Horace Gold was not merely the proprietor of a gaming establishment, he spent his days brilliantly editing *Galaxy Magazine*, and his evenings and weekends brilliantly writing stories.

The conviviality and the hard work both contributed to the magazine. It began attracting many more noted sf authors. The February issue, for instance, had "The Fireman," an excellent novella by Ray Bradbury, then at the very peak of his writing career. Bradbury's magnificent *Martian Chronicles* was already written and attracting great numbers of new readers to sf and to his work as it continued to appear. The novella in *Galaxy* later on was expanded into the well-known novel *Fahrenheit 451*. That is the temperature at which book paper catches fire. In the 1960's the book became a noted movie starring Oskar Werner.

Bradbury's work was uncharacteristically polemic in its harsh portrayal of a book-burning future and the plots of brave people to save the literature and the general culture preserved in books.

Also in the February issue is a good short story by Clifford D. Simak, "Second Childhood," which deals with the problem in a future society of rejuvenating people who have achieved immortality. The difficulty is a loss of interest in living after going on for years and years longer than normal. It is a problem of morale that is solved by returning the old person to a state of psychological infancy. How this is done is rather intriguing.

A significant reason why *Galaxy* was getting writers like Bradbury was the rate Gold was paying—three to four cents per word—as opposed to the two cents a word then prevalent in the magazine world. John Campbell of *Astounding* eventually moved his magazine's rates up to match *Galaxy*'s, and thus the two magazines continued to gather in the top talent in sf.

The March *Galaxy* carried some fine novelets and short stories. Lester del Rey's "The Wind Between the Worlds" dealt with some of the problems that could arise with interstellar matter transmission, in this case disastrous sabotage, with the wiser races of the galaxy sitting back to see if Earth's scientists and experts could figure out a solution. If the Earthmen can't, then the outworlders are going to make sure Earth is set back to a state of semi-savagery to render its natives—scientists and saboteurs and all others—harmless to the senior races of the galaxy. Earth solves the problem in the person of Vic Peters, troubleshooter for Teleport Interstellar.

The March issue is a little more oriented to chills and thrills than some of the previous ones and has less of the ameliorative psycho-sociological approach. Clifford Simak's "Good Night, Mr. James" deals with a chilling sample of duplicated identity. A sinister creature called the puudly, which can kill humans by thought power alone, is being stalked by a skilled hunter named Henderson James. He kills the puudly after taking it by surprise, and it says with its last bit of energy, "You half-thing, you duplicate."

James realizes this is true. The real Henderson James had made a duplicate of himself to confuse the puudly, and the ruse had worked. Now there is no need for the duplicate to remain alive, and it is to be gunned down as soon as its usefulness is done. The duplicate, thanks to the puudly's information, manages to get the real Henderson James destroyed. But his troubles aren't over.

The short stories, "The Other Now" by Murray Leinster and "Socrates" by John Christopher, are also of high quality. The former deals with a man who investigates another temporal dimension to get back his wife, who in this dimension was killed in a car crash. The latter is about a super-intelligent dog who tragically gives his life attempting to save a drowning victim. Luckily, highly intelligent puppies may be on the way.

The issue for April, 1951 features a story by an author who came to epitomize the *Galaxy* of the 1950's. He was C. M. Kornbluth, and we will hear a good deal more about him and his collaborator, Frederik Pohl. His story, "The Marching Morons," has been continually anthologized, and for good reason. Briefly, a businessman of our time is preserved by a medical accident. He is revived in the far future and finds himself in a very puzzling world. It is full of incompetent morons who are apparently in complete charge. In fact, a small minority of highly intelligent people are really running things, and not because they want to. They *have* to, because otherwise the world will absolutely collapse in ruin and chaos. The protagonist, John Barlow, is accused by the hard-pressed intelligentsia of having caused the current state of affairs by not having children in his own era. The smart ones didn't breed, the dumb ones did, and the result is what Barlow sees. Barlow devises a cruel plan to relieve the intelligentsia of their burden. The story begs the question at various points. The sociology seems rather awkward and the morons are all cut out of the same cloth. Even so, it is an extremely interesting anti-utopian (dystopian) tale.

"Betelgeuse Bridge," by William Tenn (Philip Klass), a short story in the April issue, is an amusing account of the swindling of Earth by giant snails from Betelgeuse IX. They give us a fine new technology in exchange for all our uranium, radium, etc. After a while it becomes obvious that this wonderful new technology has to be powered by the aforementioned uranium and other radioactive fuels. Far from collapsing in chagrin, Earth's scientists come up with "artificial radioactives" and we are off into the galaxy to even the score with the denizens of Betelgeuse IX.

The April issue of *Galaxy* contains no serial. It was Gold's policy to have an issue of complete stories between issues which carried serials. At this time Gold decided to raise the price of the magazine from 25 to 35 cents, effective with the May issue, because of "an alarming tidal flood of rising costs."

The May issue features another excellent Bonestell cover which illustrates the three-part serial, "Mars Child," written by "Cyril Judd." This *nom de plume* represents two writers, C. M. Kornbluth (whom we have just met), and Judith Merril. Also published under this pseudonym was *Gunner Cade*, a novel of a warlike future society, which appeared in *Astounding*.

"Mars Child" (reprinted as *Outpost Mars*), tells of Sun Lake City, an independent colony on the Red Planet. The colonists, ranging from laborers to scientists, seek to break away from the domination of Earth, where war is rumored as usual. However, they are reliant on imported Ox-En, which lets them breathe Martian air. A series of dramatic events ends in the salvation of the colony, the finding of native (humanoid) Martian life, and the discovery that children born on Mars can breathe Martian air with the aid of the drug Marcaine. Marcaine functions for Martians as Ox-En does for Terrestrials on Mars. Marcaine is a Martian product, and so the dependence on Earth will become a thing of the past.

Mars Child. Illustrator: Chesley Bonestell.

Also in the May issue is a fine novelet by Damon Knight called "Ask Me Anything." Knight's appearances in *Galaxy* were always outstanding, and this one is no exception. It describes a grim militaristic Earth outpost in the outer reaches of the galaxy, far in the future. There cadets are trained and turned into big armored fighting machines without emotion. But an apparition consisting of various energy fields appears to them and ruins them by stimulating their hidden or submerged human feelings, merely by answering any question posed to it. Krisch, the base commander, attempts to use this strange entity, but ends up trapped by his own cleverness and by the thing's logical, but barely informative, answers to his questions. In the end Krisch manages to become an energy-field apparition himself.

June had a fine humorous cover by Emsh. "Emsh" was short for Ed Emshwiller, who was one of the most popular sf illustrators of the 1950's. His covers always stood out and were consistent prize-winners. He won no less than five of the prestigious Hugo awards during his career of illustrating sf magazines. He is best known for his *Galaxy* covers.

The June issue is distinguished by two novelettes, both real jewels, or as George Ade might have put it, "the real goods." The first, "Angel's Egg," by Edgar Pangborn, is another of the classics which Gold was so skilled in recognizing at once. The story is haunting and lyrical, and also tranquil. Its mood is quite unlike that of most other science fiction, and quite the opposite of the hyperactive satire so many critics have seen as *Galaxy*'s hallmark.

Dr. David Bannerman, a retired teacher, finds his hen hatching a strange alien egg. When the egg opens, a tiny female figure appears. The old teacher is entranced at once, and helps to take care of the angel. He learns to communicate with her by telepathy. Soon the tiny angel has grown wings and can outfly hawks and hummingbirds. The unusual extraterrestrial has come to Earth with a serious purpose, however. Her people are a very ancient civilized race who outgrew war and violence fifty million years past. They want to encourage Earthmen to attain this level also, but they need to study humanity. They have a process which records all the brain's memories. But there is one hitch . . .

The other novelette is a typically excellent Damon Knight piece, "Don't Live in the Past." In a future where the people have ancestral totem poles and revere their forebears, a break in "temporal flow" matter transmission spills all kinds of sinister products back into our own century. This is

Relics of an Ancient Race. Illustrator: Emsh.

a disaster for them because Blodgett, the great founder of their society, lived in our time. A young man by the name of Mazurin goes back to try to safeguard Blodgett from the sinister or merely comical future goods. He ends up trapped in the Twentieth Century. Worse yet, the Blodgett he discovers is an odious tyrant. Mazurin is being interrogated by Blodgett when he notices that the dictator is about to eat something that looks like a grape but really isn't. Should Mazurin warn him? This is a story which, like most of Knight's works, stands up well to re-reading.

One problem confronting *Galaxy*'s editor from the inception of the magazine was the task of winnowing out the good stories from the chaff. Gold is quite incisive about this in his June editorial:

> [Science fiction] is still what I want, though anesthetized by the daily routine of reading and sending back duels on asteroids, alien eaters of life force in the Andes, which somehow select only lovely virgins, thinking machines that go insane when asked to solve the problem of man's survival, mutant babies that have to be destroyed because they only have ten fingers . . .
>
> No day's mail is free of these flakes of literary dandruff . . . the alleged adventures of dull lushes, humorless wisecrackers, hard-lipped Space Patrolmen, nymphomaniacal heroines who are snowy pure . . .

"Mars Child" concludes in the July issue. One of the short stories is "Syndrome Johnny," by Charles Dye. It is prophetic of present-day recombinant techniques. A virus is employed to introduce a silicon-using gene into human chromosomes. This will eventually result in a very sturdy, almost plastic human being, but in the meantime is causing plagues which will kill millions who are not strong enough to survive this virus. It is a compelling story, and rather better done than Katherine MacLean's "Contagion" in the first *Galaxy*, of which it is reminiscent in some ways.

August features Wyman Guin's novella "Beyond Bedlam." Guin was at this time the advertising director of Lakeside Laboratories, a pharmaceutical firm. His knowledge of drugs and the trend of medical and pharmaceutical research led him to think of a future society where drug-taking is mandatory. His story describes a world based on enforced schizophrenia. The drugs cause two distinct human personalities to exist in each body, a body they take turns using in five-day shifts. This has reduced the old human passions to almost nothing and the world has become a dull, although a safe, place.

Bill Walden and Conrad Manz inhabit the same body. They are quite

The Puppet Masters. Illustrator: Don Sibley.

different persons. Conrad is a bluff sportsman and Bill is something of a romantic. Bill finds love and adventure by not taking his drugs and thus usurping part of Conrad's shift to make love to Conrad's wife, Clara. Clara is the other personality sharing the body of Helen Walden, Bill's wife. The Waldens' daughter, Mary, suspects something is going on and becomes depressed because Bill has no time for her. She becomes catatonic and has to be taken in for treatment. Finally Bill is discovered by the Medicorps, the security police of this future Earth, and we see how their justice system operates.

The high quality of *Galaxy* continues with the September, 1951 issue. A new serial begins, and its author is none other than Robert A. Heinlein, Mr. Science Fiction, and the top writer of the old *Astounding SF* Golden Age. His serial is *The Puppet Masters*. It deals with flying saucers from Titan which land on Earth. The aliens aboard are not friendly. They are giant parasites, all brain and nervous system, who are fond of fastening themselves on human backs and taking over control of the human brain and body. In passing, I might point out the fact that sinister giant brains turned up now and again in the fiction and film of the Fifties. This strikes me as odd, or perhaps as somehow fitting. The 1950's were generally an anti-intellectual era. Being referred to as a "brain" before the Sputnik era was not necessarily a compliment and indeed had all kinds of unpleasant, insulting undertones.

Getting back to Heinlein, the protagonist is one Sam Nivens, who works for a secret intelligence agency headed by his father, referred to throughout as "The Old Man." They discover people acting strangely in areas where saucers were reported to have landed. Soon they find the *modus operandi* of the titans and begin killing them or capturing them for study. This is risky and they are at times taken over themselves by the "slugs." The alien infestation is too great, however, and in the end a Venerian virus called nine-day fever is induced in the general populace, since it has been found that the aliens die of it. After the victims are free of their "masters" they are given antitoxin. The slugs are an enemy fearful to encounter and well thought out by Heinlein. James Blish panned *The Puppet Masters* for being overly trendy, but I think it's more than that.

Also in the September issue is a novelette by Damon Knight called "Cabin Boy." It is what F. Orlin Tremaine of the old *Astounding* called a "thought variant" story. It is certainly out of the ordinary. The author himself says of it (in his book *In Search of Wonder*):

The C-Chute. Illustrator: Richard Arbib.

The hero of my "Cabin Boy" is an active gelatinous ovoid, who propels himself by an ion stream, and who lives with others of his kind inside another living organism who is his father . . . I thought I was writing space opera . . . But I don't know how you could ask for a clearer description of a sperm in the testis.

In the October issue, which has a marvelous pulp-type cover to illustrate an Asimov story, Gold has a forthright editorial in which he states:

GALAXY is for democracy, human decency and dignity, peace, progress, scientific advance, better standards of living, education, international and intergroup relations, and individual awareness . . .

GALAXY is against tyranny of any sort whatever, human degradation, inhuman war, repudiation of science or any other aspect of progress, lower standards of living, . . . individual unawareness, and bad stories.

It's obvious that Gold would not have gone in much for Sword and Sorcery stories. It is very refreshing to the reader to have an editor, especially the editor of a mass-circulation fiction magazine, come right out and lay it on the line to reveal clearly what he feels the magazine should be for—what, in fact, the magazine should be doing for humanity.

The Asimov story, "The C-Chute," is an interesting adventure, but that is all. The story "Pleasant Dreams" remains in my memory because of the unusually brisk way the author, Ralph Robin (a pseudonym?), disposes of one of the characters:

There were tears in the visitor's eyes as he walked into the elevator. As soon as he had entered, the door automatically closed, and the elevator automatically carried him to a lower floor, where it automatically and completely disposed of him.

The November *Galaxy* shows how the magazine continued to improve its artwork, both interior and exterior. The cover painting is on an astronomical theme, viewing a double star from one of its satellites. The interior art now includes work by Emsh and is of a higher quality than much of the work in the preceding issues by less-well-known artists.

Besides the improved artwork, the November issue had the conclusion of *The Puppet Masters* and some good novelettes and short stories. The novelette "Self Portrait," by Bernard Wolfe, has the new field of cybernetics as one of its topics. It also weaves in developments in prosthetic limbs and the sinister McCarthyite paranoid atmosphere of the early 1950's. Wolfe is a man of many talents and experiences. He had been a war correspondent, and before WWII had been a bodyguard to the late

Double Star. Anonymous Illustrator.

Russian revolutionary, Leon Trotsky. Thus, it is presumably no accident that his story also contains some legitimate left-wing history (about the Abraham Lincoln Brigade in the Spanish Civil War). It is more of a mood piece than anything else, and continues *Galaxy*'s habit of printing unique and uncommon stories.

The November issue also had a chilling short story by the noted physician-author Alan Nourse. "Tiger by the Tail" is about the way things you are looking for tend to disappear. As it turns out, they vanish into another dimension. A woman's purse is one of the transfer points. We reach deep into it to try to make contact. We do, and then begin to pull on the other universe to see something of what's on the other side. *They* pull back, and that's when the trouble starts.

At this point, *Galaxy* changed publishers. H. L. Gold tells how this occurred (in the October, 1975 *Galaxy*):

> He [Lombi, the Italian who represented World Editions] was in the U.S. on a visitor's visa. . . . One day he was called down to Washington by the Immigration Department and shown all of a letter but the signature—which stated that he was a dirty Italian communistic fascist who ought to be sent back where he came from. . . . He was sent back to Italy, his visa withdrawn.
>
> I still don't know who sent that letter, but it's no coincidence that as soon as Lombi was out of the country, internal warfare developed between the American, French and Italian offices of World Editions. . . . Strange things happened to our sales. Readers wrote in that they couldn't find us on any newsstand anywhere.
>
> The upshot was that the Riviera guy sent the head of the French office to New York to find out what went wrong. To make a short story of all this, the Frenchman cabled back to the Riviera that the magazine was a dud and should immediately be sold—to the American president and the circulation director, and their price was $3,000. I got in touch hurriedly with Lombi and told him of this. The time in Rome was 4:30 a.m., but Lombi got up and raced to the Riviera. The publisher instantly sent a cable stopping negotiations and followed up with another visit by Lombi to take care of the matter.
>
> I was told by the two American scoundrels that I was part of the deal, but I wasn't having any. Lombi arrived by plane and we began looking for a better buyer. A number of outfits here were interested, but, as I said, we were becoming great friends with the printing broker, Bob Guinn, and I got him to make a bid. . . . and no sooner had Guinn bought it than the inside job became clear to Lombi. The distribution

Season's Greetings To Our Readers. Illustrator: Emsh.

pattern had been deliberately loused up—by shipping *Galaxy* all over the South, where there was practically nobody interested in sf, and into hamlets all over the North and West.

The December, 1951 issue has a cover by Emsh, the first appearance of *Galaxy*'s four-armed Santa Claus. This extraterrestrial St. Nick lasted for a decade of December issues. Other sf magazines and the later *Galaxy* no longer had Santas of any kind, possibly for some of the same reasons that the Beatles never made a Christmas album—a general wearing away of sentimentality, perhaps.

This was a very superior issue. It contained, of course, no serial installment, but it had a Knight novella and novelettes by C. M. Kornbluth and John Wyndham. The Wyndham piece, "Pillar to Post," is a real classic of one variant of time travel, the temporal displacement of personalities; it turns into something of a thriller as a present and a future man vie for control of the temporal shifting device.

"With These Hands," the Kornbluth story, makes a statement about the growing plasticization of art in a world that has survived a major atomic war. Then, as now, the true artist is never rewarded for his or her pains, and especially so when a new technology threatens to wipe out the artist's specialty with mechanical techniques.

Fritz Leiber's "A Pail of Air" is a well done conception of possible survival in a cold and ravaged world, torn away from its orbit by a passing "dark star." The title refers to the way the characters get air: they bundle up, go out of their shelter, and scoop up some frozen oxygen. Then they merely thaw it out in the firelit interior of the shelter. They get visitors . . .

Jack Vance, in "Winner Lose All," the first of his *Galaxy* appearances, wrote of the deadly encounter of an energy being, a starship of human explorers, and a uranium-eating plant. No dull moment in this one!

4. THE HEIGHT OF THE GOLD YEARS: PART ONE, 1952–1953

GALAXY'S REPUTATION WAS GROWING FAST. Everett F. Bleiler and T. E. Dikty, editors of the hardbound anthology *The Best Science Fiction Stories: 1951*, dedicated it to Horace Gold. They said Gold:

> . . . has focused attention upon maturity and craftsmanship in modern science-fiction. We feel that the sort of story which has appeared in *Galaxy* . . . will succeed in placing science-fiction on an equal basis with any other field of modern literature.

January of 1952 saw the first installment of a new serial, *The Demolished Man*, by New York writer Alfred Bester. Ben Reich kills his economic rival, Craye D'Courtney, in a future where premeditated murder is theoretically impossible because of the development of telepathic powers in the human race. Reich is eventually tracked down by Preston Powell, a telepath of the highest order. In the process a fascinating future society is shown, with its future amusements and future crimes. The telepaths play interesting mind-word-pun games which Bester illustrates with innovative typography.

A controversy with *Astounding* arose in February's editorial, although the rival magazine's name was not used. Alva Rogers, in his *A Requiem for Astounding*, explains what happened:

> In November, 1951 a further change in [*Astounding*'s] cover makeup was made. Heretofore the cover painting covered the entire page with the title logo, date and price overprinted at the top and the featured story at the bottom. With the November issue the cover painting was bled off the right hand side and the bottom of the page and given a one half inch margin on the left and a one and three-eighths inch margin at the top. The title of the feature story, or the title of the cover, was printed along the left hand margin and the title logo across the top margin, thus leaving the cover painting entirely free of print. This lasted until January, 1954. This makeup was remarkably similar to the cover format used by *Galaxy* since its first issue, and H. L. Gold . . . was quite bitter in his condemnation of Campbell's "theft" of his format. However, Gold's argument that Campbell had "stolen" *Galaxy*'s format was somewhat weakened by the fact that *Comet Stories* used almost the identical cover format ten years earlier. From this point the rivalry between Campbell and Gold became increasingly intensified . . .

Gold's actual editorial was a bit on the sarcastic side:

> No, we're not angry, though we would like to know when we may have it [the format] back again. We are developing some other ideas; would the magazine in question prefer to have us send them over now, or wait and see how they work out after publication?

The covers and the interior art for the first two issues of 1952 are not particularly distinguished. The March cover is quite a different matter, a bit of surrealism to illustrate Robert A. Heinlein's "Year of the Jackpot." The thesis of this fine novelette is that our history is influenced by all kinds of cycles—economic, biological, you name it! One day there will come a time when all the negative cycles coincide. That day is the subject of this story. It is unusually pessimistic for Heinlein, who seems to favor in many of his works a rather up-and-at-'em, man over environment (and his fellow men) sort of attitude. However uncharacteristic, it is a good story.

There is a good F. L. Wallace story, "Accidental Flight," in the April issue. On one of the asteroids is an institution called Handicap Haven. People suffering from severe injuries or birth defects are sent there, ostensibly to enjoy the low gravity, but actually to keep them from offending the sensibilities of their fellow Earthpeople, all of whom are perfect physi-

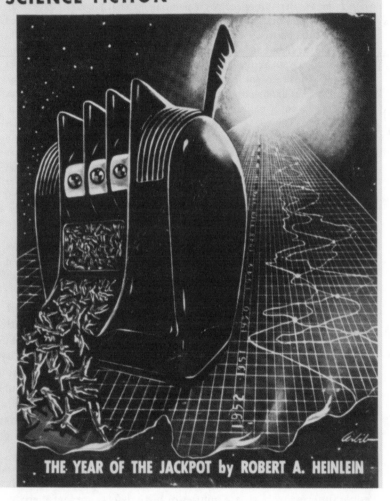

The Year of the Jackpot. Illustrator: Richard Arbib.

Accidental Flight. Illustrator: Richard Powers.

cal specimens, thanks to advanced medical science. A group of the handicapped escape from the Haven and chart a course for the stars, to Far
Centauri. They are ushered back by the armed cruisers of Earth, but their
return to the Haven proves to be short. The so-called handicapped are in
actuality perfectly adapted to space. In addition, they can live for hundreds of years, whereas normal Earthpeople have not been "biocompen-
sated" and still have normal lifespans. There is a role for them yet.

April has yet another memorable Damon Knight novelette for *Galaxy*'s
readers: "Ticket to Anywhere." Richard Falk lives in a future society
where everyone gets an "analogue," a sort of little policeman who sits in
the mind of the conditioned person and controls his activities. The conditioning did not take with Falk, and he is unique on Earth and quite
uncomfortable. He stows away to Mars and locates a man named Wolfert
who is the guardian of the Doorway, a simple and indestructible matter
transmitter, relic of a fabulous ancient race. Falk has nothing to lose. He
steps into the Doorway, pulls the lever, and visits a variety of interesting
worlds. A previous human traveler has left him a note about the route to
follow, and Falk, now more encouraged, sets off for the center of the
galaxy.

By this time Gold had edited a hardbound anthology, the *Galaxy
Reader of Science Fiction*, a big book 566 pages in length. It contained 32
stories from the magazine's first year, such as "Betelgeuse Bridge" and
"Beyond Bedlam." It was published by Crown Publishers and is now
rather hard to find. Buyers of sf anthologies really got their money's
worth at that time. The *Second Galaxy Reader*, published in 1954, was
also over 500 pages in length.

The June, 1952 issue began the first appearance of the Pohl/Kornbluth
collaboration "Gravy Planet," which later appeared in paperback as *The
Space Merchants*. Gold wrote in that month's editorial:

> The literary philosophy behind *Gravy Planet* is one I'm fond of: what
> would happen if any given situation is carried to the utmost extremes we
> are capable of imagining?
>
> The result may or may not ever come true; that's not the point.
> Neither is approval or disapproval—the situation must be viewed purely
> in terms of its contemporaries.

"Gravy Planet" is about a future world where large corporations operate like independent governments and business executives and advertising
men are the aristocracy. The main character is Mitchell Courtenay, a

Gravy Planet ("utopia" misspelled). Illustrator: Emsh.

high-ranking ad man in charge of his corporation's Venus Project, a
scheme to develop and exploit Venus. Mitch encounters strange attempts
on his life, sabotage, and a plot to change his identity to that of a very
low-ranking member of the working class. As he fights his way back to his
real identity, he becomes exposed to the Conservationist movement, an
underground group whose existence is anathema to the corporate moguls
and other supporters of unregenerate consumerism. He regains his high
position, but becomes a convert to the "Connie" cause. In the end we see
him and his wife Kathy, who had been a Conservationist all along, hard at
work developing an independent and self-sustaining colony on Venus.

Kornbluth said of this novel:

> As I leaf through the book I see that Pohl and I left virtually nothing
> in American life untransformed, from breakfast food to the Presidency
> of the United States. I see that with almost lunatic single-mindedness we
> made everything in our future America that could be touched, tasted,
> smelled, heard, seen or talked about bear witness to the dishonesty of the
> concepts and methods of today's advertising.

James Blish, in a footnote in his book *The Issue at Hand*, wrote:

> "Gravy Planet" [*The Space Merchants*] . . . is still sweeping its way
> around the world ten years later. It is easily the best anti-utopia (or
> dystopia or comic inferno—choose your own term) since *Brave New
> World*, and doesn't appear to be dating as rapidly as most members of its
> class, Huxley's excluded . . .

Blish wrote that observation in 1962, but the phenomenon of the book
still continues. It is still in print and is even recommended to collegians
in *Science Fiction: An Introduction*, a publication of the famous Cliffs
Notes. Sam Lundwall refers to it in his book *Science Fiction: What It's
All About*, and compares it somewhat fruitfully to George Orwell's *1984*.

To conclude, it would appear that "Gravy Planet" is the premiere novel
of *Galaxy*'s early years, perhaps even of its entire career. It is surely the
high point of the sociological satire so prominent in the *Galaxy* of the
1950's.

July continues "Gravy Planet" and has some good novelettes and short
stories. The notable "Star, Bright," by Mark Clifton, is a novelette about
some very bright children who discover how to enter the fourth dimension, leaving the adults behind to try to figure out how they did it. This
story also was educational for me when I first read it at age 13 or so,
because it was the first time I'd read about Klein bottles, the Moebius

strip, tesseracts, and other such dimensional puzzles.

The August issue has a typically whimsical cover by Emsh showing aliens (little green men) being tourists in a city and snapping pictures of the natives of urban Earth. This issue features a classic of a novelette, the famous "Surface Tension" by James Blish. This was to become his most popular, most anthologized story.

"Surface Tension" deals with human colonists on an alien planet. They are not the sort of colonists we are used to. They are microscopic in size and entirely aquatic; they can't breathe air. These colonists have been designed that way by a very advanced genetic engineering, because on the planet Hydrot only a human of that type and size could survive. The adventure is real as the tiny people battle rotifers, ally themselves with paramecia (one of the certainly rare instances in fiction where a single-celled animal appears as part of a noble and philosophical race), and finally build a wooden "spaceship" which can take them from water puddle to water puddle. This is a genuine "thought variant" story, as original and imaginative as anyone could desire.

Also in the August issue, the interior illustrations by Ashman are a great improvement over the wan *Galaxy* norm. His work would continue through much of the 1950's.

Katherine MacLean, by now a *Galaxy* regular, produced the most memorable piece in the September issue, which also features work by F. L. Wallace and by Gordon Dickson in his first *Galaxy* appearance. "The Snowball Effect," MacLean's story, tells about a sociological experiment which worked all too well. An old professor of sociology figures out what makes great historical movements and institutions gain momentum and grow mighty. He comes up with a formula to describe his "snowball process." The principles thus displayed are applied to a charitable group of ladies, the Watashaw Sewing Circle. By the end of the story, the organization has gone through several name changes and structural alterations and is on its way to becoming the first world government, to the intense chagrin of the sociologists who only wanted a little experiment.

Gordon R. Dickson's short story "The Mousetrap" is a grim thing about a man conditioned to act as bait by entering alien areas of space and trapping whatever forms of alien life come aboard to investigate. He is conditioned to do this even though the aliens may be intelligent and friendly. The psychological damage to the human bait is quite severe, and usually only criminals volunteer for the duty. This is a heavier sort of

Galaxy's Birthday Party (H. L. Gold, center left). Illustrator: Emsh.

story than usual for that period of *Galaxy*'s history, but is still in keeping with the magazine's ambient distrust of human motives.

A cheerful party is the theme of the October, 1952 wraparound cover. Emsh included in semi-caricature *GSF* luminaries Fritz Leiber, Evelyn Paige (Assistant Editor), Robert A. Heinlein, Katherine MacLean, Chesley Bonestell, Theodore Sturgeon, Damon Knight, Gold and Robert Guinn, Cyril Kornbluth, Willy Ley, F. L. Wallace (with a short military crewcut), Isaac Asimov, Ray Bradbury and Poul Anderson, among others. There was reason for the party to look so jolly. *Galaxy* was now preeminent among sf magazines. It had published, or would shortly print, the best and most characteristic work of the decade. For instance, in that very same October issue Theodore Sturgeon has a novella, "Baby Is Three," which is the first section of *More Than Human*, a novel published later that has been often mentioned as one of the most memorable sf books of the entire 1950's.

"Baby Is Three" is about the uniting of the minds of six super-sensitive (psionic) humans. This hive-mind is viewed sympathetically by the author, who seemed always in that period to view human loneliness as a very severe problem to which, of course, mental union was a perfect answer. The reader is drawn in as this unity becomes more mature. Sturgeon covered some of this ground in his earlier "Rule of Three" in the January, 1951 issue, but this later effort is done with a surer grasp of the psychological aspects.

Other noteworthy stories in October were "A Little Oil" by Eric Frank Russell (a sociopsychological piece about the beneficial effects of a professional clown aboard an otherwise grim space exploration ship), and "Game for Blondes" by the noted mystery author, John D. MacDonald (in which blondes from the future come back to our time on a scavenger hunt).

Isaac Asimov wrote the feature story for the November issue. His name is misspelled on the cover as "Issaac Asimov," the only blemish in an otherwise excellent issue. The cover by Jack Coggins shows some oddly spaced shuttle-like ships in orbit around the Earth as a space station is being constructed.

Asimov's story, "The Martian Way," is about a Mars colony dependent on Earth for water supplies. The Martians make a living by retrieving discarded stages or "shells" of interplanetary rockets and salvaging the metal. An Earth-first political party comes to power and soon Earth is threatening to cut the water supply to Mars unless certain concessions are granted. However, the adaptive Mars colonists fly out to Saturn and, using the same techniques they employ for snaring the space shells, rope in gigantic chunks of ice from the Rings. They bring these back to Mars, and Earth no longer has any leverage. The trip outward to Saturn is told in a realistic and convincing way without any phony heroics.

In this issue is perhaps the premiere *Galaxy* short story of the decade. This is "The Altar at Midnight," by the immensely skilled C. M. Kornbluth. Barry Malzberg says in his anthology *The End of Summer*:

> . . . "The Altar at Midnight" remains as perhaps the prototypical *Galaxy* standard of excellence; this is the kind of story which would not have existed had it not been for Horace Gold and the genre thus incalculably reduced. *Galaxy*'s legacy is persistent: the story is a shade self-conscious and creaks a little at the end . . . but it lives now as very few American literary short stories of the period live.

Kornbluth's story takes place in some ratty bars around midnight. A young spaceman, ravaged and deteriorating from the effects of the space drive used on the ships he flies between planets, is getting drunk. He is being treated badly, so the alcoholic narrator takes him in tow. They visit a down-and-out Skid Row joint where the sad spaceman disappears into a back room with one of the young ladies who frequent the place. Later the narrator makes sure the young spacer gets into a YMCA without being rolled. Then at the end of the story we find out exactly who the narrator is and why he has been so solicitous about the young spaceman.

The last issue of 1952 has an interesting photomontage cover to illustrate Clifford D. Simak's three-part serial *Ring Around the Sun*. This work by the old veteran writer, like "Time Quarry" in the 1950 issues, has a rather complicated plot. We deal again with humans, androids, and robots. This time, however, Simak has thrown in a new element, a mutant strain of humans who are telepathic in some instances and have other advanced traits. We view events from the perspective of Jay Vickers, a writer. The mutants are trying various ways to keep the humans of Earth from going to war. One method is general sabotage of national economies, to force people to form a less competitive and more peaceable world.

The mutants operate from a series of parallel Earths, the 'Ring Around the Sun,' and they are also busily evacuating humans to these safer and unpopulated worlds so humanity will survive in the event of a war. There

DECEMBER 1952
35¢

RING AROUND THE SUN
By Clifford D. Simak

Ring Around the Sun. Photomontage.

are many surprises and twists in the plot. Vickers turns out to be an android, carrying only a part of his original mutant personality. His major opponent, Crawford, an industrialist, is another. When the mutants succeed, Vickers' total self will be replaced in his human body. Finally, war is averted at almost the last moment.

Groff Conklin's book review feature, "Galaxy's 5 Star Shelf," had a new lead-in illustration in the February, 1953 issue. It was by Emsh, who also illustrated the superb story by Robert Sheckley, "Watchbird." Robert Sheckley, one of the more prolific *GSF* writers in the Fifties, was a satirist and ironist *sans pareil*. Some (James Blish, for instance) have accused him of being overly cutesy and gag-oriented at the expense of sensible plots. That view has some validity, but "Watchbird" is a gem of a story. Watchbirds are flying metallic monitors designed to prevent murder. They observe people about to commit this crime and shock them severely. If they keep on trying, the watchbirds shock them dead. In this way humanity hopes to free itself of murder. It works for awhile, but inevitably grim complications occur.

Also appearing in this issue is Algis Budrys, one of the better sf authors of the period (who has resumed his fine work at the end of the Seventies). He has an amusing short story entitled "Protective Mimicry." Baumholtzer, an agent from UnGalac, is sent to Deneb XI to find out who is making identical-copy 50-credit bills, and ends up being copied himself— 168 Baumholtzers!

Theodore Sturgeon's story "Saucer of Loneliness" is a definitive treatment of one of the themes that concerned him. A young woman is contacted mentally by a small flying saucer. This happens in a crowded park, and she is promptly taken in for questioning by the FBI. They keep her locked up and grill her, but she regards the message as deeply personal and refuses to repeat it. When she is released, people continue to invade her privacy hoping she will tell them what she heard. Finally, she writes the message, puts it in various bottles, and launches them into the ocean. Then she goes down to the beach again to drown herself, but someone has gotten one of her messages and convinces her to stay alive. Then we learn the saucer's message. It is an interesting and decidedly poetic piece. James Blish, writing as William Atheling, Jr., gives it very high honors.

Damon Knight's novelette "Four in One" is the fourth of the major items in the February issue. Blish says in his book *The Issue at Hand*:

... the major idea in this story is not only as old as Homer, but has been handled before by science-fiction writers of stature: the Proteus, the creature which can assume any shape. Knight makes no attempt to surprise anyone with this notion; even had he himself never encountered the idea before outside his own head, he is too good a craftsman to assume that an idea alone is enough. The contrasting idea is that of escape from a totalitarian society, again a piece of common coin. The result is "Four in One," which is compelling not because it contains a single new notion but because nobody but Knight ever before showed these two old notions in such an individual light, and because in addition, the light is individual throughout—the story contains hardly a single stock reaction.

At this time *Galaxy* began to run advertisements of its forthcoming sister publication, *Beyond Fantasy Fiction*.

Gold later said:

And then came *Beyond Fantasy Fiction*. It was beautiful—for ten wonderful issues. By then we had learned that there just wasn't a big enough audience to support a fantasy magazine, so it died just as *Unknown* had, a decade before, of financial malnutrition. If *Beyond* had come first, I think it would have had the same effect and same misty memories as *Unknown*.

Unknown, of course, was the former fantasy companion to John Campbell's *Astounding SF. Beyond* actually appeared from July, 1953 to July, 1955. The first eight issues were bi-monthly and dated. The last two were undated, always a serious sign for magazines. It featured such notable authors as Theodore Sturgeon, Damon Knight, L. Sprague de Camp, Fletcher Pratt, and Ray Bradbury. A number of its stories were of quite a high standard, especially those in the first issue.

Fantasy is a far more ancient genre than science fiction. It relies on magical formulae, faery lands unknown, castles, dragons, and princesses. Many writers do both; Jack Vance and Fletcher Pratt, for instance. Some magazines combine both fantasy and sf, as *The Magazine of Fantasy and Science Fiction* does. This combination seems to work, for *F&SF* is still on the newsstands, whereas the magazines of pure fantasy (and the Fifties saw a number of them) are no longer with us. I am not referring here to magazines that are half panel art of dubious politics and aesthetics and half semi-factual articles. These are based upon the French *Metal Hurlant* (*Heavy Metal*), an import of the sort which seems to soothe the souls of the sword and sorcery retinue.

The March *Galaxy* featured a novella by H. L. Gold himself. It was called "The Old Die Rich," and it spun out its story of an investigation into the deaths of old people who have perished of malnutrition even though they have several hundred thousand in cash lying around or in a mattress. The investigator finds that they are being sent into the past to make money by betting on events whose outcomes are known through history—famous prize fights and so on. A sinister woman, a professor's daughter who is ruthless (instead of frail, which stereotypical sf profs' daughters so often were), early on traps the investigator. There are some logical problems with the story, but it is thought-provoking and good adventure.

The cover of the March issue is another photomontage to illustrate the Gold story. The magazine also contains details and rules of a contest for a prizewinning novel, sponsored by *Galaxy* and the publishing firm of Simon and Schuster. The prize was to be $6500 and publication of the novel. The money was quite a lot for sf novel rights at that time. Even taking inflation into account, it would not be so much now, but then it was doubtless thought to be a sure-fire way to prompt new writers to come forward and try their luck. We shall see what became of this idea.

At this time Gold abandoned his earlier policy of running serials separated by one issue without a serial installment. Now there were simply no serials at all, and would not be for another half-year (when Isaac Asimov would check in with *The Caves of Steel*).

I rather liked the April cover by Schomburg illustrating an article by Willy Ley, "The Birth of the Space Station." Some words here about Ley—he was German-born and from very early on he had been one of the scientists who laid the groundwork for German rocketry. After a year or so of the Nazis, he got out of Germany and came to the U.S. He became the quintessential science writer and expounder of future space flight to the readers of sf and others interested in rocket travel. He was given the coveted Hugo award twice in the Fifties for his articles. Ironically, he died some months short of seeing the Moon Landing in 1969.

In this issue, old pro Murray Leinster (William Fitzgerald Jenkins) has a novelette called "The Sentimentalists," about two honeymooning aliens who help to save an Earth colony that would otherwise be doomed by huge solar flares. They also liberate the tenant farmers who are always in debt to a kind of company store. They do all this by projecting ideas of ingenious gadgets into the mind of Lon Simpson, one of the struggling

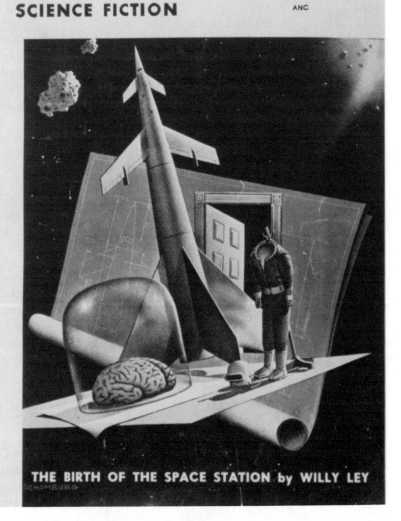

Still Life in Space. Illustrator: Schomburg.

colonists. There is also some romantic interest. Lon wishes to marry a "beamphone" operator named Cathy. He is too poor to do so until he builds a device which reproduces *thanar* leaves, a crop which produces a longevity drug. This story might strike some as being somewhat *deus ex machina*, but it is worth reading all the same.

Kurt Vonnegut, Jr. makes his first appearance in *Galaxy* in the April, 1953 issue with "Not Ready to Wear," a witty short story. It's about a future world where many people are disembodied minds who only inhabit bodies (which are otherwise stored away) on certain ceremonial days. There is much comment about what a nuisance the old-fashioned bodies used to be—how they had to be fed and so on. Enjoyable.

One of the April short stories had later reverberations and provided us with a second movie from stories originally in *Galaxy*. This is "Seventh Victim" by Robert Sheckley. It deals with a future dystopia where duels to the death are allowed. The idea is that general human aggression will be less if individuals can indulge their aggressive instincts. The high goal of those who choose to hunt and kill fellow hunters and killers is to reach seven victims. After that number, one can enjoy great social status. The narrator is after a young woman, his current target.

The movie based on this story is *The Tenth Victim*, filmed in Italy, with Ursula Andress as the woman. If I remember correctly, she has a trick brassiere instead of a trick cigarette lighter and shoots her victims with that. This caused a lot of comment among film critics, comments which mentioned Freudian psychiatric theories. It was not one of the world's greatest flicks but it *was* inspired by a very good story. When Robert Sheckley wasn't joking around with his AAA Ace stories of lovable space boobs, he could do some quite respectable things.

The May issue's cover by Mel Hunter is very effective. It is entitled "Rescue Above the Moon." The space gear depicted on the covers of *Galaxy* was beginning to be not so very different in appearance from the real space gear of the succeeding decades.

Clifford Simak has the novelette "Junkyard" in the May *Galaxy*. On an extremely remote planet the crew of an exploration vessel find the wreckage of other spacecraft from hundreds of years earlier, but with no one around on a planet that is still in the stage of early plant life. Then they find themselves forgetting things, even how to blast off again. The entity that is draining their minds is an egg-shaped alien information collector concealed in a stone tower. Whenever the explorers get near it

Rescue Above the Moon. Illustrator: Mel Hunter.

they lose all their memories and revert to a childish stage. After several crew members are made useless, captain Ira Warren gets an idea. He borrows a lot of whiskey from a continually inebriated crewman, Bat Ears Brady, and proceeds to tie one on. The conclusion is clever and amusing.

June's cover is also by Mel Hunter, showing someone in a mint green space suit discovering a hoard of glowing uranium in a cave of a distant planet or satellite.

Philip K. Dick, an author to be much heard from, made *Galaxy* with a genuine chiller of a novelette. "Colony" is premised on an adaptable alien protoplasmic form of life which is mimetic, and dangerous to the nth degree. It can imitate any kind of human equipment, microscopes and gloves, file cabinets, etc. Getting into close proximity to one of these masquerading aliens is always dangerous and often fatal, as their main goal is to disable the humans and digest them. One officer of the exploration team gets into what he thinks is his car, and finds himself being quickly digested. The exploration team uses poison gas to kill the protoplasmic entity in all its disguises, with varied results.

Beyond and *Galaxy* both appear in July. The *Galaxy* has an amusing Emsh cover showing a green-skinned extraterrestrial shaking a fist at a Terran spaceman whose rocket has accidentally landed on and killed an obviously ET purple cow. The spacer gestures helplessly. The Earthman is wearing one of the quaint bell-jar space helmets which never did get into actual use, or haven't so far.

There is another hunter story in the July issue, "Home Is the Hunter." This one is by C. L. Moore and Henry Kuttner, that redoubtable pair who had already done so much fine work in the 1940's. Their piece is about a master hunter who is at the top of his "profession." It appears that the hunters stalk each other in Central Park. The winner preserves the head of his foe in a glass case. Our protagonist has collected lots of them. But he awaits his true triumph. He knows other hunters want the prestige of getting his head, but he fools them. He invites them all into his palace and then, standing at the top of the staircase, takes poison. They can never get him now and his body will be cased in a plastic monument. This is his true triumph. One wonders if these hunter stories do not amount to some indirect commentary on the business practices of the Fifties. They certainly function as a satire on the macho big game hunting postures of the main-stream writer Papa Ernest Hemingway. In the rather repressed intellectual milieu of the Fifties, *Galaxy* really was functioning as a counter-cultural publication.

In the July *Galaxy* there is another darkly humorous classic by Fritz Leiber called "A Bad Day for Sales." This one, too, has been placed in numerous anthologies. It was one of the stories I read in that era which has always remained perfectly vivid. Robie, the vending machine robot, appears in Times Square one nice afternoon. It's on a trial run. Robie looks a bit like a small tank, a turret on a metal hoopskirt, with radar and a rubber buffer so it doesn't bump into people. A crowd gathers and it gives a little boy some candy. It announces it can also dispense intoxicating liquor, and as it does the enemy drops the Bomb. Robie is somewhat jarred but continues functioning, inadvertently acting as a guardian to a little girl who has lost her mommy. All the other people on the street have been killed or badly hurt by the heat blast, but not the girl's mother, who had been inside a nearby building. She appears and takes her daughter away. The robot, ever optimistic, whirrs off to sell soda pop to an approaching rescue squad! The story is written in an unfailingly ironic tone.

Someone by the name of Villiers Gerson replaced Groff Conklin for one review in the July "Galaxy Five Star Shelf": the book was one of Conklin's anthologies. *Galaxy*'s reviewer deserves some commentary, too. Groff Conklin compiled forty anthologies of science fiction stories before his death in 1968 at the age of sixty-four. Some of the earliest and best of the sf anthologies, those of the 1940's, were his work, and he deserves much credit for having preserved so many of the early stories in hardcover books.

In some of the issues of this year *Galaxy* referred to itself as the "aristocrat of science fiction." This complimentary term had been applied to the magazine in an article in *Life* magazine (May 21, 1951), and it was accurate in the sense that *Galaxy* had been drawing the very best writers in the field.

In the August issue, *Galaxy* has a story by the veteran Raymond Z. Gallun, who had appeared in sf magazines since 1929, when he was only eighteen. Gallun did some classic stories for the Tremaine *Astounding* in the mid-1930's, dealing with a benevolent Martian called "Old Faithful." His *Galaxy* story, "Stamped Caution," also deals with the Earth-Mars relationship. A UFO crashes, but an embryonic Martian survives, although the adults are killed. Scientists on Earth raise the Martian, Etl, to adulthood and then transport it back to its own planet. Etl goes back to its people and the Earthmen are put in confinement. Eventually they figure out a way to escape and make it back to their ship. There Etl greets them and congratulates them on having proved their intelligence to his people. A little of the interplanetary suspicion diminishes and it is apparent that Earthmen and Martians will soon begin trade with, and formal recognition of, each other's planets.

Also in August, Theodore R. Cogswell has a story, "Minimum Sentence," about an extraterrestrial from the Centauri system who looks a lot like a large cockroach (shades of Kafka!). Quang Dal has come to visit Earth and has gotten stranded. He falls into the company of some crooks who decide to use him to escape justice (they've stolen a lot of money) by going to Alpha Centauri. They think he can devise a faster-than-light drive and they never listen to him explain that FTL drives are impossible. They find themselves on a one-way twenty-year journey to Centauri with Quang Dal, who intends to nap through most of the flight. The journey's length means nothing to the Centaurian insect since his people can live for 40,000 years. This fact he was polite enough not to tell his Terran fellow passengers earlier, because he did not want to hurt their feelings.

Emsh has a nice cover for September, "Mercury's Solar Weather Station." He also did the interior art for the month's lead story, Theodore Sturgeon's "The Touch of Your Hand." A big young man by the name of Osser is tyrannizing some of his neighbors into helping him build a tower. He has seen the ruins of big cities and wants to bring back that kind of civilization, instead of the loose anarchic, rather idyllic rural existence now led by his people. A young woman named Jubilith is fond of him and tries to get close to him, but he is hard and obdurate. His tower grows. Just when it is finished and Osser's pride is great, an alien golden ship appears. The seemingly rustic people of the planet all of a sudden produce some very sophisticated weaponry and destroy the golden ship. The explosion knocks down Osser's tower, which now was looking foolish and silly. He reverts to infancy. Wrenn, an elder of the people, explains to Jubilith that Osser was an experiment. As a child he was removed from the benevolent interlinkage of minds that has so advanced the race. The result was that Osser was turning out to be dangerous, just as the explorers from Earth would have been if their golden ship had not been destroyed. Wrenn says Osser can be restored to his mind and regain all he has lost through just a touch of her hand (and a certain ring). This is another change rung on Sturgeon's theme of the foolishness of the society versus the individual, and vice versa. A better world will be one in which people seek beneficial mental communing and not one where people are consumed by egotism and personal ambition. These, Sturgeon seems to feel, lead almost inevitably to civilization-wrecking war.

There was another change in the logo for "Galaxy's Five Star Shelf." It assumed the rocket-and-bookshelf form it would retain for some years.

In 1953 *Galaxy* received one of the first Hugo awards (named after Hugo Gernsback) for the category of Best Magazine. However, it was not *the* winner, but a co-winner sharing the award with (no real surprise) John Campbell's *Astounding SF*. In some respects, this was appropriate. The members of the 1953 World Science Fiction Convention were really, it seems to me, honoring *Astounding* for all its glorious old accomplishments and honoring *Galaxy* for helping to maintain the high standard of sf.

Representative of this high standard was the publication of Isaac Asimov's *The Caves of Steel* in the last three issues of 1953. *Galaxy* had at last gotten back to its serials.

Asimov's novel was a successful alliance of the detective puzzler type of novel and straight sf. It was also rather prophetic of present concerns because it paid serious attention to the problems of over-population on Earth. Earth's population centers are large enclosed underground cities. The fine Emsh cover for October gives some idea of their size and internal arrangement. All of Earth's eight billion people are contained in such cities.

Near the future New York is Spacetown, an area for citizens of the Outer Worlds, where Earthmen can go only by special permission, and only after infuriating sanitizing of their persons. This, however, is only a sensible precaution, for the Outworlders may be sensitive to some Terran viruses, etc. There is much hostility between Earth dwellers and Spacers, but none of it is really warranted. The Spacers are introducing robots into New York and other cities in an attempt to lessen the number of jobs available on Earth, and in that way to get more people to leave Earth and settle on the thinly populated Outer Planets. The secret Earth society of the Medievalists has sprung up, however, and resists any innovations. Then one of the leading roboticists among the Spacers, a Dr. Sarton, is murdered under very unusual circumstances, and Elijah Baley of the New York Police is sent to investigate. To his surprise he is teamed with a

The Caves of Steel. Illustrator: Emsh.

Spacer robot detective, an extremely human-appearing entity by the name of R. (Robot) Daneel Olivaw. The plot then threads around ingeniously. For a while, Baley even suspects R. Daneel of doing the deed, even though that would violate one of the famous Asimovian Laws of Robotics: that no robot may by commission or omission cause any harm to come to a human being. It becomes an exciting mystery.

H. L. Gold has a novelette in the October *Galaxy*, an interesting item called "At the Post." Its premise is that people who become catatonic are actually in a sort of telepathic dimension communicating facts about Earth to a society of benevolent aliens who want to know all about Earth for the record, just in case it is destroyed in a final war. Clocker Locke, a racehorse tipster, loses his wife Zelda to catatonia. He figures out a way to go where she is, meets the aliens (who are in human form), and works out a deal with them. They will let him have Zelda back if he agrees to get more people to contact them for their project. He also convinces them that he will do his best to make the world more peaceable. The characters in this story are mainly very stereotypical, but it seems to work as a sort of gentle satire. The premise, of course, is nonsensical.

November and December *Galaxy* issues both have Emsh covers. The December cover has the four-armed ET Santa again, being serenaded in his spaceship by four carolers, of whom only one is human.

December has a good Sturgeon story, "Mr. Costello, Hero," another variation on the hivemind. Mr. Costello is a former high-ranking Earth official who is being transported into exile after a fall from grace. His problem is that he manipulates people, and does it very well. The narrator of the story is obviously rather impressed by him. Costello more or less dominates the ship transporting him. He comes to dominate Borinquen, his destination, a rather wild and woolly outpost. He turns it into a huge inhuman hive where no one is allowed to be alone for any reason and where everybody sleeps in a huge warehouse dormitory where the lights are always on. Very grim. In the end, the entire Space Navy shows up and blasts Mr. Costello out of business. He ends up on an asylum planet actually manipulating ants in an anthill—a rather shuddery scene. Sturgeon is so good that he can take even a scrap of a story idea and turn it into something creepily effective like this.

Robert Sheckley also shows up in this issue with his short "One Man's Poison." This was anthologized later in a paperback with the new title "Untouched by Human Hands" (also the title of the anthology). Briefly,

Season's Greetings To Our Readers. Illustrator: Emsh.

some space explorers run out of provisions and land on an odd planet which has a huge warehouse. They look for edibles and get themselves into alarming situations. Finally, they find a Super Custom Transport, which is actually a large (and edible) animal. I suspect Gold added the ending here, for the anthologized version does not end so cheerily. He often did that.

5. THE HEIGHT OF THE GOLD YEARS:
PART TWO, 1954–1955

KINGSLEY AMIS, IN HIS BOOK *NEW MAPS OF Hell*, quotes Gold as having written:

> We today can, in reading the science fiction of the past, get often a far clearer view of the societies they were written in than from their contemporary "contemporary" fiction and often the non-fictional examinations. Few things reveal so sharply as science fiction the wishes, hopes, fears, inner stresses and tensions of an era, or define its limitations with such exactness.

This certainly seems true of the science fiction of the Fifties. There seem to be a lot of stories which reflect an apprehension of children, at least children who have very advanced mental powers. It was, of course, my generation they were writing about. They need not have worried. We only had different priorities. Another element was sex. Stories containing up-front sexual activity were not to be found (and still are rather rare in the sf field). Instead, what one finds is a lot of peekaboo stuff. In the previous issues of *Galaxy*, men were continually coming across beautiful women as they emerged from showering. Of course, a towel was always ready-at-hand, but not before the reader could share a vicarious ogle. In some of the future societies, women didn't wear brassieres! When the topic of progeny came up conversationally between the male protagonist and his Romantic Interest, she usually tended to "blush pinkly." On the other hand, sex in the sense of biological theory and genetic engineering was dealt with in some depth.

There was of course, the continued paranoia about nuclear war, ET invasions, atom bomb bases on the moon, radiation-induced mutations, and so on. These seemed somehow more immediate in the Fifties, perhaps because World War II was still vivid and had not yet become misty and romanticized.

To continue chronologically, the next issue in line is January, 1954. The cover is a good but somewhat far-fetched scene, "Flight Over Mercury," by Mel Hunter. This issue is distinguished by an excellent Damon Knight novella called "Natural State." Future cities are in trouble. They are static and the population of the countryside far outnumbers them. In order to gain some money and stimulus, New York decides to send out an actor, Alvah Gustad, to urge the despised hicks ("Muckfeet") to purchase the goods common to the allegedly superior urban existence. Gustad has no luck, meeting only with hostility and indifference. Then his "floater" is ruined by some mysterious creatures which eat its rhodopalladium fuel nodules. He is marooned among the Muckfeet.

Gustad discovers that he has been conditioned to regard the rural people as nauseating. When he overcomes that, he finds that they are really very superior. Their civilization, too, is superior to that of the besieged cities. They breed strange new animals to replace mechanical devices and also have bred all kinds of new nutritious fruits and vege-tables. He grows fond of a Muckfoot girl, B. J. (Betty Jane), and becomes opposed to the artificial and mechanical city life himself. Finally, he aids in ending the cities, and all their population is led away to begin a better and healthier decentralized rural life-style. This story sounds as though it could have been written in the later 1960's by some member of a commune. Well, there you are, sf is often well ahead of its time, as well as mirroring more current anxieties. In addition, Gold's editorial in this issue is devoted entirely to the problem of overpopulation.

Kurt Vonnegut reappears in the January *Galaxy* with "The Big Trip Up Yonder," about a future society where everyone lives on and on, thanks to an anti-aging drug. Thus, they can watch the same soap opera for sixty years!

Emsh did the February cover showing a spaceship hydroponics room. This issue had a pleasant surprise. James Blish, who had the superb "Surface Tension" in the August, 1952 issue, returned in this one with the highly imaginative "Beep." The Secret Service of Earth has perfected the Dirac Communicator, based on a principle beyond relativity. With it, they can keep the peace by knowing the future. All the Service does is analyze the "beep" sound that is heard when the communicator is turned on, for it consists of every message ever sent on the Dirac, past and future. They are all security-related, since only the Service has the Dirac. The origin of the Dirac is portrayed in a training film for a Service recruit, and we learn about it as he does. It is a fascinating story which has all kinds of ramifications, philosophical and otherwise.

There was another story in this issue, one which more or less haunted me at a semi-conscious level for years. When I was taking some graduate classes in Iowa City, I noticed the old bound volumes of *Galaxy* in the stacks, sat down with one of them, and sure enough, I found the story! It was as good as I remembered it. The story is "The Passenger," by an author whose name has gone into obscurity, Kenneth Harmon (or it could just be another pseudonym). Lenore, a young and attractive woman traveling on an interstellar liner, is returning from a stint in the Education Service. The ship is on the last leg of its trip back to Earth.

Suddenly, she begins to hear words and see images in her mind. She hears and sees a handsome young man, Fairheart, "of the billionaire Fairhearts." He explains that he is a telepath from far-away Dekker's star traveling to Earth alone. He talks her into a date with him in his stateroom. She dresses up, takes two fancy drinks with her, and descends down, down to his room in an ill-lit part of the ship. She goes in and sees a vision of a handsome young man waiting for her. They exchange greetings and she smiles. When she reaches out to him, she gets an unpleasant surprise.

There is a somewhat silly Emsh cover for March. A blue-skinned humanoid is sculpting a statue of an Earthwoman. His model is wearing a helmet like a glass bell jar but the rest of her is quite unprotected save for a graceful dress, and there is no hint of any oxygen mask. Strange. The cover's title is a ghastly play on words which always embarrassed me for some reason: "Pygm-Alien and Galaxea." The contents are not outstanding, either, except for "Ironclad," a fine novelette by Algis Budrys dealing with a future after the atom wars. (It was expanded as the book *Some Will Not Die*.)

We follow the grim fate of Cottrell Slade Garvin, who dies of the outmoded code of Integrity. After the big war, when civilization was rebuilding, every home and farm owner had his own little armored self-protected world, guarded by his own machine guns, artillery, etc. Garvin, who is very highstrung, is humiliated by being caught spying on a girl he liked. He really meant no harm—he only watched her as she read a book—but he still felt upset at being caught. He is a young man full of complex feelings, but he relies on the old Integrity Code to provide some meaning in his life. Someone kids him about all his weaponry and indicates the code isn't all-important, and then the troubles begin. A grim tale about a still-conceivable future . . .

In the April issue is Frederik Pohl's famous story "The Midas Plague," which tells of a future society of enforced consumption of goods. Social status is inversely proportional to the amount of goods and luxuries a person is forced to eat and wear out and use up. This is because the society suffers from chronic overproduction brought about by unlimited free robot labor, advanced solar and nuclear power, and other breakthroughs in technology. The main character, Morey Fry, is a member of a lower class, so he lives in a palace and has tons of good food and clothing, entertaining robots and so on, which is the portion the National Ration Board insists that he accept. His wife is from a more elevated, simpler style of life and it's hard for her to adjust. Morey thinks of scheme after scheme until he finally gets the idea of making the robots wear out the clothes, the sports equipment and so on. This makes him a hero since he's come up with the solution to overproduction. The National Ration Board is happy and dissolves itself. Morey's wife, Cherry, is happy too. Now they have only two robots to help them consume, but then Morey sees a little third one. He knows what this means and happily hugs Cherry, who blushes slightly.

But not everyone was happy. Damon Knight (in his critical book *In Search of Wonder*) was clearly not. He felt that the story not only took too long to come up with the really obvious solution, but that the whole situation was basically stupid all along:

This is something new in idiot plots—it's second-order idiot plotting, in which not merely the principals, but everybody in the whole *society* has to be a grade-A idiot, or the story couldn't happen. Admittedly, this attitude toward amusing but intrinsically wobbly ideas gets a lot of stories written that otherwise would be discarded: but it also populates the future exclusively with lackwits.

However, the British sf critic Kingsley Amis rather enjoyed it. In *New Maps of Hell* he referred to "The Midas Plague" as a "comic inferno" and a good one. He adds:

"The Midas Plague" does not merely inform us that the results of over-production may be fantastic, or hilarious, or desperate; it also comments on the revolutions in manners which human beings will swallow—in [Morey's] world you show your politeness by letting the other fellow pick up the restaurant or bar bill . . .

So, there is a legitimate difference by two experts on the Pohl story. The reader is, therefore, left to draw his or her own conclusion. My own choice is to treat it as a light satire which provides diversion and amusement. In that respect it does well and should be regarded as a classic.

H. L. Gold brought out the *Second Galaxy Reader of Science Fiction* in 1954. This, as I have said, is a big, solid book. The fine Mel Hunter cover of the May, 1953 *Galaxy* is used as the dust-jacket illustration. The stories come from the 1951-1953 period and are well-chosen. As a preface, Gold reprints one of his editorials which had caused a lot of comment. This was an excellent spoof of the Charles Fort school of woeful prognostication from random strange facts and events. That is to say, sudden locust raids signify that they are actually being dumped down on us from some nearby heavenly body. Gold notes that he always seems to have enough paperclips and clothes hangers, and concludes that it is an alien plot. We will become so dependent on these things that we will not recognize them for the fakes they are. We will never purchase real Earth paperclips and pencils, and then all of a sudden the alien underminers of our civilization will cause all the ersatz clips and hangers to vanish and then we'll be done for. Some people actually took this seriously and got annoyed. Oddly enough, some of the points raised in this little spoof were to cast some shadows in the pages of *Galaxy*.

Gold gives another variant of this theme in his editorial for the May issue—he suggests that a conqueror might:

. . . send in experts who can maddeningly hog the road, hold up queues while fishing for change or ration coupons, tie up buses by asking questions that need complicated answers, snarl phone service with endless bright, witless gabble, bring cops and firemen to rescue kittens caught in trees, immobilize banks by depositing sacks of coins that have to be counted or by breaking big bills into infuriating combinations of smaller bills and change, holding up subway trains for friends . . . In other words, inflict our daily frustrations in exaggerated form on a potential enemy—and watch his society go edgy and begin to shake apart!

Now of course, *Galaxy*'s editor was referring primarily to urban civilization, but he is in the main correct. Even in small-town Iowa, a picky new computerized gas pump which rounds sales off to the nearest penny caused some irritation and face-slapping. The long gas lines of a few years ago produced plenty of apoplectic feeling and some gunplay. The Senate turns away in horror from the new longer zip codes. As the song says, "little things mean a lot."

Gold is making another point, though. He is basically saying that our society is highly vulnerable to disintegrative forces because of its very complexity. He has also stated that a highly industrialized nation is not susceptible to an old-style revolution by force of arms. This seems to be the case, but *personal* use of armed violence can increase and cause great strains. It does seem odd that Pohl, Kornbluth, Gold and the rest did not seem to foresee the enormous rise in urban violence that would occur in the most recent years. The Marching Morons would start shooting at each other.

The feature story in the May issue was "Granny Won't Knit" by Theodore Sturgeon. In this far-future piece, there has been a big atomic war and mankind has had to regroup in Africa until the rest of the world is once again livable. In the meantime, human society has gone rigid and become a super-Victorian patriarchy. There is a fanatical mania for privacy, and every one keeps covered up except for the face. There is also a kind of running gag: the head of the family, any respected elder male, is known as "Private"—because they remember that "Private" had been a military term of respect (!) in the old destroyed civilizations.

Transportation in this world is by "transplats," platforms on which persons and goods are teleported back and forth. Roan Walsh, the young man through whose eyes we see, is a member of the family that produced the first transplats. He is not happy, and is much put upon by his father, an old tyrant. In the normal scheme of things for that society, Roan would have eventually succeeded to the family business and maintained decorum and "the Stasis." But Roan's ageless grandmother doesn't allow this to happen. Instead of letting Roan and the rest of humanity rest in self-satisfaction, she introduces him to an alternate world and a new technology beyond the transplats, a matter transmitter which can eventually help man to reach the stars. The difficulty is mainly psychological. "Granny" has to break through a lot of conditioning to finally reach her grandson and let him know that the world must change again. She, as it turns out, was also the one who initially developed the transplats and not someone who will spend her retirement knitting.

The Pohl/Kornbluth combination was back in the June issue with the first installment of *Gladiator at Law*. This novel is in the same grand counter-utopian vein as "Gravy Planet," but examined future legal methods and the roles of lawyers and realtors instead of ad men. Charles Platt, in *Dream Makers*, his fine book about sf writers, says of Kornbluth and his work with Frederik Pohl:

> C. M. Kornbluth died in 1958, when he was only thirty-five years old. He was undoubtedly one of the finest writers in the science fiction field; he worked at a time when fine prose was rare indeed. In collaboration with Frederik Pohl he produced classic, enduring novels; since then it has become fashionable for some people—such as Lester del Rey—to suggest that Kornbluth played some kind of lesser role in the collaborations, though there is no evidence for this whatsoever. Kornbluth's solo work, especially his short stories, showed great inventiveness, meticulous writing and outstanding maturity. He is given less credit now than is due.
>
> Like Pohl, Kornbluth had a sophisticated awareness of the dark undercurrents in life and society—the elements of greed, crime, power and fear which mold much of twentieth-century America, whether one likes it or not. In almost all of Kornbluth's stories these forces shape future societies with dramatic, often unpleasant realism. The grimness of these visions may be one reason for their not being more popular now, among readers who may prefer more optimistic materials.

These undercurrents are certainly in evidence, if not in the forefront of the new novel. Huge corporations are once again all powerful. The police are thoroughly corrupted tools of the status quo. There are sharp social divisions—the most basic of which is where one lives. In a satirical inversion typical of the *Galaxy* of those days, the wealthy live in bubble homes built in the city, while the poor are forced to live in miserable, unsafe, crumbling suburbs. The one we explore is called Belly Rave (from *Belle*

Rêve). The words originally meant "sweet dreams." When people lose their valued status in the city, they get booted out to crime-ridden Belly Rave.

And it is to Belly Rave that lawyer Charles Mundin must go to track down Norma Lavin and her brother Don, who have a startling tale to tell. They actually own one-fourth of G-M-L Homes, the giant monopoly that makes the bubble homes, because their father was the actual inventor. But he was swindled and kept out of the corporation. Before he killed himself, Mr. Lavin managed to convey his share of the stock to his children. They have been persecuted by G-M-L ever since, and Mundin is the first true defender they have ever had.

The society in which this is happening is not a reassuring one. The major sport of the lower classes is watching other unfortunates butcher each other in gladiatorial conflicts. The games are updated and varied to include such "sports" as octogenarians using blowtorches in duels, Scandinavian knife-fights, Kiddy Kutups and so on. One of the most popular crowd-pleasers is the high-wire act over a tank full of piranhas. The artist is hampered by the groundlings tossing bricks at him.

The corporations are bloodthirsty, too, and Mundin has to resort to many ruses to finally get to a G-M-L stockholders' meeting where he uses keen cunning and good strategy to place his clients in the position they deserve. There are still some grim moments left, though, including one where Don Lavin is "conditioned" by his foes to do the high-wire act over the sharp-toothed hungry fish. Only the sacrifice of one of the beloved major characters saves him. In the end, all is well. The lawyer is married to Norma, and the cruel gladiatorial games are losing favor as the general public learns to disdain them. The basic message seems to be that the system, even a grossly unjust one, can be improved, although only by heroic effort.

The only quibble I have is a very small one. At one point we are told that Belly Rave has no police force; yet later on, a particularly obnoxious patrolman is transferred there. How could this be? In all other respects, this Pohl/Kornbluth work is another high standard-setter.

The June, 1954 issue also has a novelette by William Tenn. "Down Among the Dead Men" is a grim tale of the long war between Mankind and the Eoti (the Bugs) which will end only when one side is wiped out. Humanity is taking a beating because it is behind technologically and because the aliens are breeding faster. The scientists of the Terrestrial

Armed Forces have begun to solve the problem by building soldier surrogates out of the body cells and organs of the warriors who died in action. They have even advanced beyond that stage and are designing space troopers to specification, creating duplicates of famous heroes of the war. There is much prejudice against these "zombies," and the narrator, a warship commander, has to overcome his before he can deal with his new crew. They are hostile to naturally-born humans because they are aware of the prejudices around them. However, they find that they do have something in common with their captain.

The other fine June piece is a short story by Robert Sheckley, "Something for Nothing." Joe Collins, a drifter of sorts, finds a miraculous metal box in his room. It turns out to be a kind of wishing machine. Soon he is wishing for money and luxuries and palaces and other grand things. But someone keeps trying to bring the machine back into its proper dimension, and that's where the problems start.

James Gunn says about Robert Sheckley:

> Sheckley (1928—) returned to New York City after service in Korea and was graduated from New York University. He appeared first in 1952 with a story entitled "Final Examination" in *Imagination Science Fiction*, but he then immediately began selling to *Galaxy*, which was the natural home for his clever ideas and witty style. In the next decade or so he published 106 stories and three serials, all but seven of the stories and one of the serials before 1959. He was published in almost all the magazines, including *Astounding* and *F&SF*, but 63 of those 106 stories and one serial were published in *Galaxy*, under his own name and under the pseudonyms he had to adopt for *Galaxy* because he was so prolific, Finn O'Donnevan and Phillips Barbee.

As a proof of Sheckley's prolific writing, the July *Galaxy* has an excellent novelette of his, "A Thief in Time." Professor Thomas Eldridge is approached by time-traveling police who want to arrest him for alleged future crimes. They tell him also that he will invent the time-jumping machine sometime in 1962. It is also a dimension-jumper, apparently, for it carries him into alternate futures.

People are after him, so he has to keep escaping from the police or the village elders in the various time sectors. Finally he reaches an uncivilized sector where he meets the people who have been waiting for him, including a lovely young woman of the future to whom he discovers he is married. Now that he knows how and where he will end up, he goes back to where he began to do everything he has learned he will do. Eventually he will get to his future colony and wife again and will stay for good this time around.

The September issue has a strange story by F. L. Wallace entitled "The Man Who Was Six." Dan Merrol, a space liner pilot, is badly injured in a collision between two spacecraft. He is repaired, largely by parts of less fortunate crash victims. (That idea again!) He receives a rebuilt brain, too; largely his, but with parts of the brains of five other men built into it. He has lost some memory, but gains by accumulating the five new partial personalities. This in effect gives him charisma. It also makes women want to jump in bed with him almost as soon as they see him. He quits moaning about his fate (he can't remember how to run a space liner) and starts to preen himself instead. This is a story that is more boyish wishful thinking than it is science fiction.

The October cover is by Mel Hunter and shows some aliens inspecting an Earth-based (I think) rocket complex just to check out the competition. Of major interest in this issue is a novelette by the late Philip K. Dick, "A World of Talent." The Centaurian Colonies include many people with "Psi" powers—telepathy, telekinesis, and so on. The government of Earth is opposed both to psi-power and to the colonial secessionist movement. The advanced mental powers of an overweight idiot-savant named Big Noodle keeps Earth's forces at a safe distance.

There are, however, more complications. The people who have psi-powers want to dominate the non-psis in the Colonies but a new type of human is appearing, the anti-psi, individuals who are invulnerable to psychic manipulating or prying. The narrator's girlfriend Pat is one of these, and she is killed by the psi forces. But then we discover that his son, Tim, also has unusual powers and can actually change time-lines to resolve human crises, and is doing so now to end the psi controversies. He also feels sorry for his father and places him in a time-line where Pat is alive, and so a happy note concludes this piece. The message seems to be that advanced human powers must be counterbalanced by other new human powers or one group will become all-powerful.

In the *Galaxy* for November there is a novelette by Edgar Pangborn, the superb and well-remembered "The Music Master of Babylon." There have been one too many great wars and all of man's old civilization is gone except for an old Museum of Human History which contains books, art, and a Hall of Music. It is inhabited by an old man, Brian Van Anda, who had once been a noted concert pianist. He lives with the old instruments and music scores, and subsists by doing a little hunting when necessary. He has not been in the company of another human being for decades. He spends some of his time trying to play the works of Andrew Carr, the last great composer of the Twentieth Century, but one piano work particularly eludes him.

Then he is visited by a couple in their teens. To his dismay, he finds that they are barbarians. They cannot read and they know nothing of past human achievements. A part of their belief-system is that the world was created only one thousand years before. They venerate Brian at first but then distrust him and want to hear him pray. He demonstrates his kind of prayer—he invites them into the Hall of Music and plays the Carr piano piece, which he suddenly finds he is able to interpret. He is elated but the barbarians are scared away by the noise. They paddle off in their canoe with a small statue they've stolen from the Museum. Brian angrily pursues them but loses his own canoe's paddle and his strength, and finds himself drifting out to his death in the lonely ocean. Instead of cursing the young people, he hollers after them, "Go in peace!"

One of my long-time favorite stories is in this November *Galaxy*. It's "Big Ancestor" by F. L. Wallace, with fine illustrations by Emsh (who gets better with each issue). The novelette is about the search for a common ancestor by scientists Emmer, Halden, Meredith and Kelburn, who each represent a species of humanity, each more advanced than the last, Kelburn being the highest type. Halden, of our species, is only the second most developed in mental powers, visual range and so on. Yet they know they all have a common ancestor to account for humanity being found on many different worlds. Their ship is piloted by a totally alien being, Taphetta the Ribboneer, who resembles a bow on a Christmas package, a rather larger than average bow. He is a representative of one of the oldest galactic civilizations.

Humans have an advantage because of their enormous numbers. Taphetta pales to think of how many there are, and he too wonders how they originated and spread so far. The explorers soon find the abandoned cities and artifacts of a great ancient race—and then they learn the grim truth.

The year 1954 ends with another Emsh Santa (in a rocket-powered sleigh) on the December cover, and a clever novelette by Sheckley. This was one of his best years, so it is only fitting to recall "Skulking Permit" to mind. The villagers of New Delaware, a very outlying planet, hear of a galactic war, but it simply never reaches them. Then they hear from a new entity called Imperial Earth, which wants to know if they retain Earth customs and are loyal to Earth (or else). The villagers say so and try to reinstate Earth customs for the benefit of a visiting Imperial official. They even build a jail (which they've never needed) and license Tom Fisher, a kindly villager, to be a criminal. He can force himself to steal but not to kill. This latter fact horrifies the Imperial Inspector, who orders his ship off the planet lest New Delaware's pacifism spread. The planet then is left in peace.

For some reason, both the December, 1954 and the January, 1955 issues have the "Galaxy" on the spine printed in red instead of the usual black. This was discontinued after those two months.

The first issue of 1955 had stories by old favorites Frederik Pohl, Theodore Sturgeon and Robert Sheckley. The cover was by Emsh and showed a futuristic cosmetics machine readying a young woman for a date. The Pohl story was called "The Tunnel Under the World." I have always been fascinated by this account of a town held as a captive audience. Tylerton was smashed by the explosion of a large chemical plant on its outskirts. The residents who still had intact brains, and therefore minds and personalities, found themselves alive again on the day of June 15th, a day which is repeated over and over for them because in actuality they never lived to June 16th. During this day they are treated to all kinds of advertisements and techniques, ranging from the subtle to the obnoxious, and their reactions are observed by the people who have created the miniature Tylerton in which the former residents continue their existences in tiny android bodies. It is a real shock when Guy Burckhardt, the primary character, discovers the fact of his minute size.

James Blish decided to target the January issue for special attention in *The Issue at Hand*, and he took on the Pohl story first:

"The Tunnel Under the World" by Frederik Pohl continues the writer's feud with advertising into an improbable but circumstantially-told mechanical nightmare. Competent though the story is, it is spoiled for me by the excesses Pohl commits in giving samples of the ads used by the villains. The examples offered by Pohl and Kornbluth, both together and separately, in other stories have been revolting enough but remained funny because of their visible relationship to what is being committed today. "Cheap freezers ruin your food. You'll get sick and throw up. You'll get sick and die. . . . Do you want to eat rotten, stinking food? Or do you want to wise up and buy a Feckle, Feckle, Feckle—" is no longer satire, however. It is the naked hatred of the author, screamed out at the top of his voice.

On the other hand, Kingsley Amis (in *New Maps of Hell*) gives the story a good deal of respect and quotes the whole fearsome Feckle Freezers ad to illustrate the point of how such ad techniques invade our mental privacy. Amis also sees "Tunnel" as an allegory of the "thraldom of economic man." This story has been anthologized many times.

"When You're Smiling," the Sturgeon novelette, involves the attempt of a drunken sadistic slob to con a patsy friend named Henry, who is always foolishly grinning, into helping murder his wife. The sadist has some quite ingenious schemes, but they do him no good because Henry, who turns out to be a sensitive telepath, doses him instead with dicoumarin, a subtle capillary poison. Henry explains to his dying victim that the reason he was smiling all the time was the irritating mental noise that sadistic minds cause all telepaths to suffer. It was not a foolish grin at all, but a grimace of constant mental pain. In *The Issue at Hand*, Blish says of this story:

> "When You're Smiling" is a hate-piece, too, but it is never out of the author's control for so long as three words. Ted's portrait of a man who enjoys causing pain is that of a man who thoroughly deserves the author's loathing. But by taking the pains to tell the story from that man's point of view, and to convey some of the man's enthusiasm for himself and his researches, Ted has made sure that his evil character does not emerge as an unbelievable caricature.

In reference to the short story by Robert Sheckley, Blish has this to say:

> "Squirrel Cage" by Robert Sheckley is another of the interminable AAA Ace series, this time so awful as to read like a cruel burlesque of all the others. Why should a man who wants his farm decontaminated deliberately withhold crucial information about the nature of the infestation from the firm he's hired to do the exterminating? Why does this exact thing happen in all the AAA Ace stories? Why don't the partners of AAA Ace wise up?

Finally, I want to quote Blish on the novelette "Perfect Control":

> "Perfect Control" by Richard Stockham is almost as bad [as the Sheckley story]. If there is anyone in the room who believed in the "great inventions" made by the characters in this yarn, he should stay away from Fred Pohl's commercials, or he will wind up owning all the Feckle Freezers in existence.

The Emsh cover for February is one of his most memorable. It depicts a human tootling away on a clarinet in the company of five very strange alien musicians who have equally odd instruments. The scene is a precursor of the bar episode in *Star Wars* and the music is probably just as bizarre.

James E. Gunn, a prolific sf writer and anthologist, has a very effective short story in this issue. The first U.S. spaceman, Reverdy L. McMillen III, is in orbit around the Earth, perpendicular to the Equator. He falls victim to malfunctioning equipment and is stuck in his orbit, in "the cave of night"—which is the title of the story. He dies bravely just before a rescue ship can reach him. His example stimulates Earthmen to conquer space and reach the planets, but was it all as it seemed?

The *Galaxy* for March has an interesting short story by Frederik Pohl, "The Candle Lighter." An Earthman, Jaffa Doane, is appointed chief administrator of the Martian Colony. This is a remarkable appointment because Doane is the leader of the Equality League, which believes that the Martians are being exploited and kept down by the policies of Earth, and that these policies must be reversed. However, Doane soon learns the real Martian conditions and the very remarkable Martian biology and psychology. Doane had believed it was wrong for an Earthman to serve as the executioner for Martians, for instance, but Martian biology dictates that the only way a Martian *can* die is by being physically destroyed, and only an alien Earthman or a Martian of the Healer class can do this for the sick and old. In addition, the Healers suffer from the mental shock of killing their own kind, necessary though it is, and they seldom last longer than a few years. In short, Doane realizes that the very basic differences he discovers on Mars make his earlier ideological views seem very simplistic.

One of the novelettes in this issue is particularly powerful. It is called simply "Who?" and is by Theodore Sturgeon. A cadet space pilot is on l. first extended Mission, a Long Haul. He is by himself except for another cadet that he has been informed is on the other side of a heavy metal bulkhead. The two are kept separated but can be in voice communication. Finally, boredom gets to the cadet and he contacts the person on the other side of the bulkhead. He is shocked to find himself addressing a scared and sad, but hero-worshipping fifteen-year-old boy.

The cadet is at first incredulous, then enraged. He thinks the youngster is a child prodigy out to usurp his position, and he thinks of getting at him

Chamber Music Society of Deneb. Illustrator: Emsh.

and killing him. Instead, he ignores him cruelly for a long time. But finally he decides to be friendlier, and starts talking to the kid. Soon they become good friends and the cadet is eager to meet him once they get back to the base. There the cadet gets a real surprise when he learns who his shipmate is.

"Hostile Reception on Aldebaran IV" is the Emsh cover for April—intrepid spacemen are blazing away near their badly damaged rocket. William Tenn (Philip Klass, a professor at Pennsylvania State College these days) wrote a paradoxical novelette, "The Servant Problem." In this story, there is a future totalitarian society which is "served" (ruled) by a man named Garomma, the Servant of All, the World's Drudge, the Slavey of Civilization. He controls all the power of the state in a conditioned and mind-controlled society. But, it turns out, Garomma is actually under the spell of Moddo, the Servant of Education, who is a sort of grey eminence and administrative genius who once took Garomma, then a peasant lad, under his wing. Moddo, however, is under the psychological control of Loob, a Healer of minds and a minor official—and Loob has been conditioned by Sidothi, a mere lab technician. Sidothi knows that he can now relish supreme power, yet when he sees Garomma appear in public Sidothi goes into ecstatic paroxysms, as he has been conditioned to do!

There is another AAA Ace episode in this issue and it is as silly as the others (though amusing). Damon Knight (in *In Search of Wonder*) says of Sheckley:

> Sheckley's heroes weigh in at an I.Q. of about ninety, just sufficient to get aboard their shiny machines, but not enough to push all the right levers. . . In "Milk Run," AAA Ace's Arnold and Gregor ship a load of extraterrestrial animals without bothering to find out anything about them; in "The Lifeboat Mutiny," they trustingly buy an alien-built lifeboat, again without asking questions, although this same gaffe has got Sheckleymen in dire peril before.

The alien lifeboat treats Arnold and Gregor as members of the race that built it and gives them the wrong food, climatic conditions, etc., and so they have to escape from it rather than use it as a merchant ship.

The lead-off novelette for May was an odd brooding tale called "The Dreaming Wall." A civilian scientist and a military officer are sent to far distant Fallon's planet. They are members of an exploration team determined to find out why a colleague who preceded them had killed himself there. They find the camp in the vicinity of an old and circular wall which turns out to have rather strange properties. The explorers' sleep is terribly disturbed by bad and alien dreams. Finally they realize the dreams have something to do with the wall and the major blasts it down, killing an amoeba-like entity spread out within it. This being was a sort of recorder of racial memory and was also telepathic; it had been sending them past memories which they took for nightmares. Now they know why their predecessor had killed himself—he had decided that he'd been going insane because of the thought-projections from the "dreaming wall." The story idea isn't that fantastic, but the curiously heavy mood of this, so different from *Galaxy*'s then prevalent bright satire, made it effective. The tale is by a Gerald Pearce, another pseudonym possibly?

Frederik Pohl has a straight adventure story in this one, "The Middle of Nowhere." The men in the Mars colonies are being subjected to guerrilla attacks by the unseen native Martians. Sudden streams of mysterious flame appear out of nowhere and blow up Earth vehicles and burn up settlers. Some of the colonists organize an expedition to root out the Martians. They are attacked, but most of them survive, and they take some Martian natives prisoner. To their disappointment, they find that their prisoners are only the Mars equivalent of monkeys. The *real* Martians still lurk!

June began *Preferred Risk*, by Edson McCann, a four-part (!) serial, winner of the great *Galaxy* novel contest and recipient of the $6,500 prize. Remember the prize contest? What had happened was that Gold had received nothing worthy of the prize—probably just more of the alien life force eaters in the Andes or the mutant babies, etc. He then commissioned Frederik Pohl and Lester del Rey to quickly come up with a novel. The result was *Preferred Risk*.

This time it isn't the ad men or the realtors and lawyers that are running the world. Now it's a massive insurance company that has everybody covered for everything. The hitch is that there are social strata. If you are a Plan B person you get better treatment and care than a Plan C, and so on. Thomas Wills, Claim Adjuster, is an up and coming Company person, but he becomes involved with antiestablishment revolutionary types in Naples, now a war-wracked city-state. The villain of the novel is Underwriter Defoe, *de facto* company head. People who don't like the Company's rule get killed or literally put in the cooler: The Clinics, suspended animation vaults normally used for preserving fatally ill people until a cure is found. In the midst of schemes and plots, someone in the underground explodes a cobalt bomb and everyone has to get into the shielded life suspension vaults to escape the worldwide fallout.

Wills and Zorchi, a Neapolitan comrade, use the confusion of the massive movement into the vaults to seize control of the Company's headquarters from Defoe and his cronies. All the villains are put in the cooler, too, and only Wills and his girlfriend, Rena dell'Angela, will be left awake in the vaults. They will take care of everything until the suspended people wake up to a world that will be free of radiation and perhaps also ready for a saner, safer and more democratic society.

In his critical book *In Search of Wonder* Damon Knight says of this novel:

> There is a tendency for the heroes of long *Galaxy* stories to be shmoes; I do not know why, although I have contributed to the trend myself; I suspect the editor likes them and sends out emanations to that effect . . .
>
> And for whatever reason, the hero of *Preferred Risk*, a claims adjuster named Tom Wills, is a shmo to end all shmoes.
>
> "I know for a fact," Gogarty said bitterly, "that Zorchi knew we found out he was going to dive in front of that express tonight. . ."
>
> I interrupted, "Mr. Gogarty are you trying to tell me this man *deliberately* maims himself for the accident insurance?" Gogarty nodded sourly. "Good heavens," I cried, "that's disloyal!"
>
> This will give you some idea. The whole front half of the book is like that: evidence parades across the middle ground in a steady stream that the Company is run by a bunch of corrupt no-goods and tyrants . . . and Wills stomps around through it all, with a regulation smile on his face, uttering platitudes . . . he is totally unimportant to the plot.

There is another Pohl story in the July *Galaxy*, a novelette called "The Mapmakers." A meteorite has struck the *Starship Terra II* and killed Recorder Mate Spohn, the Celestial Atlas, a crewman trained in the special mental techniques needed to guide the ship in hyperspace, or rather, through hyperspace from point to known point. Without the Atlas the ship is lost and can only jump blindly and possibly end up even further thousands of light years away. However, one of the ship's officers, Lt. Groden, had been blinded in the accident. It turns out that he can now see in hyperspace, though not in normal space. With his help, the starship can return to Earth.

The other novelette for July was "Property of Venus" by the often whimsical fantasist L. Sprague de Camp, a seasoned veteran of the

Forties. De Camp was not a likely author to turn up in the pages of *Galaxy* (although, back in 1939 he had collaborated with H. L. Gold on "None But Lucifer" for the now-defunct magazine *Unknown*). De Camp's story was of the humorous and sinister effects of planting forbidden Venerian plants on Earth. There are singing shrubs and bulldog bushes, and the tree of Eden with excellent fruit which makes everyone grateful to it, which fact causes near-disaster.

The August *Galaxy* featured a new William Tenn novelette, "The Flat-Eyed Monster." Clyde Manship, an assistant professor, is suddenly matter-transported to a planet far from our solar system. He is being observed by aliens who resemble suitcases and have tentacles with eyes on the ends. They are researchers and scientists who regard Manship with even more loathing than he regards them. When he tries to make a break for a spacecraft to get him home again, an alien tries to shoot him. Manship gives the alien a fearful glance, and the unlucky recipient of this Look dissolves! Manship makes another break and again uses the Look, which seems to be powered by his fear. But he becomes overconfident. When one of the heroes of the tentacled folk approaches him, Manship is no longer frightened, and this makes a difference.

August's other long piece is by Daniel F. Galouye, now deceased, a New Orleans newspaperman and a test pilot during World War II. His "Country Estate" concerns a hardboiled Earth exploration crew who come across a group of beautiful, peaceable "savages" whose chief delight appears to be in doing extremely intricate dances in the firelight. Several of them, including a lovely young woman called Lola, are tested, hypnotized and interrogated, but the explorers can't get any clue as to why the natives behave as they do. Norton, the narrator, starts to sympathize with the "savages" and arouses the ire of the mission commander, Sharp. It soon becomes obvious that the natives are very highly evolved. They have advanced beyond eating, and Sharp's blaster has no effect upon them. They can also teleport themselves to other worlds. They are, as Lola said, tens of millions of years ahead of us on the evolutionary scale. However, they like Norton and he gets to go with them when they leave —in the analogy used in the story, like a dog allowed to wander on a country estate. This story would take any Terran chauvinist down a peg or two.

The August *Galaxy* carried an ad for a fine bargain offer. The reader could send in $3.50 for all ten issues of the late lamented *Beyond* fantasy magazine. There was a faintly regretful tone to the advertisement.

The interior art in the August issue was a little better than in previous 1955 issues, especially the Docktor illustrations to the Galouye story. The magazine covers for this year, with the exception of one or two, were not very interesting—in short, humdrum. This was a pity, since there certainly was no shortage of good sf artists and illustrators at the time. The August issue also lacked the Conklin book review column.

Groff Conklin was back in September, and his book review section covers one of editor Gold's books, *The Old Die Rich and Other Science Fiction Stories*. Conklin writes:

> Most of the tales . . . have that sensitive combination of imaginations that I like to call *science fantasy*—almost supernatural development combined with vividly alive and plausible motivation and shrewd scientific and societal extrapolation. . . . a genuinely distinguished collection.

Damon Knight does not totally agree with Mr. Conklin. In the book *In Search of Wonder*, Knight says that five of the stories in this collection are "good to passable" and six are "totally regrettable potboilers." One of the stories, not from *Galaxy*, is "Trouble With Water," and it *is* on Knight's list of all-time favorites. As for the other razor-sharp critic, James Blish, he muttered somewhere about *Galaxy*'s book reviewer being an in-law of Gold. (This is nearly correct. Floyd C. Gale, who succeeded Conklin, was Gold's brother with a slightly changed surname.) Anyway, this book is the only collection of Gold's stories ever to appear.

The issue has a rather grim novelette by Richard Matheson (who with Ray Bradbury was noted for writing sf without much s). It's called "One for the Books," and is about an old timer named Fred who suddenly knows French and after that Italian and eventually all sorts of information. In fact, the sum total of knowledge at a local university. He amazes the professors, but his glory is brief. A flickering blue light catches him on the dark campus, and he is later found wandering without any memory. Aliens had only been using his mind for a handy local reservoir. When he had accumulated enough facts for them, they "squeezed" his mind dry. This story has far too long a buildup, I think, and it's an example of the "one punch" story that critic James Blish got so very tired of.

Sheckley is back again, this time with a short story entitled "Hunting Problem." An aerial alien ovoid by the name of Drog is in a kind of ET Boy Scout Troop. To make first class, he has to get the pelt of a Mirash (a human). Drog comes across some Terran gold and diamond miners-explorers and tries various ruses on them (including a simulated girl-in-distress call) with no success. At last he tricks one of them and gets his pelt. The pelt turns out to be a spacesuit and the Earthman escapes unharmed, though shaken. Another one-puncher! This issue must have caused Blish to mutter *and* gnash his teeth!

October was memorable because that was when *Galaxy*'s original book reviewer, Groff Conklin, bade farewell:

> And so, friends, after five years of reviewing for *Galaxy*, I say "Au revoir." I'm off for a long trip to the West Coast and then down to the Virgin Islands . . . . It's been a fine five years, but now I turn the column over to Floyd C. Gale; he did some s-f writing years back and a great deal of reading since about 1929 . . . You'll like him. I do.

Meanwhile, out in the scientific world, changes were also going on. Willy Ley's October feature tells about the new Walt Disney television film *Man in Space*. This was a largely animated explanation of the state of American rocketry. I remember it as being somewhat elementary, but effective. Willy Ley describes his contribution to it and also the help given by other experts, such as Dr. Heinz Haber and the late Dr. Wernher von Braun, one of the designers of the German V-1 and V-2 weapons.

Sheckley is back again! He has a splendid novella, "A Ticket to Tranai." Young, romantically inclined Marvin Goodman longs for the excitement of the far reaches of the galaxy. He hears of an extremely remote planet called Tranai, allegedly a joyous creative utopia. When he somehow manages to get there, he finds himself on a very odd world indeed.

Tranai has no crime or taxes, Goodman is told, and the women are always beautiful. Goodman decides to stay and help design robots. Tranaians don't want super-efficient robots. They want grotesquely malfunctioning ones they can easily and satisfyingly destroy. Goodman proves good at designing these. Soon he is doing well, meets a lovely Tranaian woman, and weds her. All is idyllic for them, though he does avoid one custom of Tranai: he does not keep his wife, Janna, in a stasis field most of the time as other Tranaian husbands do—they bring their wives out only when a party or dinner date is at hand. Then the fun starts as Goodman finds out more about Tranai.

Cordwainer Smith (a pseudonym of Paul Linebarger, an old China hand), makes his first appearance in *Galaxy* in the October issue. His novelette "The Game of Rat and Dragon" takes place in his future universe of the Instrumentality, but that society is not really mentioned much in this piece. Instead, we are shown how interstellar passengers are protected from a nebulous insanity-producing monster that can move a million miles in just two milliseconds. Human and cat telepaths are used to protect the interstellar craft by setting off power flares near the ships. These flares have the effect of dissolving the "dragons." Humans see the evil things as dragons. Cats see them as large rats. Much of the interest in this story is generated by the interplay between the feline and human minds. Linebarger pursues this cat/human theme in later stories. His appearance here shows him at his best when he is telling a fast-moving story without putting it in a kind of gilded frame, as he did in much of his later work, good though it still is.

The William Tenn short in this issue is the amusing "The Discovery of Morniel Mathaway." Glescu, a future art historian, comes back to mid-Twentieth Century America to meet Mathaway, the famous painter that he's written a book about. He soon discovers that Mathaway is in actuality a hack, and his paintings do not at all look like the works of genius revealed in the 25th Century edition of his works. Mathaway then steals the historian's time machine and heads for the future, thus stranding Glescu in our time, with paradoxical results.

November was the last issue dated 1955. Gold had decided to have his magazine come out earlier, so the issue to go on sale November 22nd would be dated January, 1956. The magazine would continue without a break despite the advancement of January. The Emsh cover for November was satisfyingly surreal and psionic. It illustrates "The Ties of Earth" by James H. Schmitz, a two-part serial. This tortuous short novel is about warfare between two groups of human telepaths, the Old Mind and the nascent New Mind. They are, as the phrase goes, trying to "bum each other out."

Alan Commager, the main character, is being attacked throughout the novel by the people of the Old Mind. In the end he pretends to give in to them, while through his stronger mental powers he reaches the subconscious of the Old Minders so they will help his people without knowing it. What the New Mind plans is a gigantic all-unified Earth Mind. This is remarkable, for the New Mind was earlier derided for being overly individualistic, but perhaps that was one of their tricks on those of us who are not any kind of telepath, to set us up for a reality that is far different from what we expect. I liked Schmitz's "The Witches of Karres" (which appeared in *Astounding*) better. It too had a psionic theme, but it also had a sense of humor which "The Ties of Earth" definitely lacks.

Philip K. Dick reappears with "Autofac." This novelette deals with a future after a Big War where the surviving humans are well taken care of by giant robot factories which produce all they need. The people weary of the machine civilization and want to strike out on their own, so they get the huge robot plants to make war on each other. This stimulates the factories to evolve, to shoot out tiny embryonic factories throughout the world and perhaps into outer space as well!

6. GOLD'S SILVER AGE: PART ONE, 1956–1957

A SEGMENT OF *GALAXY*'S HISTORY I HAVE OMIT-
ted so far is the publication of the Galaxy
Science Fiction Novels. The original series
consisted of 31 novels in digest magazine format. Later on the novels
continued in paperback format. In 1959-1961 Beacon Books brought out
eleven issues with suggestive titles and covers. These novels include old
reprinted classics such as Jack Williamson's *Legion of Space* (from the
old Tremaine *Astounding*), some original novels such as *Empire* by Clifford D. Simak, and, in the Beacon series, a sexual fantasy by Philip José
Farmer, called simply *Flesh* (in 1960).

The series in magazine format was more interesting to me. I liked the
stories and the bright covers, and the size did not particularly inconve-
nience me. Some of the titles I enjoyed reading were *Odd John*, by Olaf
Stapledon, *City at World's End*, by Edmond Hamilton, and *The House of
Many Worlds*, by Sam Merwin, Jr. The latter was not on the same lofty

Season's Greetings To Our Readers. Illustrator: Emsh.

plane as the Stapledon, but it did provide intrigue and diversion, plus a particularly hateful villain who gets his.

Gold says of this initial series (in the October, 1975 *Galaxy* article):

> As for the *Galaxy* sf novel reprints—they weren't handled right as packages, being more like numbered magazines than paperbacks. I got that go-ahead just as the paperback market broke, but it was too late.

In the last years of the decade *Galaxy* was also on the radio. An NBC ad in the June, 1956 issue announced that *X-1* [pronounced "X Minus One"] was on the air every Tuesday night. This show dramatized *Galaxy* stories (often short stories by Sheckley), and was prefaced by a countdown and blast-off. Roughly, it was a good radio equivalent of TV's *Twilight Zone.*

Emsh has his Santa Claus on the cover of the January, 1956 issue. A bewildered Mr. Claus is puzzling over star charts and interstellar navigation. Behind him are immense computer banks holding the names of those who have been either bad or good. The physician/writer Alan Nourse has a novelette, "Brightside Crossing," about the perils of crossing Mercury at perihelion, with the sun always beating down and the temperature at 770 degrees Fahrenheit. A survivor of one ill-fated mission is talking to a confident member of a new one just about to go out. The survivor went through a terrible time but in the end he wants to volunteer for the new attempt. This story hasn't worn too badly over the years, and the names of two explorers sound rather familiar: There is a Carpenter and an Armstrong!

In a fine editorial in the February issue, Gold strikes back at some of the academic critics of sf:

> After writing and editing science fiction for a couple of decades, I really ought to take a moment to see if it's Literature. The reason is that in a few months, some imposing name is going to be induced to make an equally imposing ass of himself on just that question—attacking science fiction as non-literature has joined the robin and the crocus as a sign of spring. . . .
>
> The trouble is that I have no idea of who will draw the assignment this year. If I knew, I'd be able to map out my counter-strategy in advance, for the campaign on the other side is inevitably shifty, being unhampered by knowledge or calm judgment. . . .
>
> Well, no matter who gets the short straw this year and whatever the weapons to be used, we know in advance the outcome—science fiction will be declared a grimy aggressor into the field of Literature.

A Hot Welcome on Mercury. Illustrator: Emsh.

Then why bother to defend ourselves? I'm past that stage and I hope
you are, too—a viable art form can't be destroyed by criticism any more
than a moribund one can be revived by praise . . .

Frederik Pohl begins a three-part serial in the March *Galaxy*. It is *Slave
Ship*, and Emsh did the March cover for it. He also did the interior
illustrations for the novel, and incorporated photos into his line drawings,
a technique I rather liked but which was not used again.

The Pohl novel deals with a future in which the West is aligned against
an Asian enemy, the Caodai militant religionists, who originated in Indo-
China and whose leader is Nguyen Yat Hugo, an old man who vaguely
resembles Ho Chi Minh. The Caodais have overrun Asia, Oceania and
Africa. The protagonist is Lt. j.g. Logan Moeller, U.N. Naval Reserve;
he is sent to Project Mako, which involves learning to talk with animals in
their own languages. The idea is that the animals could be useful in future
guerrilla operations on Madagascar, where the Caodais are reported to be
operating a sinister weapon, the Glotch. This is a sudden attack of burning that hits telepaths, often fatally. Moeller himself is almost killed by it.

The cold war continues to heat up, and so the big sub *Monmouth* is
ordered to take Moeller and some other agents to Madagascar to harass
the enemy and find out the secret of the Glotch. But the mission is
betrayed and Moeller is captured and made to talk by truth serum. Then
he and his comrades, one of them a nice Russian who is a sort of proto-
typical Ensign Chekov, are interviewed by Hugo himself. It turns out that
the war is worsening (with satellite bombs and so on) because the Glotch
is attacking both sides, and each side feels the other is responsible. The
truth is very different.

L. Sprague de Camp returned in the March issue with "A Gun for
Dinosaur." The novelette's thesis is that it *is* feasible to travel to the past
and hunt and do other relatively transient things to the environment
without changing our present at all. This is contra Tenn and Bradbury,
whose stories of this type show enormous and often unpleasant changes
resulting from even the destruction of some ancient arthropod or insect,
a trilobite or a butterfly. Not so with de Camp—his hardy people lead
safaris into the age of large and aggressive dinosaurs. However, one trip is
spoiled by the ill behavior of a rich playboy, Courtney James, whose
random and hasty shooting jeopardizes everyone. I enjoyed this story.
It was fast-paced and I felt I could almost sniff the spring-like air of the
Cretaceous.

A short called "Flat Tiger" by Gordon R. Dickson also appeared in March. This one is a satirical little fable about Earth's initial contact with the Galactic Confraternity of Races. The highly civilized aliens want us to join, but a sacrifice is demanded. The President and the other major world leaders get together to see if they can accede to the request of the alien emissary (Captain Bligh by name!): The people of Earth must all agree with the principles of the Confraternity—and must also undergo a simple process which will turn them into eaters of energy. No more steak? No more wine? Earth objects!

The writers who had emerged after the war were now showing signs of burning out. At least, they needed a breather. There were new writers appearing in *Galaxy*—Gordon Dickson, Philip K. Dick—but these were still a ways from producing their greatest works. For reasons of this sort, *Galaxy* began to slip from its eminent position. Alexei and Cory Panshin, in their February, 1973 *Fantastic Stories* article, think that Gold had simply dwelt too long on social satire at the expense of the imagination and the sense of wonder:

> Through the Fifties, satire—realistic and didactic stuff by its nature—
> was a minor industry in sf. In *Galaxy*, it was a major industry, with
> Frederik Pohl the leading manufacturer. That *Galaxy* continued to con-
> centrate on satire and contemporary realistic stuff in the middle Fifties
> when the other magazines were tempering their didacticism with at least
> a minimum of aesthesis may explain why *Galaxy* gradually lost the
> power and importance that it had had . . .

True, there was to be continual satire and jabs at various socially obnoxious groups and customs. Still, I found plenty of sense of wonder in the *Galaxy* of the later Fifties, plenty of the sort of thing that grabs your collar and makes you say, "I'm *here* again! (wandering in deep space)."

In the April *Galaxy*, the story "Swenson, Dispatcher," by R. DeWitt Miller, is not really a deep-space adventure. It could have been set on Earth and involved a trucking company instead of the offices of a space-ship line in the Twenty-Second Century. Acme Interplanetary Express is running out of credit and some of its ships have been impounded in order to pay debts. A crew on one ship is about to mutiny when in comes Swenson, the legendary dispatcher. He saves the little firm from the clutches of some sinister bigger companies by sending the Acme ships where they will do the most good. He drinks beer, bends the rules here and there, tries a shrewd bribe or two, outwits the government officials and the bigshots of the competing companies, and lo and behold, Acme is soon solvent and clicking cheerfully along, thanks to the brilliant but eccentric dispatcher.

The story is amusing and the reader keeps wondering how Acme's irons will all be pulled out of the fire, but it really is not a story that absolutely needs to be told in sf terms.

In the May issue *Slave Ship* concludes. The cover is one which many might think typical of the *Galaxy* of that period. Tocchet, the artist, depicts a woman operating some sort of future antigravity vehicle—she's arguing with a policeman who has pulled her over with a similar vehicle. In short, today's problems and little headaches in futuristic guise; and to a great extent and by design this was true of *Galaxy*. But not entirely true. In this issue, Wyman Guin (of "Beyond Bedlam" fame) reappears with a novelette called "Volpla."

A wealthy Californian, somewhat of an eccentric, decides to play a joke on mankind by producing a new race, the volplas. Created by mutation and the use of a "metabolic accelerator," they are winged and intelligent and can speak English. They are charming little individuals. The Californian wishes to plant them in the wild and have them tell the people who discover them that they came from the stars. This was to have been a grand joke, but of course it backfired. The little creatures prove to be very intelligent indeed. They commandeer a probe rocket bound for Venus and take off in it, thus turning the tables on their creator with no little irony.

Venus was a lot easier to write about before it was known how impossibly hot the place is. Far too hot for winged volplas or for anybody else except perhaps for life based on other basic structural principles than ours—the Abyormenites of Hal Clement's *Cycle of Fire* come to mind. Mars is a different matter. Mars stories can still "work."

Evelyn E. Smith, a writer not much active since the end of the Fifties, appeared constantly in Gold's *Galaxy*. She was not much beloved by James Blish, who felt her stories were not carefully enough thought out. Her novelette in the June issue is "The Venus Trap," a reference to the plant, not the planet.

The Earth has just colonized Elysium, a far distant planet, and found it excellent, although the plants have bluish and not greenish foliage. The intelligent life on Elysium consists of large talking trees. James Haut, a settler, has built his house close by one of the big trees, a female whom he names Magnolia. The tree has a definite personality and regards James' wife, Phyllis, as an unworthy match for him. Phyllis is easily upset and also pregnant, yet more complications! Soon she and Magnolia are jealous of each other, as ridiculous as that sounds. The situation is resolved when a little male shrub from Earth arrives to be a future consort for Magnolia and his green shrubbery begins changing to blue. It's funny sf isn't more popular, since stories like this are on the same intellectual plane as *Gilligan's Island*. Undoubtedly, Evelyn Smith wrote better than this. Perhaps the use of the name Magnolia rubbed me wrong. The only Magnolia I ever envision is Magnolia Ravenel, *née* Hawkes, of *Showboat*.

The July issue was far more auspicious. Virgil Finlay, the very superior sf artist, appears as the interior illustrator for the Theodore Sturgeon novelette "The Skills of Xanadu." Finlay did illustrations for at least ten sf magazines and had even done covers for the great old fantasy magazine *Weird Tales* in the Thirties. His style was painstaking and unmistakable for that of any other artist. Gold did well to get him.

Sturgeon must have gotten some message from "The Ties of Earth," because his novelette is about a shared world consciousness, not omnipresent but something that can be produced by concentration and a special aura-casting garment. Each person on the planet Xanadu can draw upon the skills of others. Bril from the Kit Carson system has been sent to underpopulated Xanadu to see how easy it will be to conquer and be made a dependency. In the end, the aura-garments are introduced on Kit Carson and the peaceful and liberating world-mind comes into existence there also. The spirit of Xanadu prevails.

I'm not personally so sure about all this Sturgeonite or Olaf Stapledonian shared consciousness. In the main, I don't think a person would benefit so greatly. Most minds seem to be most ordinary and humdrum. Sharing consciousness with them would be worse than current television programming, or perhaps it would be the *same* as current television programming.

There is a fine James Blish short story in the July issue. Blish appeared in *Galaxy* now and then just to show the other sf writers how it should be done. His "Writing of the Rat" is a quite serious tale of the encounter of the human race with six-foot-tall rats who are twice as intelligent as humans and far more civilized. One rat scout is tortured to death by a sadistic colonel of intelligence. Then an emissary of the rats appears on Earth to explain what his race is really up to.

September Morn, 1999 A.D. Illustrator: Virgil Finlay.

The August, 1956 *Galaxy* has an all-star batting order: William Tenn, Robert Sheckley, Theodore Sturgeon, Clifford D. Simak, Damon Knight *and* James Blish (both sharp-eyed sf critics—quite a haul!). Tenn's work is a novelette called "Time in Advance," set in a still recognizable future. The law permits felons to do prison time first, then allows them to commit their chosen crimes—murder, rape, etc. People who choose murder have to serve seven years on hellish worlds readying them for human colonization. This story starts with two such "pre-criminals" returning (rather unusual) in good health from their pre-murder stints. The obvious actions are changed by some shocking discoveries.

"Honorable Opponent" by Clifford D. Simak is an amusing tale about the big war Earth is waging with another civilization, the mysterious "Fivers." Whole Earth fleets disappear and Earth is feeling powerless and frustrated. Then a general learns that the aliens' idea of war is very different from ours.

The James Blish story, "Genius Heap," is about an artists' colony on Callisto, one of Jupiter's moons. The artists get on each other's nerves. They then discover that they are part of an experiment to see if Earth can actually live without artistic geniuses. The artists revolt and plan to return to Earth where their creativity *is* needed.

"Seeing-Eye Dog" is an interesting short story by Daniel F. Galouye in the September issue. It tells of a future advance in aid to the blind: mental telepathy allows humans to see through the eyes of their specially trained dogs. Curt Markson is slowly achieving rapport with Brutus, a 200 pound beast. The dog keeps becoming agitated and rather dangerous to both Curt and his friend Alex. Curt suspects something is fishy when he discovers the dog had been ordered in *his* name, rather than in the name of Alex, who had actually gotten Brutus from the special kennels. After Curt comes across a gardener's rake with sharpened tines he realizes he is being set up. Rather than allow himself to be murdered, he gets Brutus to trust him again (although surreptitiously so Alex will not suspect), and this turns the tables.

The September Willy Ley article was about Project Vanguard and the upcoming International Geophysical Year, in which scientists of all nations would join together to gain more knowledge of the Earth and its outer atmosphere. Ley discusses the plans for orbiting satellites shot up into space by rockets firing in stages. The sf world was well aware of the non-fictional plans for space exploration.

Alfred Bester, who had given *Galaxy* the superb *Demolished Man*, now returned. The October issue featured the first installment (of four) of the innovative and legendary work *The Stars My Destination*. Teleportation ("jaunting") is a major feature of Bester's future world. Most people can jaunte; some can do so for up to a thousand miles, as long as they know exactly where they are jaunting to. They would not survive simply jaunting into the unknown. Common spaceman Gully Foyle is marooned after a disaster to his ship, the *Vesta*. He sees another spacecraft approach and fires his distress flares. The other vessel, *Vorga*-T:1339, ignores him, in a memorable scene, and grandly moves on. This one unbelievable act of inhumanity causes Foyle to become a new man, a "Tiger," a powerful figure yearning for revenge.

Rescued by asteroid savages, Foyle makes his way back to civilization. At first he tries to destroy *Vorga*, but this does him no good. He is captured and intensively interrogated by the Earth's security chiefs and minions of Earth's corporate elite. They are determined to get hold of *Vesta*, which was carrying twenty million credits worth of platinum bullion to the Mars Bank. Far more important, *Vesta* was also carrying twenty pounds of pyrE, a substance which Earth hopes to use in its war with the outer planets of the Solar System.

Foyle is no help. He is placed in an underground cave prison so secure he cannot jaunte out of it. But the redoubtable Gully Foyle does find a way out, with Jisbella McQueen, a female convict. They help themselves to a spaceship and head straight back to the *Vesta*. Foyle gets away with the bullion and the pyrE, though Jisbella gets caught by Earth Security. Back on Earth, Foyle disguises himself as wealthy eccentric Geoffrey Fourmyle and enters polite society, determined to discover the truth about the Presteigns, the plutocratic family that owns *Vorga*-T:1339.

He uses connections to track down former crewmembers of the *Vorga* and finally finds out that the beautiful, blind Olivia Presteign of the Presteigns gave the order to pass him by. The *Vorga* had been carrying refugees from the Outer to the Inner Planets. Its crew had taken all the valuables from the refugees and pushed them all out the airlock. Busily pursuing this villainy, they did not need to take someone aboard while they were throwing their passengers to their deaths.

Foyle confronts Olivia (whom he has grown to love!), and they agree that they are revengeful monsters whom the world should not be saddled with. Foyle realizes that much of mankind's problems are due to the

The Stars My Destination. Illustrator: Emsh.

secret ruling circles of the oligopoly who have always had things their own way. He decides to change the world by changing the balance of power. PyrE is a very powerful thermonuclear explosive which can be triggered by psychokinetic thought alone. Foyle was able to set off a few minute pieces which caused great damage; the harm that can be done by twenty pounds of the stuff is mind-boggling. Foyle jauntes all around the world, tossing out vials of pyrE to waiting crowds while exhorting them to take some responsiblity and bring themselves up to their full capacity as he has. Then Foyle dares them to follow him, and he jauntes to distant *stars!*

There are some subplots I have not covered, but Bester is the kind of writer who can juggle flaming swords, as it were, and keep you on the edge of your seat, despite some complexity. Bester himself admitted that the basic plot for this novel was *The Count of Monte Cristo*. Others have referred to his novels as being related to the English Renaissance revenge tragedies (*The Duchess of Malfi*, etc.). Whatever its ancestry, Bester's creation stands on its own for inventiveness, vivid action, and of course, wit.

The October and November covers were by Emsh, who also did a brilliant job on the interior art for *The Stars My Destination*. Virgil Finlay did a fine cover for the December *Galaxy*. It shows a kindly robot giving a coin to a blind begging spaceman, doubtless of Earthly origin. A space helmet serves as his begging bowl.

Robert Sheckley is back in form in the December issue. His novelette "The Native Problem" deals with the plight of Edward Danton, one of Sheckley's usual social misfits who seeks grandeur off-Earth. He goes to Hedonia but that world is too sybaritic. He settles on New Tahiti, an unpeopled lush world which he has all to himself until a ship full of colonists lands. By this time he is eager to see other people from civilization and he makes haste to greet them. They turn out to be the Hutter People, a religious colony who greet Danton with mistrust and hostility. They are convinced he is one of the natives and wonder where all the others are. Things get complicated after that.

William Tenn has a short zinger in December called "Of All Possible Worlds," which has been often reprinted. A guided nuclear missile will explode in the Brazilian jungle in 1976, producing a blight which will destroy most of the food of the world. The people of 2089 have perfected a time machine which will go back, intercept the missile, and make it explode in the atmosphere. However, if it explodes in the air, an epidemic will result which will reduce man's reproductive capacity almost to the

Help for Mankind. Illustrator: Virgil Finlay.

vanishing point (somehow that doesn't sound like such a disaster today) and produce a future society which will create a time machine to intercept the missile and make it explode in the jungle. You see the difficulties.

In a recent anthology of *Galaxy* stories entitled *Galaxy: Thirty Years of Innovative Science Fiction*, some of Gold's authors reminisce about his *modus operandi*. For instance, Philip Klass (William Tenn) writes:

> The complex of buildings had been put up just north of Manhattan's Fourteenth Street by a big insurance company after World War II. You went into the street entrance that looked like all the other street entrances in the huge complex, you rode up in a bright, plastic-looking elevator, you walked out into a bright, plastic-looking corridor, and you came to a bright, plastic-looking door. All around you were apartment doors behind which people lived and cooked and slept, behind which they yelled at each other and murmured at television, but this one door was different. Behind the door was a cave, and in the cave Horace L. Gold lay hidden from the day while he went about his business of sending writers to the outermost edges of time and the universe. . . .
>
> You discussed a new idea with Horace in a corner of his entrance hallway or you argued a revision with him in the tiny kitchen area— because Horace couldn't take you out to lunch as other editors did. You debated Vaihinger's philosophy or Sapir's linguistics around Horace's dining-room table where you were playing fifteen-cent-limit poker . . . You worked out deadlines and word rates and similar business problems near the coffee table in his living room during an evening party . . . because Evelyn, Horace's wife, was determined that Horace would have a full social as well as a full professional life, agoraphobia or no agoraphobia.

Alfred Bester recalls (in the same book):

> Horace used to give dos at his apartment near New York's SoHo, and I went occasionally. He was always casually dressed: a biggish man, broad, balding, skin white, almost transparent from his years spent indoors. He would joke, laugh, express his strong opinions and criticisms. Some of the writers there were too much in awe of his personality and powerful buying position to dare disagree with him. Not me . . .

Thus, the business of *Galaxy* was carried on and the years slipped by. Now it was 1957, a year that was to be particularly significant and ominous for science fiction. *Galaxy* began it with another of the inimitable Emsh Santa Clauses on the January cover. This time the dear old four-armed saint is balancing human and ET children on his knees and hearing what they want for their various Christmases. Two arms are folded benevolently and the hand on his lower right arm is reaching for a lollipop. When did sf magazine covers lose their sense of humor? One wearies of posturing lunks in chain-mail skivvies and the dense-looking, somewhat plump damsels lying, usually, at their feet.

The January issue has the novelette "Butterfly 9" by Donald Keith, in his only appearance in *Galaxy* (if the name is not a pseudonym—they were always using those). An electronics firm in a parallel world needs someone to help them develop color television (!) and one Greet Snader kidnaps pleasant young Jeff Elliott from our U.S.A. into the other Earth. They go via a weird time-traveling device which inside looks like a railroad passenger car with a curiously flattened perspective as one looks down the aisles to the future and past terminals. Elliott eventually outwits Snader and agrees to work for the eager firm—but on his own terms.

The short story "All Jackson's Children," by Daniel F. Galouye, takes place on a distant planet where spacemen McIntosh and Drummond land in search of wrecked spacecraft to salvage. They find a wrecked Vegan robot carrier and a large group of activated robots who have been carrying on their mechanical life for years. The robots have also acquired religious faith through a battered Bible left in the wreck of their ship. They, however, worship "Jackson," a man whose picture was preserved in the old Bible. The robots have evolved a faith in Jackson the Supervisor. Unfortunately for the two spacemen, the robots can worship only one Supervisor. Will it be McIntosh or Drummond?

The reader who is unfamiliar with *Galaxy* will be startled to find some very familiar illustrations in the February issue. "The Bomb in the Bathtub," by Thomas N. Scortia, was illustrated by Don Martin, who later became renowned for his hilarious work for *Mad Magazine*, quite a different market. His *Galaxy* illustrations are just as zany as any of his later work. The story illustrated is a bit of wacky fluff about universe-destroying bombs that talk and a Saviour from "Messiahs, Incorporated —You Too Can Save a Universe."

The cover art for 1957 was not particularly distinguished, though there are a few exceptions. The February cover is not one of them. The issue does have a good novelette and novella. The novelette I particularly enjoyed was by Christopher Anvil. A pseudonym for Harry C. Crosby, Anvil is a name more usually associated with John Campbell's later *Astounding SF* magazine. The story is "Advance Agent," nicely illustrated by Virgil Finlay.

Dan Redman, an advance agent for the trading firm Galactic Enterprises, is sent to the far planet Porcys to investigate its society for a possible trade agreement. Porcys has a lot of edible seafood in its large ocean (its people live only on the one small continent). Galactic Enterprises wants to import the seafood to Earth by "subspace mataforming." But first they must make sure the Porcyns have "a proper mercantile attitude." Redman also has to discover how the Porcyns keep their population down, and why another world in their system is called "Vacation Planet" and what function it has in their society. Disguised as a Porcyn, he enters their chief city and soon finds astonishing answers to his questions. The sheer oddity of the Porcyn society made this enjoyable.

The novella in the February issue is "My Lady Greensleeves," by Frederik Pohl. The title refers to a prison uniform which has green sleeves. In the society that Pohl describes, people are rigidly bound to categories of work. Civil servants will have nothing to do with clerks and mechanics, and the professionals—doctors, architects, etc.—are the highest ranked of all. What is different is that the old racial and religious prejudices have been transposed into intercategorial contempt. A mechanic is a "greaser." A laborer is a "wipe." In the course of the story, there is a riot in a prison for those who have tried to "pass" out of their job and hierarchical positions. But nothing comes of it because the prisoners of different job-types can't get together, and often can't even understand each other. At the end we realize that all this is good, because with such a general lack of social cohesion all over the world, war will no longer be possible.

In *In Search of Wonder*, Damon Knight goes after this Pohl story:

> In its own corkscrew fashion, I suppose this is intended as a contribution toward racial egalitarianism. But it seems to me that rubbing the reader's nose repeatedly into racial hate-words in this way is the worst possible way to go about it. The story is such a mishmash of viewpoints that it's impossible to tell where (if anywhere) the author's sympathies lie . . .

Pohl was merely continuing a trend set earlier, as the Swedish author Sam Lundwall says in his book *Science Fiction: What It's All About*:

> The sociological satire was foremost represented by Frederik Pohl and C. M. Kornbluth's stories about the advertising-industry-or trust-ruled future. Time for the grand views again, with the emphasis on the change of society on account of certain stimuli: unlimited power; religion coming into full undisputed power . . . the American Way of Life *in absurdum*. The writers created their societies with great care, incorpo-

rating the characteristics they needed, stocking them with people and examining the result.

The interior art in the March *Galaxy* causes one to sit up and take notice. The team of Leo and Diane Dillon (who were to win a Hugo award in the future) appear and illustrate four stories, no less. Jack Gaughan, another future Hugo winner and also a future art director for *Galaxy*, appears with illustrations for "An Eye for a What?" by Damon Knight. The magazine's interior artwork had never been shabby, but it had often been indifferent—now it was of a very high quality indeed.

A classic Theodore Sturgeon short story appears in March—"The Other Celia." A man who is just kind of loafing around lives in a cheap hotel. Time weighs heavy on his hands and he is also constitutionally curious, so he passes his time peeping and spying on the building's other residents. He investigates the rooms of the other tenants and finds them all expressive of individual personalities—except the room of Celia Sarton. Her room has nothing in it but the furnishings. No toothpaste, no soap, the bed is not slept in, and so on. Our man is puzzled that the only item in the room actually of Celia's is a large traveling bag. He concentrates his spying on this strange person and finds that Celia is really some kind of alien being who inhabits a human body—two human bodies, actually, one at a time. Celia flows from one body to the other every day, then takes the empty body, folds it up and hides it in a hollowed-out ream of typing paper which she keeps in her traveling bag. Our hero is naturally startled to discover this, and he starts shadowing her-it, learning only that Celia lives chiefly on lots of milk. But Celia is even more surprising than that! He hides her second body, just to see what will happen. He finds out in a very spectacular and final way.

Clifford D. Simak was back in the April issue with a rustic sort of thing, "Operation Stinky." This one does not have the mind-numbing plot I have associated with Simak. A friendly creature that looks like a skunk visits an oldtimer who mainly lives in a shack and sips booze. The skunk does something to the man's ancient touring car which soups it up and eventually causes it to fly. The alterations are thought highly interesting by the Military (of course), and the skunk is brought in to make its mental changes in some of our latest jet fighters. It obligingly does so, and then does more besides, some of it quite unsought.

A short story in this issue, "Army Without Banners," is one of the shadows cast by Gold's earlier editorial about how easily civilization may be disrupted. A strange driver is irritating the hell out of another more hotheaded one and there are some heated words from the latter. The offending driver grabs the angry man's necktie and starts driving away. We don't see what happens next but switch scenes to an alien spacecraft near Earth. We discover that the odd driver is actually an alien agent sent to Earth to cause accidents, infuriation, and as much highway disruption as possible. This is a direct echo of what Gold thought would be a good tactic against an enemy country. The aliens plan to keep it up until we are more or less paralyzed, then they will step in and take over. The author of this story is Edward Wellen, better known for his humorous non-fact articles in *Galaxy*, such as "Origins of Galactic Slang."

April also brought another Sheckley story, a typically inverted satirical piece, "The Victim From Space." Richard Hadwell, a free-lance interplanetary explorer, lands on a relatively uncivilized world with the usual native tribes, or so he thinks. The people he runs into have rather curious folk mores. Their highest award for anything is an excruciating death administered by the priests of their religion. The most painful is called the Ultimate, involving a sinister-looking machine set up in a holy place. This is reserved for Hadwell, though he doesn't know it yet. How the tale ends involves a good deal of rather satirical paradox.

The May 1957 cover is a particularly nice one called "Port of Entry—Phobos," by (first name not given) Pederson. That practice of giving the artist's last name only is one of the few irritating policies of *Galaxy* at that time. I suppose it can be traced back to the old *Astounding* of the early Thirties where the artist Hans Wessolowski was simply known as "Wesso." All the same, it dooms lesser *Galaxy* artists to oblivion.

The May *Galaxy* features "Survival Kit" by Frederik Pohl. The hero is another one of the unlovable social rejects that the pages of Gold's *Galaxy* absolutely teem with. This one, Howard Mooney, is a greedy scheming misfit who meets up with Harse, a stranded alien who has to get to Brooklyn on a certain day to travel back into his own era in a time nexus that will occur on that date. Harse has a survival kit with little spheroids full of gold, gems, radium, rations, etc.—everything needed to survive among a primitive people. Mooney tries to winkle it away from Harse, but Harse outwits him, or uses a mysterious weapon to make the people Mooney has hired to mug him disappear. Finally, Harse gets away in a ship of his own peers, leaving Mooney with the odd weapon. This has unfortunate repercussions.

Port of Entry—Phobos. Illustrator: Pederson.

There is an intriguing Fritz Leiber novelette in May, "Time in the Round." In a peaceful future when warfare has been outlawed, one of the pastimes is to go to the Time Theater and observe past civilizations of barbarian times by means of a time-traveling viewer. They watch real and life-sized past events. Children under five years old aren't allowed in the theater, and a little boy nicknamed "the Butcher" is not pleased at that. With his "uninj" (for "uninjurable") robotic dogs, he sneaks in anyway just as the viewers are watching a Viking encampment. Either his presence or the mumbo-jumbo of a Viking warlock cause the protective bubble around the stage to dissolve, and out come the Vikings looking for adventure. They snatch up a young woman sitting in a front row. They are about to do more when Butcher sics the uninjes on them. The uninjes show surprising capabilities!

June's issue has a rather colorful cover by a certain Kirberger. It's called "Portrait of a World." A baldheaded artist in space suit is daubing away at a canvas on the surface of a colorful but apparently lifeless planet with brightly colored rings around it. The issue is chiefly distinguished by a fine article by Willy Ley, "Tribes of the Dinosaurs." He gives an excellent short history of the ancient reptiles and also gives a good putdown to those who think of the dinosaurs as evolutionary flops. He points out that they existed for 140 million years and that we who are so judgmental have been on the scene for barely one million years.

The July *Galaxy* has several fine stories. Poul Anderson is there, Avram Davidson has a novelette, and the redoubtable Robert Sheckley has *two* stories, one ("The Deaths of Ben Baxter") under his own name and the other, a short story called "A Wind Is Rising," under the pseudonym Finn O'Donnevan.

Davidson's novelette, "Help! I Am Dr. Morris Goldpepper," is one of the few sf stories to deal much with dentists and dentistry. The Goldpepper of the title is a fine dentist who has been kidnapped to a distant world to make teeth for otherwise toothless natives so they can masquerade as humans. The other dentists find out about his plight in a message he has concealed in a plate worn back to Earth by one of the aliens. The American Dental Association vows to rescue him. This story is unique also because I can't think of any other sf piece that mentions the works of Ruskin, Elbert Hubbard or Edna Ferber. These are recommended by one of the dentists as "rich treasures of literature." I guess one reason I've always been fond of this story is that my grandfather was a dentist for almost sixty years and so I got to know a little about the profession.

"A Wind Is Rising" is about two humans on the planet Carella. Members of the Advance Exploration Corps, they have four months left before they will be relieved, and it doesn't appear that they will make it. On Carella a wind of 82 mph is regarded as a mere breeze, and their heavy steel shelter has almost blown away in a storm. Now the natives approach to tell them that the *real* storm season is coming on, when even the Carellans retreat to caverns. The Earthmen can't follow them because of a lack of a stored oxygen supply. And outside a wind is rising! This story was made more memorable to me because it was also turned into a play for the radio show *X Minus One*.

The August cover is by Coggins and depicts a spacecraft much like those that had graced the covers of pulp magazines of the Thirties. It shows spacers snaring a large space squid. The cover has nothing to do with the contents of the magazine, which are rather fine. Silverberg and Galouye have stories, but the featured work is "Time Waits for Winthrop," a striking novella by William Tenn (Philip Klass), well illustrated by Virgil Finlay.

The Earth of the Twenty-Fifth Century invites a representative group of Twentieth Century Americans to visit the future. It turns out that the future is a world that looks like it has been designed by Salvador Dali, Wilhelm Reich, and the proponents of Primal Scream Therapy. (There is, for instance, Shriek Field where the future folk go to shout and scream and let off their tensions.) The rooms are vividly colored and flow around those inside them; floors flow up to form seats if anyone wants to sit down. The food is strange to Twentieth Century tastes, involving a lot of extraterrestrial cuisine. Only Winthrop, an old derelict type, really gets into the spirit of the future; the other Americans, being more middle class, are squeamish as hell and hate the future. The story's problem is how to persuade Winthrop to go back; if he refuses, then for temporo-physical reasons, *all* must stay.

The September *Galaxy* has a fine cover by Virgil Finlay, "Capt. Ahab of Space," depicting a crumbling statue of an explorer on an apparently deserted planet. This issue is also superb. Sturgeon, Simak and Tenn are contributors. Willy Ley has an interesting column in which he answers readers' queries about robots, fresh-water sharks, "footless" birds, and magic magnetic mountains of legend.

One story, "Doat Age" by John Boland, deals with an animal invented

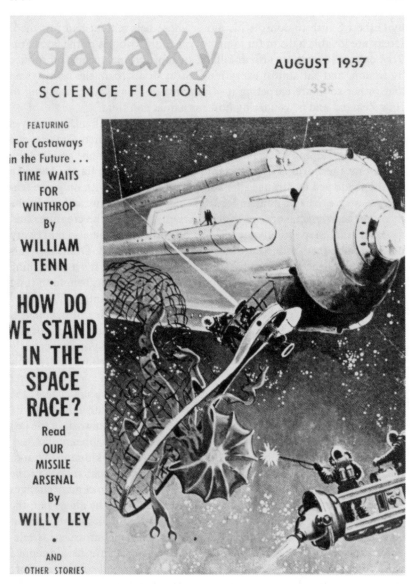

How To Use A Space Net. Illustrator: Coggins.

by Gilbert Smith to console his aunt, whose beloved cat had just died. Doats are lovable balls of fur, a prototype of the tribbles of the later *Star Trek* episode. Doats are also unkillable by most normal means, reproduce by fission, and eat almost everything. Stray doats roam the countryside and rather soon are carpeting it. The narrator tells us he is escaping to New Zealand and is wondering how far a doat can float.

Clifford D. Simak's novelette "Shadow World" was delightful, and was satisfactorily illustrated by the Dillon team. Robert Emmett Drake is one of a team developing a new planet. Drake is a conservationist and is along to see that the world is treated right and not ruined like Earth. The men are all shadowed by strange silent shrouded creatures with only one feature, a large eye like a camera lens. They are very curious and study the men and their machinery very intently. Drake studies the creatures and discovers that they actually are viewing machines that can also make very detailed miniatures of the Earthmen and their equipment. Drake inadvertently stops his personal shadow from duplicating him. It's a good thing he does, as he learns when he finds out what the real aliens behind the odd shadows are up to. They view the colonists as entertainment. They send payment to encourage the colonists to stay, but their idea of payment is different from ours! There is also a strange and illegal viewing device called a "peeper" that figures in the story; it involves you in perfectly realized dreams and visions and is highly addictive psychologically. This story has Simak's usual high quota of imagination.

The two-part serial *Wolfbane* begins in the October issue. This is the final serial collaboration of the famous Pohl/Kornbluth combination. It is illustrated by Wallace Wood, an artist who did much work in the last years of Gold's *Galaxy* and who, like Don Martin, also appeared in *Mad Magazine*. The novel is about the Earth after it has been kidnapped out of the Solar System by huge mysterious blue pyramids that reside on the Moon, although there is also one on Mt. Everest. As the climate changes and food becomes rare and mankind's efforts to fight the aliens fail, the number of humans dwindles and human culture embraces a rather fatalistic and mystical world view. Glenn Tropile, a nonconformist, is teleported to one of the Moon pyramids to be plugged into its kidnapped work force. Tropile is trained by stimulus/response and becomes no more than a component before his nonconformity asserts itself again. Then he plunges into conspiracy and sabotage, and at last the pyramids are gotten rid of and humanity is free to plan its own destiny again.

BEGINNING
A GREAT
2-PART SERIAL

WOLFBANE
By
**FREDERIK
POHL**
and
**C. M.
KORNBLUTH**
•
HUNTING DOWN
THE DODO
By
WILLY LEY
•
IDEAS
DIE HARD
By
**ISAAC
ASIMOV**
•
DOUBLE
INDEMNITY
By
**ROBERT
SHECKLEY**
AND
OTHER STORIES

OCTOBER 1957
35¢

Wolfbane. Illustrator: Wallace Wood.

There is quite a lot more to *Wolfbane* than that summary can show. Damon Knight says in his book of sf criticism that:

> ... in *Wolfbane*, by Pohl and Kornbluth, you ... get a brilliant analysis of the Oriental life pattern, developed and projected onto a future civilization on this continent (1,500 calories a day: slouching gait, politeness, minuscule sub-arts—Water Watching, Clouds and Odors, Sky-Viewing ... people named Tropile and Boyne, in towns called Wheeling, Altoona and Gary, walking through an elaborate life-long ritual, purely and simply because their diet permits nothing better) ...
>
> *Wolfbane* ... is one of the most entertaining jobs Pohl and Kornbluth did together. For breadth of conception, for the intellectual brilliance with which it ranges over Zen Buddhism, higher mathematics, machine shop practice &c., &c.; for occasional fruitful ironies (e.g., the robots who wire people into the circuits of their computers); and above all for the unsentimental clarity with which it views mankind, the novel is a rewarding experience.

October also has a novelette by Isaac Asimov, "Ideas Die Hard." The reactions of two men on the way to the Moon are analyzed by monitors back on Earth. The men become strained by the exploratory trip; one becomes withdrawn and the other becomes rather quarrelsome and aggressive. The last straw comes when they catch a glimpse of the back of the Moon and it is all wooden framework and canvas. They think the Moon is a fake and go bananas. In this story fact is as strange as hallucinatory fantasy.

There is another Asimov novelette in the December issue, "Galley Slave." It involves Susan Calvin, U.S. Robots, Inc., the Three Laws of Robotics and a proofreading Robot EZ-27. Northeastern University has rented EZ-27 to do routine proofreading and other mundane tasks for the professors and their graduate assistants. Ninheimer, a professor of sociology who had originally opposed the renting of EZ, now decides to have the robot proofread his book before it is sent out to the publisher. The book is panned by other sociologists and Ninheimer takes U.S. Robots to court, alleging that EZ ruined his book by inserting alien views and making changes in accordance with the Robotic Laws, laws that do not apply to humans.

U.S. Robots and its counsel are at a loss for a while, but then they hit upon how to use the Laws. When Ninheimer is led to say how much the publication of the book is hurting him and wrecking his reputation, EZ-27 speaks up in court and tells some startling truths!

7. GOLD'S SILVER AGE: PART TWO, 1958–1959

WILLY LEY HAD BEEN WRITING ABOUT SATEL-
lites and the space program for some years
and he must have had some inkling of what
the scientists of the U.S.S.R. were up to. What they were up to was
Sputnik, which went up on October 4th, 1957, and the world was
changed. All of a sudden, the United States became concerned about its
loss of preeminence in space and solicitous about its resident "brains"
who had earlier been neglected in the postwar boom times. Science
courses and projects began to be funded and the latent American technical genius began to lift up its head.

However, 1958 began with some rather depressing U.S. space failures.
Here the Russkis were, orbiting dogs (which did not return) and everything, while our Vanguard rockets were falling right over on the launching pads and blowing up then and there. A lot of us continued to have
faith, and much of this faith we owed directly to sf. We knew we could
do it. Hadn't we been reading all about space exploration for years
already?

Galaxy continued on course this year whatever the vagaries of our space program. There are some who hold to the dictum that the longer Gold was editor the worse *Galaxy* got, that the magazine was more and more out of touch with the sf readership. This view, quite fashionable in the Nixonian era and the Seventies, simply is itself out of touch: out of touch with reality. In 1958, *Galaxy*'s contributions to the field earned it *two* of the highly coveted Hugo awards! One went to Fritz Leiber for his novel *The Big Time* and one went to Avram Davidson for his short story "Or All the Seas With Oysters." *Galaxy* was as glorious as ever.

The January issue had the Emsh Santa once more. He is on his way through space and has just come upon a cheerful, tentacled ET Santa going in another direction. The two are exchanging holiday greetings.

There is a good Simak novelette in the January issue, "The World That Couldn't Be." It takes place on a far planet which Earthmen are just beginning to colonize. Gavin Duncan is annoyed because some critter called the Cytha has been eating up his *vua* plants. This is too much for him and he sets off to hunt this creature, though it is taboo to do so. His native guide is a little too "native" to suit me. The guide, Sipar, says "mister" all the time, gets scared and rolls its eyeballs up so just the whites show, etc. Oh well. The guide also kills itself rather than continue to hunt the Cytha. Duncan finds out why later on when the Cytha has him trapped.

The reader will have noticed by now that the stories in *Galaxy* deal a lot with colonization of planets which have less-developed "savage" tribes on them. Sheckley, especially, was always doing something with the tribal theme, although very tongue-in-cheek. These stories seem to reflect the colonial or territorially expansive era which by then had long been over for the countries of the West. In view of today's emergence of the Third World, some of the stories of this ilk strike one now as being rather strange.

The February issue has always been one of my favorites. Lloyd Biggle, Jr. has a very fine novelette, "The Rule of the Door." This was later the title of a book of his collected stories. Skarn Skukarn, a prominent scientist in an old and far-flung interstellar empire, is ordered by the Emperor to visit an uncolonized planet and send back a specimen of its life by applying the Rule of the Door. The planet turns out to be our own, and Skukarn ends up in Centertown, Indiana. He has an irritating, meddling assistant by the name of Dork Diffack. The object of this team is to occupy a nice house, achieve community recognition and good will, and then entice one of the Earthpeople into using the Door, which is sort of an interstellar matter transmitter and instant specimen pickler, disguised as a closet. It also is a thought-analyzer and is so designed that it will not accept as a specimen any individual being possessing any good moral quality. They have an open house and people try the Door out of curiosity, but none is accepted. Dork grows annoyed. Next Skarn asks in the town's so-called bad characters—the town drunk, a supposedly crooked sheriff, and so on, but no one is taken. But the Door does finally act—to our surprise!

"Graveyard of Dreams" by H. Beam Piper, which is one of his Terran Federation stories, doesn't have much of a plot, but it's a rather charming and haunting mood piece. Conn Maxwell is returning to his frontier world, Poictesme, with sad news. The Poictesmeans had sent him to study on Terra in hopes that he could learn the location of the legendary Brain, a supercomputer supposedly hidden away somewhere on Poictesme for military use during an interstellar war forty years before. Conn has discovered that there is no Brain. It was all a hoax. However, he has found out where all the stores and provisions left over from the war are located on Poictesme. He also has schemes to more efficiently market some of the other products of the planet so new dreams will replace the forsaken old ghost-dreams. Conn's generation will bring Poictesme forward. The story is well matched by haunting Dillon illustrations.

The February issue sees Harry Harrison's first *Galaxy* appearance (though he is mainly thought of as an *Astounding/Analog* writer). His short story, "The Repairman," is a good one. It involves a repairman who must put an interstellar beacon back into service. The beacon has been made useless by a tribe of reptilian creatures who think it is a holy shrine. Its interior is now a holy-of-holies. The wily way he adopts to get the beacon functioning and how he uses the natives' religious prejudices to do so make the story entertaining.

The year 1958 brought many new writers to *Galaxy*, new writers who would go on to do prodigious work. The late Frank Herbert, author of the *Dune* series, first appeared in Gold's magazine in April of 1958. Rosel George Brown of *Galactic Sibyl Sue Blue* fame made her sf debut in September. These all were writers who would achieve great stature in the next decade—Herbert, for one, achieved virtual cult status. The fact that Gold could see what these people had and the fact that he quickly signed them on go far to refute the charge that *Galaxy* was simply stagnating in its last years and merely repeating itself over and over.

But the year also saw the loss of Cyril Kornbluth, who was only 35 years old. He died of a heart attack in March and the fine Pohl/ Kornbluth team was broken up forever (although there were still some stories from their collaboration that hadn't yet seen print). Kornbluth was the master of the piercing satirical short story. Had he been a mainstream author, college freshmen would have read one or two of his stories and maybe Public Television would have done a screen-TV adaptation of his work. "The Altar at Midnight" would be most compelling. He himself was always a realist about the actual social effect of his sf, or any sf. In the Advent book *The Science Fiction Novel*, he says at the end of his essay (which had been a speech at a University of Chicago seminar):

> In this essay I have tried to show that science fiction novels, on the record, have not been measurably effective social criticism. I have speculated that the reason for this is a sort of embarrassment of riches—that nothing in the science fiction novel is what it seems, that there is no starting point for social change resulting from social criticism. As social criticism the science fiction novel is a lever without a fulcrum, a single equation with two unknowns. The science fiction novel does contain social criticism, explicit and implicit, but I believe this criticism is massively outweighed by unconscious symbolic material more concerned with the individual's relationship to his family and the raw universe than with the individual's relationship to society.

It is my belief and the belief of many others that attention should be called to Kornbluth's work, and it should be read and reread and not permitted to vanish into the obscure shadows that have hidden F. L. Wallace and Mark Clifton, just to name two Fifties authors who are also gone.

The March *Galaxy* featured the work of a writer who is, happily, still with us. This is Fritz Leiber, who now is largely ensconced in the sword-and-sorcery end of the sf/fantasy spectrum. His two-part serial is the previously-mentioned Hugo Award-winning novel, *The Big Time*. This was the second novel appearing in *Galaxy* that had gotten the prestigious award. The first had been, of course, Alfred Bester's *The Demolished Man* in 1953. Like Bester's novel, *The Big Time* is a sheer imaginative *tour de force* and has nothing at all to do with sociopsychological heavy irony, except in the broadest imaginable way.

The Big Time has another of those mind-stretching plots which must have been a minor specialty of *Galaxy*. The various characters are from all eras of history: a Roman legionary, a British WW I officer, a Mississippi riverboat gambler, a Cretan warrior woman and other assorted human types, plus two ET's from billions of years apart. These are all on the side of the Spiders in the great Change Wars which occupy billions of years and the entire galaxy. The warriors travel in time and try to win battles which will change history in favor of the mysterious Spider overlords and against the foe, the Snakes.

The action occurs in the Place, a sort of rest and recreation area outside of time. The Place also functions as a field hospital. There is an attempted mutiny by Bruce, the Britisher, who objects to being recruited after his death during the Battle of the Somme in 1916 to serve as a time-traveling ghost soldier sent here and there throughout all time. His actions are countered by Erich, a former Nazi. In the confusion, a nuclear bomb in an ornate chest is triggered off, and this while the Place has been "introverted" and moved even further away from regular time. The Place is eventually brought back from drifting into the Void and the bomb is disarmed. There is a bit of philosophy by Illy, a tentacled ET, about how the Change Wars are primarily part of a vast galactic evolution to a higher phase. Then all is back to "normal" again and the r & r goes on as before.

March also has a good short story by Joseph Farrell, who has to be one of *Galaxy*'s more obscure writers, right up there with Ralph Robin. His piece is called "The Ethical Way." A team of somewhat benevolent Galactics shows up just as Earth is finishing itself off in a nuclear war. They carry off a thousand Earthpeople for use as "servants," since the Galactic religion forbids robots or androids. The Galactics wonder if maybe they shouldn't have intervened earlier to stop the war, but then realize that such interference would not have been "ethical." In the end, the former slave-servants outbreed their masters and take over, since the Galactics are too scrupulous and civilized to really take advantage of the former Earthlings. Luckily, the kindly Galactic civilization has rubbed off on the onetime slaves, so now they are also ethical.

The April cover is by Dember and shows a moon rocket in flight, its innards revealed by a cutaway view. *Galaxy* was getting serious about the space race now.

This issue has the Frank Herbert short story "Old Rambling House." The Grahams, a young couple, are pressed for space. They see an ad for a large house and visit it. The owners are in a rush to get rid of it, and want the Grahams to take it over at once in exchange for the Grahams' cheap trailer! There is a hitch, naturally enough. The Grahams discover that the house is actually a disguised interstellar vehicle used by tax collectors in thrall to a superior Galactic race. Earth will now be taken over, while the Grahams are bound to the house and must move along with it on the interstellar tax collection route. It's not a great story but it is a significant first for *Galaxy*.

May has another fine Mars cover by John Pederson. This one has no title but a rather technical explanation instead. We know his first name now because he was careful to print his name clearly in small, light letters over the black of space.

Robert Silverberg's "The Iron Chancellor" (illustrated amusingly by Wood), is one of the highlights of the May issue. Sam Carmichael, a pudgy business executive with an equally chubby family, is determined to lose weight. He purchases a new-model roboservitor of an imposing size and programs it to serve meals according to a rather strict diet. Soon the whole family longs for indulgent mealtimes once more, but "Bismarck," the robot, won't oblige. It has been programmed to get them all down to a certain weight. Then they may eat more again. Foolishly, the Carmichael son tampers with the roboservitor and the results are disastrous. Bismarck takes complete charge, seals the family off from the world, tells Carmichael's firm that he wishes to retire, and proceeds with the starvation rations again, this time with no limit as to how little they all should weigh, since that part of its memory was destroyed in the tampering. A repairman from the robot sales service happens by and stops Bismarck with a "neutralizer." But then he gets curious and tampers too. This is most unwise.

Another story in the May issue is one of the long shadows cast by Gold's whimsical editorial commenting on how clothes hangers seem somehow to multiply. Avram Davidson's short "Or All the Seas With Oysters" (the Hugo winner I mentioned earlier) takes up this theme to chilling effect. Ferd and Oscar run a bike repair shop. Oscar is a lusty, beery person who likes to take female customers out on bike rides in order to seduce them, mostly with success. Ferd is a brooding, thin, melancholiac who is not interested in such proceedings. He is a fine repairman and tends mostly to business. One day he happens to notice that his drawer is full of an awful lot of safety pins. Then they are suddenly gone and he wonders what happened. Oscar hasn't moved them. Also puzzling is the sudden appearance of many clothes hangers in one of the shop's closets. Suddenly, Ferd knows what is going on. The so-called hangers, etc., are actually alien creatures capable of changing form and evolving from simple device to complex machine. An example of a complex machine is the French racing bike that Ferd doesn't dare ride because it somehow throws him off and hurts him. The aliens are now on to Ferd.

I referred to the May artwork as good, but once again I failed to mention the man responsible for all the *Galaxy* art of this period. This was W. I. Van Der Poel, Gold's Art Director, who deserves considerable praise for his discovery and nurture of fine new talent, and the acquisition of the services of artists like Virgil Finlay, the old-time sf master illustrator.

The June issue is remarkable because it has two Sheckley stories and two stories by Frederik Pohl—*Galaxy* was becoming a real cottage industry for those two! Pohl uses the name Paul Flehr for his novella "Mars by Moonlight." A man named Hardee is one of the people confined on Mars in a penal colony, a rather dispiriting place. His son is there with him and they live in a house toward the edge of the colony. Hardee makes a living by harvesting nearly-grown skitterbugs, curious spider-like metal creatures that grow in the desert. He begins to suspect that the place is not what it seems when he comes across a dying man out in the desert. He wonders where this man could have come from, for he knows of no other penal colonies on Mars. Soon the truth dawns, partly through the agency of the old tavernkeeper Tavares. This is not Mars at all, but part of a western state. The penal colony is actually an assemblage of the few humans not dead or knocked out by an alien sleep ray. The invading aliens, who look like large bronze skulls and use the skitterbugs for personal transportation, know that Hardee and some of the other colonists are now dangerous because they know the truth about what has happened. Hardee, his small son, and some others finally escape the colony and get to an urban area where they find there *is* a resistance movement, literally underground, and they join it in hopes for the future of humankind. This is a good adventure, and is probably the only sf story to ever involve in its plot an ancient Ford tri-motor aircraft, used by the escapees to put some distance between them and the pursuing aliens.

The other Pohl story (under his own name) is a novelette, "The Gentlest Unpeople." It was unusual for Pohl in that part of it is seen through the eyes of some highly mannered Venusians who are somewhat

Galaxy
SCIENCE FICTION

JULY 1958

35¢

BULLET WITH
HIS NAME
By
FRITZ
LEIBER
•
THE BACK
OF
OUR HEADS
By
STEPHEN
BARR
•
IGY
ROUNDUP
By
WILLY
LEY
•
INNOCENT
AT LARGE
By
POUL & KAREN
ANDERSON
And Other Stories

First Manned Satellite (A Projection). Illustrator: Dember.

surprised to find one of their friends dead at the hands of a slob Earthman. They handle the affair politely, however.

In June, Sheckley is represented as himself and also as Finn O'Donnevan. The novelette "The Minimum Man" is under his own name. It concerns the misadventures of one Anton Perceveral, a typical *Galaxy* schnook hero who is a terrible accident-prone. This quality is desired by the Planetary Exploration & Settlement Board which recruits him to be the primary explorer and settler on a promising planet in the East Star Ridge. The theory is that if *he* can survive, with only substandard equipment, then *anyone* can survive on the planet. The scheme will save everyone except Anton a lot of trouble. He muddles along from scrape to scrape, and then finds he is getting more competent and less accident-prone. The PE&SB has compensated for this by making Anton's robot become more accident-prone, and even dangerous, the more Anton improves. The situation deteriorates rapidly.

The Dember cover for the July issue shows a huge Sputnik-type satellite with a spaceman hard at work inside it, doubtless analyzing significant data. The most significant work in this issue is "Bullet With His Name," by Fritz Leiber.

Ernest Meeker is an unassuming Chicago man, unmarried, living with his sister: a confirmed bachelor, as the phrase used to go. He is chosen by some benevolent aliens hovering above Earth to be the recipient of some big and little gifts. These include: ever-lasting razor blades, a powder which mixed with water produces fuel for cars, flashing eyes, instant comprehension and retention of printed pages, mind-reading (to an extent), precognitive ability to keep him safe from accidents, and even immortality. Then we see what he does with them.

The *Galaxy* for August has an interesting Wood cover showing firemen of the future putting out small industrial nuclear blasts with some sort of "damping" effect. Also in August, Theodore Sturgeon reached an apotheosis of mind-sharing. The lives of various people of different types are detailed for us in the novella "To Marry Medusa." A bum, Gurlick, is contacted by the Medusa, an intergalactic conquering composite mind. He is to unite the minds of Earth so that they may more easily be absorbed into the Medusa. Earth becomes united all right, but united humanity first defeats the Medusa on Earth and then absorbs it through the Galaxy and beyond. A new race of star-men of star-minds is created. All the old differences that have divided mankind are erased and human-

ity reaches for a glorious future—all except for Gurlick, who is actually
so happy being a bum that the world continues to treat him as before.
There are some rather good sensual scenes in this novella, and it is also
well-crafted. The Dillon art accompanying it is also excellent.

Frederik Pohl, writing as Paul Flehr, did the month's sole novelette,
"Seven Deadly Virtues." This is another Venusian story; most of it takes
place in Grendoon or in the hot murky swamps around the settlement.
Oliver Sawyer, a settler just recently of Earth, comes to Grendoon. He
meets Diane, who is the wife of Albert Quayle, the local strongman.
Oliver takes a liking to Diane and takes her away from Quayle, who has
been mistreating her. Everyone has supposedly been conditioned against
violence, but there are ways around that. The Grendoonians, under
Quayle's thumb, promptly ostracize the two and they will eventually die
of hunger or drown in the swamp. Then Oliver discovers that Quayle has
been running knives to the Venusian natives. This provokes a confrontation.

Damon Knight is back in the September issue. His novelette, "Thing of
Beauty," is interesting. Gordon Fish is a middle-aged phony and fraud, a
denizen of Southern California. He is the "lucky" beneficiary of a sudden
time slip which causes a drawing machine from the future to be accidentally delivered to his address. He discovers what it can do, though only
after he has thrown away the instruction book (which is written in Swedish, as we find out later). Fish uses the machine to get himself an un-
deserved reputation as an artist and teacher of drawing. He collects advances and then has trouble delivering because he has not been using the
machine correctly. Instead, each drawing it does for him further depletes
its memory bank. The final scene is rather memorable.

There was one change in the September issue. The cover and spine had
earlier read *Galaxy Science Fiction*. Now the official name of the magazine became just that: *Galaxy Magazine*. There was no longer any mention of science fiction on the cover or the spine. Interestingly enough,
there was a *Galaxy Magazine* in the Nineteenth Century. It was a good
magazine, too, a rather high-toned sort of thing with original stories and
articles of a literary-historical nature.

As earlier mentioned, Rosel George Brown makes her first (out of two)
appearances in *Galaxy* in September, a novelette called "From an Unseen
Censor" on the contents page and "Unseen Censor" on the cover, so I
guess we can take our choice. It is a good story, however. The narrator's

Uncle Isadore, a colorful character, has died on a remote planet and his wrecked rocket ship is soon found. Isadore's body won't be, as a note reveals, and neither will his vast wealth, unless his nephew uses a little ingenuity. With the aid of electromagnetic cuff links, intriguing clues, and dodo birds that recite Poe's poetry, the legacy is at last located in the form of rare and very valuable perfume trees!

In October a four-part serial began. This was the noted "Time Killer," by Robert Sheckley—his first attempt at a form longer than a novella. (The novel has been reprinted as *Immortality Delivered.*) Thomas Blaine, a young yacht designer, is killed in a car crash and wakes up in a different body 158 years later. In the rather episodic course of the story we are introduced to all manner of psychic phenomena which are now real and verifiable, such as life after death, poltergeists, zombies, ghosts, and in particular, reincarnation, by means of which Blaine has entered the future America. There is a Hereafter Corporation which guarantees life after death. Blaine's problem is that he wasn't supposed to be reincarnated at all, and in fact took away a chance for an important past religious leader to be re-embodied. Blaine has many enemies, including the afore-mentioned corporation, which feels he is not an asset to their guaranteed life after death offer, since he has no knowledge of the 158 years he spent in the land of the spirits. Finally, he "body-jumps" his way across America and into the Marquesas Islands. One of the bodies he briefly inhabits is a young woman who is about to have her first sexual intercourse (under-water yet), and we share her mind while she and her soon-to-be lover swim toward an underwater cave. This was decidedly erotic. I was not the only one to take note of this. Science fiction writer Hank Stine also mentioned this section of the novel in an interview with Charles Platt in *Dream Makers.*

Sheckley himself has this to say about his first novel (in *Galaxy: Thirty Years of Innovative Science Fiction*):

> My most exciting time with *Galaxy* was writing and publishing the four-part serial "Time Killer," . . . One of my life goals had been to do a four-part serial. . . . The writing of "Time Killer" didn't come easily. I started working on it in Acapulco, typing on tortillas since I was too poor to afford paper. Perhaps that's why it was proclaimed The Most Edible Science Fiction Novel of the Year, although some reviewers thought my guacamole was in poor taste. Horace and I shared the Nobel Prize that year, and our subsequent history as members of the Ferrari racing team is too well known to repeat here.

In January of 1958 *The Third Galaxy Reader* made its appearance.
This was not as grand a book as the previous readers. It was only 235
pages in length, though it did have some fine stories. The editorial comment at the beginning was also interesting. Gold was full of conquering
zeal:

> [The] countries of the world are uniting in the most massive assault
> yet on the mysteries of this planet of ours.
> The land and the air and the sea are being invaded in force, and the
> chill and challenging void above the air and the fiery metal under the
> land and the restless black deeps beneath the sea, and the news of
> victories will explode on the front pages like daily communiqués in a war
> that can only accelerate, never slow down.

This was a reference to the International Geophysical Year, when
American and Soviet scientists, among others, cooperated on various experiments on and above the planet's surface.

Alan Arkin, now a famous actor, wrote some short stories in the
1950's. He sold two to Horace, and one of them, "People Soup," appeared in the November issue. The story is about two kids, Bob and his
sister, who are in the kitchen trying out a formula (animal serum or
people soup) which Bob has whipped up from various items in the
kitchen: cocoa, sardine oil, aspirin, powered mustard, etc. They swallow
some of the concoction and the little girl turns into a chicken and the
little boy into a St. Bernard. They eat some more of it and change back.
The experience doesn't greatly impress them, so the next day they plan to
make an atom bomb, but first they have to get hold of a couple of onions.

Jack Vance has a novelette in the December issue, "Ullward's Retreat."
This was the second and last work he did for the Gold *Galaxy*. When I
asked him what his thoughts were of that era of the magazine, he replied,
"Vituperative!" Vance, like many other writers, didn't appreciate Gold's
rewriting of sections of stories he was going to use.

Vance's novelette takes place in a crowded future where people have to
be put on waiting lists before they are allowed to have children. Bruham
Ullward is a wealthy man in a crowded world. He has a space of almost
three-quarters of an acre in a large many-storied building. In this space
he has a real oak tree and a pond. He is proud of this and loves showing
guests around, and they are always very appreciative. However, something gnaws at him. He hears of a newly discovered world called Mail's
Planet. He finds he can rent half a continent from Kennes Mail, its dis-

coverer and sole inhabitant. Of course it's not the best part of the continent, but it is roomy. Ullward invites his friends from Earth, but instead of being appreciative, they always want to go to Mail's half of the continent, which is strictly forbidden. Ullward grows distressed at this and returns to his former dwelling, where he finds new people to visit him. They are always very appreciative.

It is fitting that I end the account of 1958 with December's Pohl/Kornbluth short story, "Nightmare With Zeppelins," which is usually included in anthologies of their work. An old man, Harry Lewes, is remembering an African expedition he made in 1864. His recounting takes place in World War I London, just then being bombed by Zeppelins. In the Belgian Congo he had found a Swiss, Herr Faesch, operating a mine with native help. The mine produced certain varieties of uranium which Faesch had refined into metal spheres. Lewes tries to examine them, but a worried Faesch takes them away, saying the small spheres must not be allowed to touch each other.

A final 1958 note: *GSF* was going bimonthly in 1959 and would cost fifty cents. There would be no January Santa issue, either. This news dismayed me.

One benefit of the bimonthly *Galaxy* was the larger size. It had increased by forty pages and so had room for more short stories, another novelette, and so on. In other respects the format was unchanged (except for cover blurbs which proclaimed the new size). In fact, Wood did four of the 1959 covers (February, April, August, October); the other two (June, December) were by Emsh.

The February, 1959 issue led off with a novella by Clifford D. Simak called "Installment Plan." A followup exploration and trading team land on Garson IV to trade for *podars*, the chief crop grown by the native humanoids and the only source in the galaxy for a near-perfect tranquilizer. Steve Sheridan and a band of multi-talented robots constitute the would-be traders, but they can't get the natives to do any trading, not even for all the fine glittering Earth products. Attempt after attempt fails and Sheridan grows discouraged. Then he discovers the horrid reason why the natives could not trade.

"Insidekick" by J. F. Bone is an excellent novelette in February. Earth Central investigator Albert Johnson is on the planet Antar trying to find out if local agents and subsidiaries of the giant Interworld Corporation are defrauding the central government by raising tobacco, a crop legally

A Full House Beats Togetherness. Illustrator: Wood.

monopolized by the state. (This seems to be an agrarian issue.) Johnson's life would be forfeit, but an unseen entity has gotten inside him and into his nervous system. It gives him psionic powers with which he gets crucial evidence against Interworld, despite its attempts to kill him.

If, a science fiction magazine that had begun in 1952, now became a companion to *Galaxy* after its original publishers sold it. Gold took over editorial duties for *If* and continued with it and *Galaxy* until his departure. This magazine was only so-so under Gold and it can be assumed that his main interest continued to be *Galaxy*. However, *If* was destined to do great things in the upcoming decade when Frederik Pohl was at the helm.

Wood's April cover is amusing. It shows a group of ET's, a robot, and a bespectacled Earthman playing poker. Some are in space helmets, some can apparently breathe the atmosphere. A birdlike creature is holding a blaster contemplatively and looking at the robot which has been winning all the chips. A very tiny alien is holding four aces, so perhaps the outcome may be different. The quality of *Galaxy*'s art continued to be good.

Spherical alien beings of pure energy have taken over all the cities of Earth. Men are forced to skulk around the various energy and force fields of the reconstituted cities, leading lives much like our present-day cockroaches and rats. They are also regarded as such by the aliens. Bruno, a young man from one of the tribes of humans who live undisturbed in the forests, comes to the city to try to contact the chief Spheres. The other humans laugh at him, but he escapes being blasted by the aliens long enough to convince them of his intelligence. This doesn't help. The last thing they need is intelligent vermin. He barely escapes back to the forest with his life and Sal, a nice young woman he met in the city. There are some interesting imaginative sections in this April novelette, "The City of Force," by an author we have encountered previously, Daniel F. Galouye of New Orleans.

Cordwainer Smith was the pen name of Paul Linebarger, who had spent many years in the China of Chiang Kai-Shek and had worked as a U.S. advisor to that regime. He was back in the April issue with an odd short story, "When the People Fell." The story takes place some centuries in the future and tells how one day the Chinese decide to occupy Venus. They fall from the Venusian sky by the millions and then surround and starve to death the native Venusian life forms, the "loudies" or "ancient ones." The Party officials are in charge of the Chinese influx and are ruthless and calculating in carrying out the operation. The story is made more interesting by being told to us by an old man, wonderingly recounting the events.

There is also a fine novelette in April: "The Man in the Mailbag," by Gordon R. Dickson. The story was later incorporated into a book called *Spacial Delivery*. John Tardy, an emissary from Earth, is on the planet Dilbia to hunt down one of the giant bear-like natives who has abducted Miss Ty Lamorc. She is called "Greasy Face" by the Dilbians, who give themselves and Earth people descriptive nicknames—a Dilbian had seen her putting on makeup. The Dilbians are gruff, boisterous, and intelligent, if technologically unadvanced, and like to twit Earthlings for their small size. They are only impressed by courage and strength, and so far they have not been impressed enough by Earth folks to want to have much to do with them. Tardy changes this by licking the big mean Dilbian kidnapper, the Streamside Terror, in an underwater fight in which the advantages of Dilbian size are minimized. Miss Lamorc is rescued and the Dilbians become more kindly disposed to their offworld guests. The title comes from Tardy travelling across Dilbia carried by a native postman. This is an excellent story and the Dilbians are quite believable characters!

Gold was getting more earnest about the hardbound and paperback anthologies. In April of 1959 Doubleday issued *The Fourth Galaxy Reader* in hardbound. Permabooks would bring it out in paper the following year. In the editorial commentary Gold mentions how the Soviet Embassy approached his magazine seeking a sort of cultural exchange, a swap of a *Galaxy* story for a Soviet story. Pretty soon Gold was getting all sorts of stories from the U.S.S.R. These stories had one thing in common: they were all unimaginative and uninteresting. Timid, in fact, and worried about any possible slights to the Perfect Socialistic Society. Gold thought this was due to the rigidity of a totalitarian state. Apparently the situation hadn't improved much in the Soviet Union. There *has* been some decent Soviet sf in more recent years, however.

In his *Reader* introduction, Gold also mentions the various countries where *Galaxy* was then appearing: all over the British "Empire," France, Belgium, Switzerland, Italy, Germany, Sweden, Finland, and of course, Canada. It had gone international in a big way!

In the June issue Avram Davidson had an interesting novelette, "Take Wooden Indians." Don Benedict is an artisan who travels from our time back to the 1880's where he works for the C. P. Hennaberry Company. He carves wooden Indians. He's also a member of the modern Wooden Indian Society, which seeks to keep the Good Old Days alive by sabotaging any competitors to the figure carvers, particularly a place named Demuth's which is about to manufacture metal Indians. Don's scheming brother-in-law, Walter, finds out about the time traveling and forces Don to take him back also. Walter intends to start patenting modern inventions, but the Hennaberry people, with Don's consent, find a good contemporary method of dealing with him. The cheery 1880 world is safe again.

In August, two of the novelettes have a rather grim tone. The first is "Mugwump Four" by Robert Silverberg. It has some fine comical Don Martin art to illustrate it. The story itself is about how a man of our time is caught in a war between two parallel future Earths, one populated by short, fat mutants and the other by tall big-chested super people, descendants of us but with all our imperfect genes removed. The unfortunate Al Miller, another *Galaxy* schnook, is calling his loan company to get another extension and dials as far as MUrray Hill 4 when he is accidentally connected with the short mutants at their private MUgwump 4 exchange. When they find out he is not one of them, they paralyze him (over the phone) and then show up at his place, rip his phone apart, and drag him away. They suspect he is on to their plots and send him forward to the 25th Century to the Earth of the super people. *They* fear his recessive genes and germs, so they shunt him over to the Mutant World, where he is arrested as a spy. They are about to do unpleasant things to him when the super people arrive. They've started to win the war and magnanimously decide to send Al back to his own time. Precisely to his own time, which produces another big problem for Al.

The other novelette, "The Malted Milk Monster" by William Tenn (Philip Klass), is about a greedy fat little girl who is a student in a class taught by Carter Broun's girl friend. Carter is made aware that the fat little girl has extraordinary mental powers. He is on his way home from a date with the teacher when he suddenly finds himself somehow transferred inside her childish mind. He is engulfed in her mental world, where she forces him to play with her and some other little kids. He eventually tries to escape being sexually forward with her mental image of herself, but that proves unwise.

Wood has a rather nice cover for the October *Galaxy* which illustrates the lead story, the novella "Someone to Watch Over Me" by Christopher Grimm. There is an excellent and moving piece by Clifford D. Simak in this issue, the novelette "A Death in the House." It takes place in the rural Wisconsin country Simak loves so well to describe. A strange alien creature has crash-landed on a remote farm and is discovered by the owner, old Mose Abrams. The half-plant and half-animal alien has been hurt in the crash and Mose takes care of it. He is all alone on the farm, without even a dog, so no one but a doctor ever sees the extraterrestrial. It dries up and dies and Mose gives it a dignified burial in his garden. However, it regenerates, a new alien grows up during the year and soon comes into the farmer's house. It wants to reconstruct its spacecraft. Doing so uses up most all of Mose's hoard of silver dollars (he doesn't trust paper money). Then the alien leaves, but first it gives Mose a smooth, round marble-like thing. It is what the alien thinks of as a Companion and it makes one feel always that one is with a group of friends. Mose is happy with it. Though the alien is gone, Mose will never feel alone again.

John Brunner, an author who will be much heard of in the approaching years, made his first *Galaxy* appearance with the novelette "Silence." A man named Hesketh is rescued from the Charnog enemies of Earth after 28 years of captivity. His rescuers attempt to snap him out of his psychological doldrums rather too soon, with serious results.

Elisabeth Mann Borgese appears in *Galaxy* for the first and last time in the October issue. She is a daughter of the late very famous German writer and anti-Nazi, Thomas Mann. Her short story "True Self" is hard to describe. I guess the closest I can get to it is that it is what a beauty parlor would perhaps seem like to someone who has been busily sniffing glue. It may also be some kind of put-on. I wish I knew for sure but I'm not going to lose any sleep over it.

In the fall of 1959 Gold came out with an anthology of nine novelettes called *The World That Couldn't Be*. It was published by Doubleday, and came out as a Permabooks paperback in 1961. In the preface Gold comments on various of the novelettes, as usual saying some interesting things along the way. For instance, he has this to say about a particularly grim sub-genre of sf, the Armageddon story:

> One of the most commendable achievements of modern science fiction
> is the virtual embargo that has been placed on post-atomic-doom stories. Not that the things aren't getting written, and by the thousands, and

all but exclusively by what often seems to be the entire science fiction readership; the theme has grown so stale through repetition that even Hollywood, infatuated though it is with mass horror, recognizes this one as box-office fallout.

In Gold's editorials he largely seem to hold to a belief in scientific progress and human advancement that is straightforward and not a bit naive. Whatever else the Fifties were, they were not naive. The world had just experienced the horrors of death camps and nuclear weapons. However, it was also an optimistic time and in this day of fashionable doom-saying, such optimism may *seem* naive. They, and we the Activists of the Sixties, always knew the odds, and the possibilities.

December once again has a Santa cover by the redoubtable Emsh. Two BEM children are watching the four-armed Kris Kringle as he delivers gifts. As fine as the cover were the contents of the issue. For instance, there was an excellent Sheckley novelette: "Prospector's Special."

Tom Morrison from Earth is hunting for valuable goldenstone on Venus. He has used up his cash and his credit prospecting in the hot Venusian desert. Then he wrecks his sandcar and has to hoof it with just a few supplies, with sinister Venusian wolves tailing him. He has a revolver to keep them away, but is running out of ammunition. He could get out of the scrape by using his portable phone to call in and declare bankruptcy. He knows he will find the goldenstone, and so he does, but it might not do him much good since he's out of water. He is desperate. His phone has just been cut off for non-payment. Just then the Venus mail robot happens by and he commandeers its emergency phone, a strictly illegal act. The wolves start closing in at the same time that he realizes he has a rich claim. A tense situation develops.

Rosel George Brown makes her second, and last, appearance in *Galaxy* with an idiosyncratic short story, "Flower Arrangement." A woman has to make a flower arrangement for an upcoming garden show. She wants to make something memorable and unusual. She enlists the aid of her six-year-old son, and he makes it memorable and *very* unusual by including a balloon which derives an antigravity force from the fourth or some other dimension. Everyone is naturally interested—except the child, who has either forgotten how he adapted the balloon, or is in fact too preoccupied with a new project. There is not much science to this story but it is amusing all the same.

George O. Smith, a veteran sf author (and not normally a *Galaxy* writer), checks in with a psionic thriller called "The Undetected." Police Captain Schnell has psi ability and he knows what he is up against when he is tracking Wood, a psionic killer and robber. The policeman's problem is that he cannot reveal any evidence of his own psi ability or he would get into serious trouble because the public is dead set against any kind of mind police. How he entraps Wood as a psionic criminal and remains himself undetected adds much interest to this novelette and makes it well worth reading. This was Smith's first *GSF* appearance. It is well illustrated by Virgil Finlay.

The Fred Pohl short story "The Snowmen" is a strange little piece. It deals with heat loss. The dwellers of Earth are using an energy device which keeps them warm enough but is slowly taking all the heat out of the atmosphere. All is frozen when an alien lands. He picked the wrong period in Earth's history. His vehicle is stripped for parts, and since food is also getting hard to find, he ends up in a freezer. The people that do this are not in the slightest remorseful—a dark, moody kind of story.

This marks the conclusion of Gold's Silver Age and it was a fine era after all. Other sf magazines, especially in the aftermath of Sputnik, were folding right and left, but Horace kept charging bravely on. He was even picking up fine new writers, keeping the good old ones, and getting stories from writers who had been around awhile but hadn't done work for *Galaxy* yet. It was altogether a most commendable effort, and the entertainment value of the magazine continued to be very high.

8. FINAL GOLD: 1960–1961

*G*ALAXY BEGAN ITS SECOND BIMONTHLY YEAR
with the February, 1960 issue. Emsh was back
with a comical cover, just like the old days.
It depicted a junkyard for used spaceships and second hand robots pre-
sided over by a chubby middle-aged woman in curlers.

The issue also had an imaginative story by Fred Pohl, "The Day the
Icicle Works Closed." This novelette is about the Icicle Works on Altair
Nine and those who depended on it for jobs. The works took healing
Altamycin from the atmosphere and stored it in multi-colored icicles
which were shipped out for medicinal purposes throughout the galaxy.
When word comes that the once-unique drug is now being synthesized,
the Icicle Works close, ruining the planet's economy. As lawyer Milo
Pulcher struggles to keep some of the unemployed Altair Nine young
folks out of prison, he becomes aware of many abuses, not the least of
which is rental to tourists of live and healthy Altairean bodies. It is about
the only way the natives can make any money. Their minds are trans-

Home on the Rocket Range. Illustrator: Emsh.

ferred to underwater mining machines while off-world personalities use—and often misuse—their bodies. When Pulcher opposes this, he rubs the local big shots the wrong way. They strike back—and so does he.

The noted chronicler of the People, Zenna Henderson, makes the first of her two appearances in *Galaxy* with the short story "Something Bright." Back in the Depression, little Anna lives in a tenement with her mom and four other children. To relieve the crowding and also to pick up a little change and some good food (or food, period) the little girl now and then stays with a mysterious hulking old woman named Mrs. Klevity to keep her company when her husband is away. The Klevitys are seeking something mysterious in their own house, which puzzles Anna. It turns out that they are aliens disguised as humans. They are waiting for an interdimensional nexus which they can pass through to get back to their own people. They long to go back, for this time and place is not their own. Then one day Anna discovers "something bright" under the bed, and the Klevitys quickly disappear through it. Anna sees their world in the dazzling light and sees the Klevitys in miniature as they resume their young and silvery elfin forms. Then the bright gateway and the silvery world vanish. Though the Klevitys have left all their possessions to Anna, she goes back to her own apartment feeling some sadness at not ever being part of that dazzling world she has just seen.

The Emsh cover for the April *Galaxy* shows a handsomely built brunette spacewoman stranded on Venus. She is sitting on a beach wearing only her bra and panties, while overhead her somewhat tattered spacesuit is raised as a flag of distress. Offshore, two alien eyes on the ends of tentacles or pseudopods, more amusing than frightening, ogle her. She looks very thoughtful, as anyone would in such circumstances.

April is chiefly distinguished by another Cordwainer Smith appearance—the novelette "The Lady Who Sailed the Soul." Helen America is a remarkable small brunette young woman whose one desire is to be an interstellar sailor. She would fly a starship whose billowing miles-long sails catch and channel stellar energy. The flights take forty years but appear as a subjective month of time, due to operations done on the sailor before the trip begins. After the voyage to another star and the delivery of thousands of colonists in cold storage, the sailor is distinguished by a unique young-old look. Helen loves another sailor, Mr. Gray-no-more, who has completed an interstellar trip. They become lovers, but then the young-old man "sails" off to New Earth and the two are parted. Helen

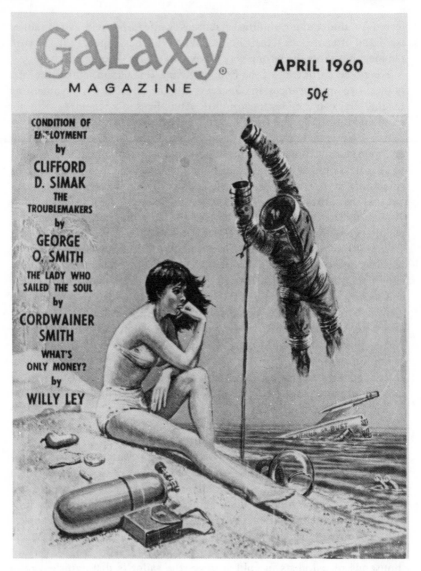

Have Spacesuit, Can't Travel. Illustrator: Emsh.

arranges to take thirty thousand colonists there, and all arrive safely forty years later. Now Helen is a young-old sailor herself. She meets her former lover in a joyful reunion. The novelette is really much more subtle and mannered than this description conveys, a situation almost always associated with the sf of Cordwainer Smith. "The Lady" is illustrated elegantly by Dillon in a manner most evocative of its mood.

April also has "The Power," a quickie by Fred Brown (back after a seven year absence). This has appeared in various collections and is almost of a folk-fable quality. A common crook tells a bookie to drop dead and the fellow does, over the phone yet. The crook soon uses this power to take care of a number of his enemies. He also finds he can tell people to lend him money and then forget about it. Lovely women go along with his every suggestion, and so on. He starts to feel almost god-like, and this proves to be his undoing.

June saw the beginning of Fred Pohl's two-part novel *Drunkard's Walk*. Cornut, a young math teacher in a heavily populated future, accounts himself a reasonable success. His only problem is that lately he keeps trying to commit suicide for no discernible reason. Sometimes he nearly succeeds. Master Carl, an old and respected mathematician, is his mentor at the University. Carl and Cornut are working on a problem involving a complex equation on the statistics of population. The work is in progress when St. Cyr, the odd and aged president of the University, orders a team, Cornut among them, to go out and bring back several natives of a Pacific island. This is unusual and mysterious, but everyone does what he is told.

Some time later, Cornut marries Locille, a pretty undergraduate, partly to safeguard his life: she stops him before he can have a successful suicide. While they visit her family on a Texas tower offshore (living space is short), Master Carl continues work on the demographic equation. When he seeks certain information on the aging elements of the populace, St. Cyr has him killed. Carl was about to discover that a number of people simply have not died. Some are quite ancient; they have placed themselves in positions of power and in fact control humanity. They have now decided to limit the numbers of ordinary short-lived people by having a plague—smallpox which had been brought in by the unwitting Pacific aborigines. When Cornut discovers all this, the ancient ones resume sending him thoughts urging him to kill himself, for they fear him also. The conclusion is exciting.

The lead-off novelette of the August *Galaxy* is "Mind Partner," by Christopher Anvil. It is a rather confusing piece about a captive alien who is forced to imprint very realistic hallucinations in the minds of people who are unwarily patronizing a certain old mansion in search of new kicks. They have no notion that the alien is there and that what it does is addictive (not to mention illegal). The people running this racket are very quick to move along when they detect any police interest in their activities. Investigative agent Jim Calder enters the house and is promptly subjected to all kinds of mind trips, some lasting an apparent lifetime. Finally he escapes, and comes across the alien by re-entering the building through an upstairs window. The building is invaded by the police and the alien is taken away to begin curing the minds that had been distorted. Calder wonders at the end if he is still hallucinating, but decides that even if he were in a nightmare again, it wouldn't last forever. This is a more speculative story than most; philosophical, in fact.

In October, Allen Kim Lang, the author of only a limited amount of sf, has a rather good novelette, "World in a Bottle." This is about a group of "Lapins"—people who have been raised from birth in a germ-free environment—and the problems they have in handling their lives as time passes and the world outside their own sterile "Big Tank" becomes more interesting to them. The germless humans are supposed to be part of a life-long experiment, but some of them grow weary and two actually leave. This is invariably fatal, for they fall prey to the first germs to reach their defenseless systems. Finally they attain their true destiny. A radio signal from Alpha Centauri is detected and an expedition is planned. All the Lapins are to be the crew of the first starship. They are all brilliant and multi-talented people and can learn to handle a starship, but one of the most important factors in their selection is that they cannot transmit any dangerous disease to the alien society. An interesting movie on this theme was made some years ago, with John Travolta as one of the germless test subjects.

The last Emsh Santa appears on the cover of the December *Galaxy*. The sf Santa looks startled and puzzled to see a robot Santa carrying toys for robots. The metallic St. Nicholas is wearing a red Santa cap and a false white beard.

As an example of how Gold was continuing to draw in top new writers, R. A. Lafferty makes his *Galaxy* debut with the novelette "Snuffles." The exploration team that has landed on the puzzling small planet Bellota finds the highest life form is a gentle and amusing pseudo-bear whom they call Snuffles. The world is interesting and pleasant. Bellota suffers short rapid rainstorms. One of the explorers observes that it doesn't rain on Snuffles, but all around him. Snuffles is a creator-god in embryo. The foolish humans continue to resist and ridicule him.

The February 1961 issue has a weird cover showing deep-frozen humans moving through space in transparent cylinders, presumably on their way to colonize a new planet. The sf old-timer Murray Leinster (Will Jenkins) has an excellent novelette, "Doctor." Doctor Nordenfeld aboard the space liner *Star Queen* is concerned about the spread of the dread virus chlorophage. It wipes out any plant or animal life it contacts. A little girl comes aboard ship who has been exposed to it. The plants near her begin to die, and soon all other life on the ship will die—*but* the doctor notices that some other plants on the space liner are immune. He experiments in a last-ditch attempt to save the ship and passengers.

Gold's editorial for February is quite interesting. He discusses all the psionic stories that he keeps getting and which he dislikes. Then he tells of some of his own "psi" experiences during World War II. He somehow got into the prediction business in his unit of Combat Engineers. He made guesses when the war would be over in Europe, when it would end in the Pacific, and the month in which he would be mustered out of the service. The first he missed by more than a week. The second he missed by only a day and the last one he got right. Gold thinks, though, that if he did have some sort of prescient powers the phenomenon was caused mainly by a deep-rooted anxiety, and not by any great superpowers of the mind. In short, he remains skeptical.

The April *Galaxy* has a Mel Hunter cover, "A Derelict in the Void," which is rather effective. Fred Saberhagen has a long novelette, "Planeteer," in this issue. This was his second *Galaxy* appearance—his first was "Volume Paa-Pyx" one issue before, February 1961. "Planeteer" deals with the experiences of a planetary contact team from the cruiser *Yuan Chwang*, who seek to establish friendly relations with the humanoid natives of the planet Aqua. When Boris Brazil makes contact he finds a situation where a red-haired warrior tribe has enslaved a tall, blond, and slightly more peaceable group. The Earthmen must find a more just way of life for the Aquans.

Somewhat more sadly, I conclude my mission. The April 1961 issue was the last one bearing Gold's name as editor. He was injured in an

A Derelict in the Void. Illustrator: Mel Hunter.

automobile accident and gradually lost weight until he was forcibly hospitalized. Gold said of his last months at *Galaxy*:

> *Galaxy* was me. I was it, and it was me. Anything that threatened it threatened me. Anything that threatened me threatened the magazine. Complete Identification. Total.
>
> If I were to edit a magazine now (which I wouldn't!), I don't think I would have that sort of damn near total identification. It almost killed me.

William Tenn (Philip Klass) writes of Gold in *Galaxy: Thirty Years of Innovative Science Fiction*:

> Before *Galaxy* I wrote science fiction. After *Galaxy* I wrote only *my* kind of science fiction. And for that, I must admit, the responsibility lies with one of the most irritating and aggravating men I've ever known. From deep within his editorial cave, Horace Gold somehow changed me. I believe he changed us all.

What irritated so many writers about Gold's editorial practices was his habit of re-writing sections of the stories. In the introduction to *The Fifth Galaxy Reader* (which came out in March of 1961 and was the last one he edited), he defends himself against that charge:

> There's a great deal to be said for integrity of material, and don't think it's not being said at stupefying length, and any good editor sweats at keeping that integrity, especially when the author loses hold of it here and there. The integrity as the editor sees it? No, as the material demands . . . And just as a writer can goof, so, as noted before, can an editor—but not being emotionally involved, he's less likely to, and he's also more likely to admit it if he does.
>
> To writers who haven't gone through the open hearth of story conferences, there's something frightening in the eagerness of editors out after a smash of a story. As Pohl said of *Gravy Planet*, . . . "It would have been a better story if you hadn't interfered. It wouldn't have been written, but it would have been a better story." Aside from not liking to read unwritten stories, I can't put out a magazine with them, can I?

To pinpoint one of Gold's achievements, he kept *Galaxy* going in a time of disaster for pulp and digest-sized sf magazines. In 1957 there were 29 sf magazines. By 1962 there were only seven. Gold guided *Galaxy* safely through most of this time of troubles and handed over a healthy magazine to Fred Pohl.

Another accomplishment is recognized in *Science Fiction: History-Science-Vision*, an academic study by Robert Scholes and Eric S. Rabkin. They state that:

By the mid-fifties there were well over thirty American magazines devoted primarily to science fiction, but *Astounding, F&SF*, and *Galaxy* still dominated the field. Most of the major works of science fiction that apppeared in the fifties were first introduced in one of these three journals—and among the three *Galaxy* seems to have held an edge.

Algis Budrys says in a memoir in the book *Galaxy: Thirty Years of Innovative Science Fiction*:

> The people who had put *Galaxy* together—essentially, Horace Gold and W. I. Van der Poel, the art director—had consciously set out to trespass on everything that was known about the production and packaging of topflight sf. What was known was that only John W. Campbell, Jr., had a license to do it.
>
> The situation is hard to grasp now because *Galaxy* succeeded in its controversion. The feat was roughly comparable to what would be accomplished if Pepsi-Cola ever outstripped Coca-Cola in popularity.

Barry Malzberg says of the sf of the Fifties in his fine anthology *The End of Summer*:

> ... virtually all of the great innovators of the eighties will carry on their work, careers, and lives as if the people of the fifties had never been. . . .
> That decade, thirty years in the past, will, for most intents and purposes, appear to have been for naught.

This history of *Galaxy*'s Gold years was written in part to make sure Malzberg's gloomy prophecy will not come true. The writers will be remembered in all their original glory and splendor and their editor, Horace Leonard Gold, will be remembered and honored for his marvelous magazine.

At last report, Gold is now the literary editor for Questar and is also back to writing fiction. This is most encouraging news, especially for those of us who grew up with *Galaxy*.

Also in *Galaxy: Thirty Years of Innovative Science Fiction*, Alfred Bester concludes his memoir:

> But this remembrance has a happy ending. I was attending an sf convention (to prove that I was still alive) and was exploring the rare-book-and-magazine stalls when I came face to face with a biggish, broad, balding, mellow-voiced young man who beamed at me and confessed that he was Horace's son. We embraced and I sent my eternal love and gratitude to Horace, as indeed I do now.

Indeed as we all do now!

PART TWO:

FREDERIK POHL AND HIS SUCCESSORS

INTRODUCTION

WHEN THE CHANGE OF COMMAND AT *GALAXY* became effective, I was not aware of it. I was deeply involved in the activities at the Lake Mills (Iowa) High School, activities mostly straight academic or musical, and I had long since been introduced to mainstream fiction. I also spent much time reading and trying to write good poetry. So it became the singing of Bach and madrigals, the reading of William Faulkner and Sinclair Lewis and T. S. Eliot and the usual struggles of the later teen years that preoccupied me. *Galaxy* drifted out of my sight. The drug store where I had, in effect, a private subscription to the magazine burned to the ground along with a pool hall in the summer of 1961. And soon it was (too soon, it seems to me now) that I was through my senior year and was one of the graduating class of 1962, a peer group since well memorialized by the movie *American Graffiti*, though the Norwegian Lutheran tradition I grew up in was very different from California. Still, the basic circumstances involving the protagonists of that film involved me too. I graduated from LMHS and left for college. In fact, my whole family left town and we resettled in Decorah, Iowa, where I attended Luther College.

Now I was totally engrossed in college activities. Existentialism and a belated beat element proved interesting, so I read the beats and also a great amount of Kierkegaard, Nietzsche, and Martin Heidegger. I can't imagine any works—except possibly economics textbooks—that were and are more alien to the precepts of science fiction, even the dystopian sf works like those of Pohl and Kornbluth alluded to in Part I, *The Gold Years*.

While I was absorbed by existentialism/phenomenology, modern poetry, and Lutheran theology, I drifted far out of the sf orbit. I remember that during my college years the only notice I gave to sf was when *Analog* (the former *Astounding SF* magazine) suddenly appeared in a larger format which proclaimed some series about "Dune." I didn't buy them.

But I would have given too much time to that magazine or *Galaxy* if I had bought and read them now and then. The societal background noise was growing so loud that even my immersion in metaphysics was disturbed. It became harder to concentrate. In my sophomore year JFK was killed, and the further disasters of the Sixties followed like more and more railroad cars derailing. The greatest of the disasters, Viet Nam, kept unfolding and I became involved in what was then called the Movement. During a lull in radical activities—in the summer of 1968, of all years— I noticed *Galaxy* again. A Vaughn Bodé cover intrigued me into buying a copy and I liked the stories inside. The sf New Wave was in full stride and part of it was linked to one of the esthetic philosophies I had been reading about, surrealism. It proved to be an excellent antidote for all the rather sterile Left "isms" that were then raging around me. I began to rebuild my *Galaxy* collection (I had sold my original one in my existentialist days), and I also became aware of the excellent paperback anthologies which were then profuse. A lot had changed since the times of H. L. Gold. This second part is an account of these changes and the magazine's later years.

9. FREDERIK POHL (I)

GALAXY BEGAN TO FEATURE FREDERIK POHL'S name as Managing Editor in the issue of June, 1961. In Pohl's autobiography *The Way the Future Was*, he describes the circumstances of his assuming editorial control:

> He [Horace Gold] was in constant pain. And toward the end of 1960 it became clear that his life was in danger, and that he was simply too ill to continue with the magazine, or indeed with any activity not directly aimed at getting him better.
>
> With Horace's approval I went downtown to see Bob Guinn, the publisher of *Galaxy*, offering to fill in for Horace on a temporary basis until things clarified themselves.

Guinn thought about Pohl's offer and then gave him the green light.

> I stayed with *Galaxy* for just about a decade. The pay was miserable. The work was never-ending. It was the best job I ever had in my life.

The June, 1961 issue included stories by the late Mack Reynolds, R. A. Lafferty, Fred Saberhagen (who was beginning to make a name for himself), and Poul Anderson (a veteran by that time). There was a short story by Pohl and Kornbluth—the latter half of that fine writing team had died in 1958 at the age of 35, but luckily there was a reserve of stories the two had collaborated upon which had not yet seen print. The old China hand Cordwainer Smith, aka Paul Linebarger, was back again with a truly horrific novelette called "Mother Hitton's Littul Kittons."

The Smith tale was one in the series of Norstrilian episodes dealing with this interesting and sinister planet which alone produces the longevity drug called stroon. It told of Benjacomin Bozart, a galaxy-class thief who planned subtly and carefully to get his hands on some practically priceless stroon. Thousands before him had tried to do the same, and had all mysteriously vanished, never to be heard of again. Bozart met no better fate than the others, but the details of *that* I shall leave to the reader to discover. In some anthologies there is actually a word of caution about this novelette to keep it from the too young or too impressionable.

Cordwainer Smith was to be a regular in *Galaxy* for about five more years, until he died rather prematurely in 1966. He was an assembler of theme-related legends and tales after the manner of Heinlein and H. Beam Piper, who had integrated future histories into which their stories could be fitted. Such integrated stories could be joined to make a single novel-length work, or a novelette extended into a novel. It is, by the way, interesting that this seems so commonplace in science fiction—both the construction of future histories and the elongation or joining together of stories to make a whole. There were and are extended historical series in mainstream fiction, but the phenomenon of splicing stories together does not seem as usual.

Cordwainer Smith had a consistent though fragmentary future of some 10,000 years from now when the Lords of the Instrumentality ruled all, but were consistently faced with rebellion by the underpeople, genetically tailored humanoids combining the traits and appearances of humans and other mammals, or even birds in the case of the winged undermen. We shall spend more time on Smith's future worlds as the Sixties progress.

The Pohl/Kornbluth short story in the June issue is of the "one-punch" type that James Blish so abominated. Well, *Galaxy* had not exhausted its supply of them. In "A Gentle Dying" an old chap named Elphen DeBeckett turns over a lot of money to study and protect children. He has apparently been sheltered from the world, for on his deathbed he wonders what became of his charitable donation. We are swiftly disillusioned of any cheery social progress brought about by his money. In fact, a sort of ageist fascism has sprung up, with grim consequences.

Frank Herbert, no stranger to *Galaxy*, has a novelette in this issue, "A-W-F Unlimited." This story has some of the old *Galaxy* hallmarks. It derides the military and advertising and is another one-puncher. The key to this one is literally a key to unlock people from their space battle armor. Romantically inclined male and female space warriors can exchange their keys so that some sexual interest can be included in the grotesque suits they must wear outside their spacecraft. It all reminds one of the old jokes about chastity belts, brought back to serve as a rather mild satire. Frank Herbert hadn't quite hit his stride yet, or else he had figured out to the millimeter one of the types of stories that *Galaxy* would take.

Pohl himself, as noted earlier, was a great practitioner of this sort of sf social satire, so the continuation of it in the *Galaxy* of the Sixties should surprise no one.

Emsh (Ed Emshwiller) was still doing *Galaxy* covers and interior art as he had done for Gold. [Emshwiller would cease sf magazine work in 1964 and go on to successful experimental film-making.] A cover of his appears on the August, 1961 issue.

In August, Jack Vance really begins to shine forth. He had done some good stories for the 1950's *Astounding* and one or two short works for *Galaxy*, but not ever a novella like "The Moon Moth." Vance is an absolute genius at constructing believable alien societies, though they do tend to be a little on the medieval side. His first book, *The Dying Earth*, which was initially published in a short-lived paperback series from Hillman, was also reminiscent of medieval and romanticist adventure. That book appeared ten years before "The Moon Moth," and Vance had lost none of his ability, but had in fact gotten even better at inventing alien societies. Xenography, alien biology and history, seem to be his specialties.

In this particular novella, which is also a detective tale, Edwer Thissell is a Consular Representative for the Earth-worlds. In the course of his duties he has to capture Haxo Angmark, an interplanetary villain. The problem is that the planet Sirene has an incredibly complex society which makes the Japanese ritualisms in *Shogun* seem like kindergarten stuff.

Each of the native Sirenese must wear an individualized face mask, and can communicate with others only after mastering six or more basic instruments. The more ornate the mask and the more sophisticated the musical accompaniment, the higher is one's social rank. Only slaves get by without musical abilities, but a slave would never get into a position to learn much, so Thissell must master Sirenese customs and costumes. To add to the difficulty, the sinister Angmark has already spent some five years on Sirene, whereas Thissell is a newcomer who begins by committing grievous *faux pas*. The reader is held enthralled while Thissell engages in a duel of wits with Angmark and with the highly refined Sirenese culture.

For an example of Vance's literary style and the care with which he builds his alien societies, here is a section where another outworlder gives Thissell some pointers:

> "I suggest that you learn the following instruments as quickly as possible: the *hymerkin* for your slaves. The *ganga* for conversation between intimates or one a trifle lower than yourself in *strakh* [Sirenese social prestige]. The *kiv* for casual polite intercourse. The *zachinko* for more formal dealings. The *strapan* or the *krodatch* for your social inferiors—in your case, to insult someone, since you have no inferiors. The *gomapard* or the *double-kamanthil* for ceremonials."

Vance has been compared to various authors, and has even admitted to being influenced by such writers as James Branch Cabell (H. L. Mencken's "last aristocrat") and the 1930's *Weird Tales* author Clark Ashton Smith, who also wrote of advanced and often decadent societies. In the context of *Galaxy* alone, I find that the two best conjurors of wonder are Vance and Cordwainer Smith. Smith's Lords of the Instrumentality and his "underpeople" are as strange as anything Vance has come up with, but with a difference: Cordwainer Smith uses live ammunition whereas Jack Vance dazzles with magical verbal fireworks. This is to take nothing away from Jack Vance, for his worlds are more detailed and engrossing.

An excellent resource work is *Jack Vance*, part of the 21st Century Writers Series edited by Underwood and Miller (Taplinger, New York, 1980). It is a collection of essays about Jack Vance's work, and reasonably thorough. For instance, Don Herron's essay "The Double Shadow" compares the "strange, evocative names" found in the writings of Vance and those of Clark Ashton Smith (referred to humorously by H. P. Lovecraft as Klarkash-ton). Some of the names are:

Jack Vance's	*C. A. Smith's*
Ulan Dhor	Manghai Thal
Rogol Domedonfors	Zon Mezzamalech
Quantique	Zothique
Olliphane	Ouphaloc
Hildemar Dasce	Theophilus Alvor
Parsifal Pankarow	Satampra Zeiros
Tschai	Tasuun
Dadiche	Evagh
Pandelume	Fustules
Skerde Vorek	Kronous Alkon
Pharode	Phandiom
Robin Rampold	Allan Octave
Pallis Atwrode	Aristide Rocher
Rundle Detteras	Tirouv Ompallios
Jad Piluna	Ux Loddhan
Sibot	Saddoth
Vogel Filschner	Jasper Trilt
Hygen Grote	Avoosl Wuthoqquan

At the time I *did* notice the cover of the October, 1961 issue of *Galaxy*. It is by Finlay and illustrates "The Beat Cluster," a short story by Fritz Leiber, another good old *GSF* standby. It tells how the Beatniks and drifters who would otherwise have been "on the road" have instead opted for living in Earth orbit in a colony of connected bubble-like structures. There they are free to play guitars, study Zen Buddhism, and carry on various creative projects. Certain Earth politicians don't like this phenomenon much—and also the Beat colonies smell! However, they turn out to have been performing a useful colonizing role in space after all, and are allowed to stay in their blissful orbit.

This story illustrates that the alternate sf worlds could even accommodate current, rather mild, social dissidents. Judith Merril, in an extended essay in the anthology *SF: The Other Side of Realism*, says:

> The Beats seemed to me a crude, sometimes grotesque, malformed variety of Establishment Litterateurs. I have no doubt at all that that is exactly how science fiction looked when viewed from North Beach. Oppositely oriented, there was not sufficient interest in either rebel camp to discover how similar our views of the middle really were. To the literary-artistic *avant garde*, science fiction's struggle for literary respect-

The Beat Cluster. Illustrator: Finlay.

ability, for acceptance by the very Establishment they had contemptu-
ously abandoned, gave us a clownish aspect; their attempt at total rejection of modern technological society made our determined involvement
with its dynamics look like a crude, sometimes grotesque, malformed
variety of 19th century "materialism." They were too involved with the
dynamics of meaning and expression, and the search for new modes of
language and literature appropriate to the ambivalences and relativistic
realities of modern life, to concern themselves with unorthodox experiments in interpretation of these realities, or with any philosophy more
complex than existentialism. Our rockets and planets and alien creatures, unconnected with their immediate realities, appeared as absurd
caricature-symbols of (not just "neurotic" but) childish "escapism." To
us, their howls and bongo rhythms and cut-up-fold-ins were, just as
obviously, the rococo entertainments of sterile decadence. We were
much too intent on communicating our intellectual insights to have time
or patience for experiments in unorthodox form.

This was the unfortunate status quo of the early Sixties. Had any of
either group known—and it is surprising none of them did—of the horrors their society, and the world, were going to be put through, they
would certainly have made common cause earlier, whether or not such a
confluence would have made any difference. Certainly, by the end of the
decade, the situation was very different—but we will not jump ahead so
far.

The October issue also contained "A Planet Named Shayol," a grim
novella by Cordwainer Smith. On this prison planet the inhabitants are
assaulted by dromozoa, wild cells that cause them to grow into grotesque
shapes—some grow extra heads or arms, and one has turned into a gigantic foot. Finally the Lords of the Instrumentality end this brutal punishment and retrieve those who can be made more or less human again.
Mercer, through whose eyes we see this prison planet, is one of these
fortunate ones. Those who have grown brainless will be painlessly disposed of. Smith, as usual, is not pulling his punches.

In the December, 1961 issue Frederik Pohl discusses the many possible
worlds in the galaxy, and also touches on a point that various astrologers
and assorted soothsayers were making much of at the time. Jupiter and
Saturn had made a rare eclipical conjunction in the constellation of
Capricornus and would be joined in February of 1962 by the faster-
moving heavenly bodies, Mars and Venus. This was thought by many to
bode some dire catastrophe, so even the residents of Lake Mills, Iowa,

who paid attention to the Des Moines *Register* expected something sinister to happen. I recall going to a comical Danny Kaye movie the day all the planets got together—an event, ironically, which we could not see because the sun interposed itself. But not much of anything happened except that I chanced to get a seat in the theater right behind a girl I was fond of at the time. She laughed so at the film that I thought she would also be a good enough sport to go on a date with me. She wouldn't—so, disaster enough for me!

The main feature of this issue is the first part of a novel by Poul Anderson, whose work we have encountered before, most notably in the later Fifties. He had also been doing some very good pieces for *Astounding/Analog*, for example, *The High Crusade*. His new *Galaxy* novel "The Day After Doomsday" (reprinted as *After Doomsday*) deals with a grim situation. Earth has just begun interstellar exploration with expectations of great discovery and trade—and suddenly Earth is destroyed, "murdered." The all-male crew of the interstellar ship *Benjamin Franklin* sets out to find what planet or race was responsible.

They have "countless thousands of races" in the galaxy to deal with; the friendly trading Monwaingi, the warlike Vorlakka, the sinister Kandemirians, and so on. They also have to eventually link up with the ship *Europa*, with its fortunately all-female crew. Because the now-homeless Terrans are possessed of more panache side by side with greater technological prowess than the somewhat more decadent races they encounter, they at last win through to gaining a new planet. But the story ends with a question: will the interstellar war grow larger? They have started something akin to the pressure on the African tribes of the western coast when white settlements began pushing inward.

The December issue also has a splendid short story by Algis Budrys, one of sf's most underrated writers. This is the much-anthologized "Wall of Crystal, Eye of Night," which in its extreme surreal subjectivity anticipated the New Wave authors by a good four or five years. It is also found in the book *Galaxy: Thirty Years of Innovative Science Fiction*, prefaced by Budrys recounting some anecdotes of his sf apprenticeship in the days of H. L. Gold. Budrys had previously worked for the short-lived Gnome Press, which produced hardbound sf books that are now almost uniformly scarce.

The February, 1962 issue dealt with the national mania for bomb shelters in "Critical Mass," a Pohl/Kornbluth satirical piece which somehow still seems appropriate. To shake the public's false sense of security in fall-out shelters a fake incident is arranged by some newly-graduated dissidents. They show up the war planning for the big fraud it really is, and also push the country toward a less bellicose set of preconceptions. It is still relevant, although I believe it would be written very differently today.

Floyd C. Gale was holding over as book reviewer from the time of H. L. Gold. He missed the April, 1962 issue but was back again in June. So were writers of such stature as Budrys and Blish (actually a Blish pair, James and Virginia), as well as Wallace West and R. A. Lafferty (who was doing a short piece for *Galaxy* in almost every issue). There was also Robert Silverberg, who was at that time still making a name for himself (and still unmellow and living in New York, according to a 1979 interview with Charles Platt in *Dream Makers*).

The Blish novelette, "On the Wall of the Lodge," shows an odd sport of the future in which city residents chase after a Clown, someone involuntarily drawn into their cruel game after being set up in a contrived car wreck. After some conditioning, the Clown begins to enjoy his role. The deserted streets and squares of the future city through which the hunt is conducted give the tale a distinctly haunting quality, as does the sinister impersonality with which the hapless Clown-to-be is processed.

The June issue also has an interesting Wallace West short story, "Dawningsburgh," about a Martian tourist trap staffed by robots. Real Martians, of course, are not seen by the regular tourists, but a frustrated Earthwoman ignores the rules of the place and goes out into the forbidden night. She encounters a real Martian who is about to avenge the desecration of his planet's old city by having the Earthlings done in by real non-robot Martians the next day. The tourist informs him that Earth will surely retaliate with cobalt bombs, and she suggests an equally cruel but non-fatal punishment. The Martian princeling agrees to it, but will not permit her to escape the same fate, saying that perhaps it will make a good Martian of her after all, not at all what she had desired.

The August, 1962 issue confirmed Fred Pohl's excellent editorial work. He managed to secure a prize short novel by Jack Vance, the famed Hugo-winning "The Dragon Masters." It takes place on one of the planets colonized by Earthmen during their sweep outwards. Richard Tiedman, in his essay "Jack Vance: Science Fiction Stylist" in *Jack Vance*, summarizes it:

The Dragon Masters. Illustrator: Gaughan.

Joaz Banbeck leads a progressive and scientifically regimented state at Banbeck Vale [one of a number of human settlements on the world circling the sun Skene], while the "jocose and wrathful" Ervis Carcolo foments his imperialistic design from the euphemistically named Happy Valley. Before the coming of the Basics, unhuman aliens from space who periodically raid the vales for captives, the Carcolos had enjoyed a dominance over their neighbors. Their reign of power now interrupted, Carcolo plots to regain the former ascendancy of Happy Valley. Both sides are now aided by dragons—Juggers, Fiends, Blue Horrors, Long Horned Murderers, each bred from Basic captives into specialized species. A third factor is the native Sacerdotes, whose pacific creed forbids action even against the Basics, but who have designs of their own. "Beyond caution or dismay," Carcolo sends his men and dragons against Banbeck Vale in ventures foredoomed by his obstinacy and lack of foresight. Indeed, the character of Carcolo could easily be read as a satire on dictators. During his misadventures the Basics return, throwing the critical situation into chaos which resolves in Joaz Banbeck's favor.

Tiedman's essay also gives us hints as to some other influences on Jack Vance's prose style: E. R. Eddison and Abraham Merritt, and also the 19th Century notable, John Ruskin, who wrote much on the art of the Renaissance.

Norman Spinrad, in his *Jack Vance* commentary, says:

To enjoy Vance, you have to enjoy words as sculpture on paper, reality as a baroque landscape, and sardonicism for its own elegance. . . .

And why not? This stream of literature has always been with us and always will be.

I neglected to mention the art. Jack Gaughan did the cover and the interior work for the Vance novel, and his depiction of the various species of dragons was most satisfactory. *Galaxy* was keeping the standards of its artwork high. Considering that Pohl was also editing *If*, he was doing very creditably indeed. In *The Way the Future Was*, Pohl himself says generally of the era:

In the decade of the 1960's I published a lot of science-fiction stories, by a lot of writers. Among them was nearly every writer of any importance in the field. For many of the best, I published all or most of the work written in that decade: Robert A. Heinlein, Cordwainer Smith, Harlan Ellison, Larry Niven, R. A. Lafferty, Fritz Leiber, Jack Vance, and a lot of others. Many of the stories, including many of the best, would never have been written if I hadn't encouraged, coaxed, and

The Ballad of Lost C'mell. Illustrator: Virgil Finlay.

sometimes browbeaten the authors. And they were mostly pretty good stories. This is, of course, my subjective opinion. But I think it's right.

In a footnote he mentions Volume Two of Isaac Asimov's *The Hugo Winners* as giving a strong hint of *Galaxy*'s ascendancy: stories from *Galaxy* gathered in nine Hugos, compared to two Hugos garnered by all the other sf magazines *combined*. To give further perspective on its accomplishment, it should also be taken into consideration that the magazine was published only bimonthly for much of the decade.

The issue of October, 1962 features the first of a two-part novel by Pohl himself, "A Plague of Pythons," and a story by Ray Bradbury, whose stature in the sf world was probably surpassed only by Heinlein himself. There is also a fine novelette by Cordwainer Smith, "The Ballad of Lost C'mell."

Smith's story is another of the Underpeople series and a crucial one. It is elegantly illustrated (the cover, too) by Virgil Finlay. One of the rulers of Old Earth, Lord Jestocost, is in love with justice and is well aware of the low status and discrimination suffered by the underpeople. He makes contact with C'mell, a beautiful red-haired cat-woman who is a receptionist and hostess for off-world visitors. She in turn serves as a telepathic conduit for the E-telekeli, the deathless guide and spirit of the underpeople. A meeting is arranged in which C'mell appears before the gathered Lords and the Lady Johanna Gnade on a false charge. She is quickly released, but not before a crucial telepathic link is made which shows the E-telekeli the secret ruling devices of the human Lords. The secret of what Lord Jestocost and C'mell managed to do was carefully kept, but hinted at in an obscure ballad sung by the now jubilant underpeople, who at long last were approaching equality with the hominids, the true humans.

The Ray Bradbury story is a rather good one too. Typical of his work, it is more impressive in mood than in plot, certainly no drawback if you can pull it off. It is a tale of odd cosmic dust, an invasion of Earth slowly but surely happening through a most innocuous and even gastronomically pleasing way—but very chilling all the same. It's called "Come Into My Cellar," and of course has long since been anthologized.

And now we have reached the year of 1963, which, so dire in so many ways, was a rather good year for *Galaxy*. As I have earlier mentioned, science fiction is not immune to the social events surrounding it. Sword and Sorcery fantasy, of course, is quite impervious, but the sort of socially

Space Station. Illustrator: Dember.

conscious and socially satirical sf *Galaxy* specialized in for so long was bound to be hit by some of the shrapnel.

No, 1963 was not a year like all years. It was a year after which most people realized that it wouldn't be business as usual for a long time, perhaps forever. Even in the spring of the year, Joan Baez, Bob Dylan, and Phil Ochs were singing anti-war protest songs and there were anti-Bomb rallies, and even so it took nearly twenty more years for a truly massive anti-nuclear war movement to develop. In 1963, an aging and angry Iranian imam, Khomeini, left Iran—the Iran of our ally, the late Shah—for exile in France.

In August, hundreds of thousands of marchers came to Washington, D.C. and heard Martin Luther King Jr.'s "I Have a Dream" speech, delivered, we now know, *extemporaneously*. The first stirrings of anxiety about the problems of the regime in South Viet Nam were surfacing amid worries about our intentions in that part of the world. And then that regime fell! Ngo Dinh Diem was assassinated by officers of his own army. And not so long after that, around noontime on a cold Friday on my college campus in Iowa, all unsuspected and unimaginable to us came rumors of some shootings in Dallas. I walked downstairs in the Student Union to the room that had a TV set and knew at once, as the British say, that it was all up. JFK, who had given us such hopes and who had set our sights toward the eventual Moon landing, was gone. No, there was to be no escaping the effects of 1963, not even for those born later.

Still, despite the hopes and the disasters, *Galaxy* continued to be a beacon of good sense and good writing. It began the year with a fine February issue. Cordwainer Smith had a mesmerizing novella, "Think Blue, Count Two," dealing with the earlier times of mankind's outward spread to farther stars. It begins:

> Before the great ships whispered between the stars by means of plano-forming, people had to fly from star to star with immense sails—huge films assorted in space on long, rigid, cold-proof rigging. A small space-boat provided room for a sailor to handle the sails, check the course and watch the passengers who were sealed, like knots in immense threads, in their little adiabatic pods which trailed behind the ship. The passengers knew nothing, except for going to sleep on earth and waking up on a strange new world forty, fifty or two hundred years later.
>
> This was a primitive way to do it. But it worked.
>
> On such a ship Helen America had followed Mr. Gray-no-more. On such ships the Scanners retained their ancient authority over space. Two

hundred planets and more were settled in this fashion, including Old
North Australia, destined to be the treasure house of them all.

However, there were sometimes problems. The space-sails ripped, some
of the crew woke up too soon and then had all the sleeping people at their
mercy. Veesey has been programmed for this, and when trouble begins
after she wakes, her conditioning and some very high technology come to
the rescue; it is all quite as intriguing and strange and evocative as the
opening paragraphs above. This story is also part of Smith/Linebarger's
20,000-year human (and underpeople) history.

The Willy Ley science article for February of 1963 is on the history of
manned rocketry. It carries developments up to the February 20, 1962
Mercury capsule flight of John H. Glenn (of continued fame), and that of
Malcolm Carpenter in May, 1962. Ley also mentions Soviet advances of
the time. There is a photograph of an astronaut on page 87. It is "Astronaut Grissom in training (centrifuge) for sub-orbital flight." Like Ley,
Gus Grissom was not destined to see the Moon landing.

The February issue also has the first *Galaxy* appearance of British sf
writer Brian W. Aldiss, later to be one of the mentors of the New Wave.
His novella "Comic Inferno," a title he borrowed from Kingsley Amis, is
about the future development of robots who are outstripping the human
race in numbers and also in philosophy. It is presented as not so bad after
all, and anyway there's not jolly much we can do about it, what? So
humans decide to give robots equal rights. The continual talk of "rights"
in these sf works can hardly be considered apart from the social struggles
then taking place in the United States.

Galaxy pioneer Clifford D. Simak also has a novelette in the February
issue, "Day of Truce." It is reminiscent of the Pohl/Kornbluth *Gladiator
at Law* of the earlier Fifties. It is definitely dystopic, dealing with the
disintegration and violence of suburban life—a family has fences and
dogs and finally even rattlesnakes to defend itself from the horrible gangs
of young punks. It has been over twenty years since Simak's piece, and
the Minneapolis suburbs where I have relatives seem much the same as
ever. They have, in fact, grown. They are no less middle class than they
were, so all that sf business about new suburban jungles has turned out to
be, no offense intended, piffle.

Sol Cohen became the new professional publisher of *Galaxy*; his name
replaced Robert M. Guinn's on the masthead of the December, 1962
issue. In August of 1963 Theodore Sturgeon substituted for Floyd C. Gale

as *Galaxy*'s book reviewer. Sturgeon gave a highly praiseful review of Kurt Vonnegut's sf/non-sf novel, *Cat's Cradle.* Vonnegut, it might be recalled, had been a *GSF* contributor in the Fifties before he decided to avoid calling his science fiction science fiction. The tactic worked beautifully. His works are nearly all still in print. One cannot say the same for his sf colleagues who were more forthright, including Sturgeon and Pohl themselves.

Wallace Wood was continuing to do some fine interior art. In the June and August issues he illustrated a fine Simak novel, "Here Gather the Stars." It is an excellent work. Enoch Wallace is a Civil War veteran who appears to his rural neighbors as a lonely eccentric. Actually, he has been given longevity and is the keeper and station-master for a trans-galactic transfer point for teleporting aliens. He is drawn into some of the interstellar conflicts by virtue of his position. What has been especially remarked about this work is the excellent depiction of the rural scenes, a specialty of Simak. This novel was released in book form as *Way Station*, and was another Hugo award winner for *Galaxy*!

Hal Clement had in the August issue a fine novelette, "Hot Planet," about surveying on Mercury. Clement has always been noted for his expertise at "hard" science fiction, meaning that he is always careful not to violate any laws of science, while at the same time writing fine—and in this case, tension-filled—stories. While the science team is on Mercury, volcanoes begin to erupt and they must use every skill to escape.

William Tenn (Philip Klass) was not as active a writer in the Sixties as he had been before. The preceding decade had seen collection after collection of his fine stories. He did appear, however, in the October, 1963 issue with a novelette, "The Men in the Walls" (expanded into a book in 1968 as *Of Men and Monsters*). A miserable remnant of humanity still clings to existence on an Earth totally controlled by huge aliens who live within their immense cities protected by technology of a very high order. Humans are to them mere vermin—mice or cockroaches. A tribesman named Eric the Only dares to enter Monster territory and even to use Monster weapons, and with Eric the human race begins to lift its head again.

This issue also contains a pleasant novelette by Cordwainer Smith, "On the Gem Planet." Casher O'Neill, nephew of a noted deposed dictator, finds himself on Pontoppidan, the Gem Planet, which really does consist mostly of gems valuable on other worlds and is thus enormously wealthy (but not as wealthy as Old North Australia where the immortality drug stroon is manufactured). Casher becomes the guest of Philip Vincent, the Hereditary Dictator, and his niece Genevieve, who is titular ruler of the gem planet. Casher is trying to liberate his world from its cruel current ruler, Colonel Mizzer, a totalitarian dictator of the sort we have grown familiar with in our own Caribbean. Casher has to solve the problem of what to do with an old but stroon-immortalized horse—a real one, not a horse underperson. The Pontoppidians have never had one on their planet before and don't know what to make of it. O'Neill must also submit to a mind-probe by Vincent. He passes both tests and gets a gem weapon, a green ruby to make a super-laser, to use against Mizzer. He wants to leave with Genevieve, but that he cannot do. He departs, having been assured of his future success and urged to rule wisely, and knowing he has made the old horse happy by means of a dog underperson who has won the horse's confidence. This novelette was later published as one section of *Quest of the Three Worlds*, a book which ties together all of O'Neill's adventures.

Floyd C. Gale is back as *Galaxy* book reviewer in this issue, but in the December issue he is displaced for keeps by Pohl *and* Sturgeon. Then the book review feature disappears altogether until February of 1965 when Algis Budrys is recruited for the task.

The October, 1963 issue is the last one which has, to my eye, the fine appearance of the classical old-time *Galaxy*; the interior art, with some excellent pages by Virgil Finlay, is still sharp and clear; and the cover is still splendidly glossy, at least on the copy I have. In his memoir, Frederik Pohl explains the financial considerations involved. In the competition for keeping such excellent writers as Galaxy had, something had to give. The magazine's production costs had to be kept competitive. Reason was still prevailing. Now we see elegantly produced and illustrated large-size paperbacks with astronomical prices filled with repetitive fantasy-fluff which will leave the reader poorer but none the wiser. *Galaxy* would have none of that.

10. FREDERIK POHL (II)

WITH SOME PRIZEWINNING ISSUES TO HIS CREDIT, Frederik Pohl had reason to be pleased with his magazine. *Galaxy* paid well enough to attract the best writers. But, according to Pohl in his autobiography, money was only one part of the formula for a top sf magazine:

Speed of reporting was almost as important, and so I made my first order of business every week to read and respond to the incoming manuscripts, not only the professional submissions but the slush pile as well. It was easy to beat out the competition in that arena. John Campbell ordinarily took a month or more to report. Horace had sometimes been far slower than that. Most of the other magazines had a two-tier system, preliminary reader and then editor; I did all my own reading, and I did it fast, and for at least ninety-five percent of the manuscripts either a buy or a bounce was on its way within forty-eight hours of the time I first saw the script. Of course, most were bounces. I trained my secretaries and assistants, when I had any, to open all incoming manuscripts, put a rejection slip on each one, and put it in an envelope stamped and addressed to go back to the writer. In the event I bought the story, that effort was wasted. But that only happened to one manuscript in twenty or fewer; and for all the others I could read them on the train on my way home to Red Bank [New Jersey] and drop them off in the mailbox at the station when I arrived.

. . . Some good stories slipped through my net. When they were good enough to make me covetous, I tried to let the author, or his agent, know how I felt, hoping that the next one would come my way.

. . . It was *Galaxy* that I was trying to make the leader in the field again. *If* was only a stepsister, but I had a good use for it. Most writers are in-and-outers, something good and then a few that are not so good. The best I wanted for *Galaxy*. The others I didn't. It's hard to deal with that sort of writer when you have only one magazine. You can't publish everything without sacrificing overall quality. But you know perfectly well (assuming the author is as good as you think he is) that someone else will publish the ones you turn down. There is always the risk that the suitor who soothes his feelings by buying the one you bounced will win him away with the next good one, too. *If*, with its lower rate, gave me a perfect dumping ground for the stories I didn't want to print in *Galaxy* but didn't want anyone else to have, either. *If* was also a good place to try out new talent.

There were, at least in my head, significant policy differences between the two magazines. Good gray *Galaxy* was the class leader. It paid a lot more for what it published, and took a lot more planning and care. *Galaxy* was edited for the mature, sophisticated science-fiction reader. If you could read only one magazine in the field but wanted to be *au courant parfaitement*, *Galaxy* was the magazine to read.

If was for the younger reader, and the newer, and the less involved. Editing *If* was almost recreational. If I had a whim not solid enough to call an inspiration, I tried it in *If*. In terms of literary quality and significance, I have no doubt that *Galaxy* was a better magazine than *If*, but *If* was a lot easier to turn around. . . . I was able to make *If* show a profit long before *Galaxy* did.

The December, 1963 issue had the first part of Jack Vance's novel, *The Star King*, and February of 1964 saw its conclusion. It appeared in April, 1964 as a Berkley Medallion paperback in a slightly altered version. This was just the beginning of Vance's famous "Demon Princes" series. The second novel also was printed in *Galaxy*, but the subsequent three appeared in book form only. In fact, the final book did not appear until January, 1981, as a DAW paperback. The concluding books were long awaited by Vance devotees.

The five are: *The Star King*, *The Palace of Love*, *The Killing Machine*,

The Face, and *The Book of Dreams*. The "star kings" are not human but assume human shape. A human avenger, Kirth Gersen, is after all five of those who had participated in a slave raid in which his parents had been killed. Gersen was brought up wisely by his grandfather, Rolf Marr Gersen, and was taught well. He has a list of names: Grendel (the Monster) [renamed Attel Malagate (the Woe) in the book version], Viole Falushe, Kokkor Hekkus (the Killing Machine), Lens Larque, and Howard Alan Treesong. He proceeds in a truly epic manner to track them down through the galaxy, "The Oikumene and the Beyond," and destroy them, one by one and in the order above.

In the *Galaxy* novel he hunts down Grendel. On an outpost world, a space explorer (doomed to death) tells Gersen of a lovely virgin planet that is coveted by the Star King, Grendel. From the records of the dying explorer, Gersen finds the names of his sponsors, seemingly philanthropical men, Kelle, Detteras, and Warweave. One of these is Grendel and an inhuman monster. Gersen calls upon all his training and wits to make the murderous Star King unmask himself, in an entertaining adventure in Vance's best baroque style and the first of a fine set of books.

The April, 1964 issue contained a complete short novel, "The Boy Who Bought Old Earth," by the redoubtable Cordwainer Smith. About his negotiations with this author Pohl says:

> Once or twice I lost out on a story I really had every right to expect, and that was painful. Cordwainer Smith was one of my favorite writers. He was also a recluse, who didn't want too much contact with the science-fiction world, but we had become friends and he had voluntarily promised to give me first look at everything he wrote. Unfortunately, he had taken on an agent. The agent was willing to live by Paul's* commitments, but he also had certain standard rules of procedure. One was that he never under any circumstances submitted two stories by the same writer to an editor at one time. When Paul happened to finish two scripts on the same day and sent them off to the agent in the same envelope, the agent sent me the one he liked best and mailed the other off to *Fantasy and Science Fiction*. By the time I found out about it, they had already accepted it, which is why I didn't get to publish "On Alpha-Ralpha Boulevard"; but I then persuaded that agent to change that rule.

* "Paul" because his real name, of course, was Paul M. A. Linebarger. Until his death he was a professor of political science at Johns Hopkins University and a frequent consultant on sensitive Far East matters for the State Department—one reason for his keeping his real identity secret.

Grandmother Earth. Illustrator: Emsh.

But he did publish "The Boy Who Bought Old Earth," and that was a significant achievement. It was to form the first section of Cordwainer Smith's only novel, *Norstrilia*, where it was redubbed "The Planet Buyer." Rod McBan, whose real name is considerably longer, is a Norstrilian (a native of Old North Australia) and a sheep ranch owner. He is, of course, very wealthy since his huge misshapen sheep produce stroon, the longevity drug, but he has a problem. He is very poor telepathically and thus could be judged a freak. A society such as Norstrilia does not need freaks, since so many sound people are around for hundreds of years, and so his life hangs in the balance. He is to be judged by a commission, and soon becomes aware that the head of Norstrilian government, the Onseck (short for Honorable Secretary) wants his life terminated. The Onseck is jealous because he cannot take stroon and thus has become a bitter old man.

Rod McBan has a way out that is full of peril, but also high-tech wizardry. In a scene eerily prophetic of the movie *War Games* and the current depredations of computer amateurs who penetrate even such secret and sacrosanct data banks as those of Johns Hopkins University and the Los Alamos atomic research institute, McBan uses his family's secret forbidden old computer for economic war and succeeds in practically cornering the market in the nearly-priceless stroon. But his troubles aren't over by any means. He makes enough to buy fabulous Old Earth, and there is one tense moment after another, and many plans made by the ruling all-planet Instrumentality, before he can get there.

Once Rod McBan arrives on Earth he is awaited by various assassins, but he is well disguised and the person (underperson) who is to be his special guide is none other than the cat-woman C'mell. The *Galaxy* section ends with their meeting, while we wonder what will become of them.

Galaxy continued to be a bi-monthly publication. Pohl mentions how he often spoke to Robert M. Guinn, the head of Galaxy Publishing Corporation, about going monthly again, and would receive only spicy jokes and noncommittal replies. The publisher, Sol Cohen, would also be noncommittal. And then both Guinn and Cohen were downright opposed. But then came a surprising twist of events, according to Pohl:

> ... But if you are all that ape-shit for a monthly magazine [said Guinn and Cohen], we'll tell you what we'll do. We'll start a third magazine for you. We'll make that one monthly.
> That took me aback. The last thing I wanted right then was another

magazine. It seems to me that a magazine, any magazine, is or at least ought to be a living creature. It should have a personality and an identity of its own. Not part of a litter; an individual. I was a long way from attaining that with either of the two magazines I already had.

. . . So I accepted the deal and got to work. We picked out a title: *Worlds of Tomorrow*. We designed a logo. I bought the stories. We signed a distribution contract. We sent the issue off to the printer. . . .

By then I was beginning to see flaws in my rosy reasoning. Suppose it *did* work as a monthly. I had had no luck at all in getting Bob and Sol to change the frequency of *If* or *Galaxy*. Just what would be my chances of getting them to *kill* a moneymaker in order to merge it with another book?

But in the long run it didn't matter. The problem never came up. By the time *Worlds of Tomorrow* came out, Bob and Sol had had another failure of nerve. The test project designed to establish the potential of monthly publication, too, was a bimonthly

Worlds of Tomorrow lasted several years, and even published some good stories that I might not have been able to get into either *If* or *Galaxy*. In order to distinguish it from the rest of the herd, I had decided to feature long complete-in-one-issue seminovels, and there were some fine ones by Gordon R. Dickson, Philip K. Dick, and others. But I had also decided to try to include some material on extrapolative science— not exactly fact but not exactly science fiction either . . .

Pohl mentions in a footnote that he did eventually get both *Galaxy* and *If* on a monthly schedule, but not for a few more years. "It made little difference one way or another to the sales," he said. That strikes me as remarkable, since sf is bought by the same devoted crew (or at least what looks like the same devoted crew) year after year, a crew whose numbers don't suddenly and startlingly shrink, at least not since the late 1950's debacle. It would seem *Galaxy* should sell each and every month, and perhaps it did sell more frequently, but apparently never to more than the initial group of *Galaxy* fans. At the time I was more concerned with Aristotle's and Bertrand Russell's philosophies and so on, and only now and then noted the appearance of *Galaxy* in a Decorah tobacco and magazine establishment (which also had a splendid soda fountain and counter, but has now vanished).

It was at this place, which also had the latest paperbacks and copies of *Playboy*, that I noticed the sudden expansion of *Analog SF* into its "bedsheet" size, not knowing it had undergone a similar odd metamorphosis in World War II. I think that might have helped overshadow

Galaxy for me to some extent. And none of my friends talked about science fiction. I think it's only in fairly recent years that I've heard some of my acquaintances admit that, yes indeed, they had read this or that story and it was a science fiction story. One has to accept as indubitable fact that the Sixties collegians were no more serious about serious, "heavy" sf for most of the decade than their predecessors of the 1950's.

The April, 1964 issue also had Harry Harrison back again. He had appeared once in the Fifties and was not a frequent *Galaxy* contributor, apparently reserving his heavier stuff for Campbell's *Analog*. His novelette "Final Encounter" is fairly straightforward. Various species of humans and humanoids of Earth ancestry discover each other while looking for some *real* aliens. One species is really different—breathes a different atmosphere, has a totally different alphabet, and so on—but can still be traced back to Earth origin by its fully human genetic code. All is not lost for the intrepid explorers, however. There are always the neighboring galaxies. This is a more optimistic story than "Big Ancestor," the November, 1954 piece by F. L. Wallace which showed the various types of humans found in the galaxy as descendants of some prodigiously multiplying vermin scorned by vastly superior species.

Interestingly enough, in the same issue Philip José Farmer, in his initial *Galaxy* appearance, also deals with planetary colonizing. In "The Blasphemers," Earth of the Nineteenth Century is about to be settled by an alien multi-sexual species who are aggressive, aristocratic, and also egg-layers like certain terrestrial mammals but much more rapidly breeding. However, they notice Terran statues which look astonishingly like the sacred ones of their revered ancestors, so for religious reasons they decide to leave Earth people alone even at the risk of running into their more advanced descendants later. Farmer was not to appear often in *Galaxy* but he was nevertheless a distinguished find. His subsequent career includes many distinguished books, primarily the "Riverworld" and "World of Tiers" series, and he has a considerable fandom. His major year for *Galaxy* seems to have been 1964, for he appears in two more of the year's issues. He had been writing sf for some time, but really achieved major fame in the Sixties and Seventies.

The question of Earth origins, in the sense of stories tracing the galactic appearances and beginnings of humankind, seems to have been a major preoccupation of this period. It is perhaps one of the basic questions of all of science fiction, as it is indeed of philosophy and theology. It is no

AUGUST · 1964
50¢

THE WATCHERS
IN THE GLADE
by
RICHARD WILSON

THE DELEGATE FROM GUAPANGA
by WYMAN GUIN

THE DEAD LADY
OF CLOWN TOWN
by
CORDWAINER SMITH

Illustrator: Pedersen.

accident that religion appears in the Farmer story in April and also in Cordwainer Smith's work, where a hidden and long-lost Christianity is hinted at in "On the Gem Planet." Of course Christian utopias were one of the ancestral contributors to sf; James Blish has much to say on the topic in his essay "Cathedrals in Space" (written under the name of William Atheling Jr., in *The Issue at Hand*). This sort of speculation in its more sophisticated forms adds a dimension to sf that is too often neglected, but was not neglected in *Galaxy*.

In the June issue, veteran writer Poul Anderson has "To Build a World," a short novel about terraforming the Moon with the help of friendly Martians. The job is straightforward until sabotage kills one of engineer Don Sevigny's crew. He is sent to Earth to investigate, and the story turns into a manic chase thriller with most of the important Earth politicos opposed to the Moon project. It is complicated by the fact that Sevigny is a Cytherean (as the human settlers of Venus call themselves) and not protected much by Earth laws. How he finally sets things straight calls for a lot of good old-fashioned derring-do. Anderson was a heavy contributor to rival *Analog*, but wily Pohl was able to snag him once in a while. Harry Harrison and Philip José Farmer also appear in this issue, adding to its luster.

The August, 1964 issue once again contains a very interesting and grim short novel by Cordwainer Smith. "The Dead Lady of Clown Town" is one of the more moving episodes in the upward struggle of the under-people. This time their leader is D'joan, a dog-girl who leads her people—bear-people, fox-people, and so on—in a mini-revolt which is animated primarily by love, or shall we say humanized by love (if that makes any sense in this nightmarish century). D'joan appeals to the basic love in all sentient creatures.

> Joan said, "Love is not something special, reserved for men alone.
> "Love is not proud [a Pauline echo]. Love has no real name. Love is for life itself, and we have life.
> "We cannot win by fighting. People outnumber us, outgun us, outrun us, outfight us. But people did not create us. Whatever made people, made us too."

Her band attempts to overcome human and robot armed forces with love, with alarming effect. Some of the robots self-destruct and even the soldiers waver and wonder, but in the end the love-bringers are all killed and D'joan, like a famous earlier Joan, is burned at the stake by a Lord of the Instrumentality. But D'joan's memory is retained by the underpeople and her heritage is ultimately brought to triumph by C'mell the cat-woman and her human sympathizers. There is, of course, more than an echo of the methods of Mahatma Gandhi and Martin Luther King Jr., both so recently and movingly memorialized, in the struggle of the under-people. In a short three years from 1964 antiwar demonstrators at the Pentagon would be placing flowers in the rifle barrels of the troops sent out to defend the nerve center of America's military establishment. That any of the demonstrators were conversant with science fiction is not material, but there is a very striking synchronicity.

Keith Laumer and Roger Zelazny both made their *Galaxy* debuts in 1964. Laumer appeared in February with "A Bad Day for Vermin," a short story about the unfortunate consequences of too hastily killing an extraterrestrial—somewhat *ex post facto* consequences, as it turns out.

Zelazny has a short-short in the June issue called "Collector's Fever," about the ill consequences of too eagerly collecting rocks, in this case an alien rock that turns out to have an agenda of its own. Roger Zelazny was later to become a much more significant contributor to *Galaxy*. He and Samuel Delany were acclaimed by Alexei and Cory Panshin as major forces in American New Wave science fiction. It is a matter of regret that Samuel Delany never published anything in *Galaxy*, particularly in view of his excellent, if somewhat diffuse, collection of critical essays entitled *The Jewel-Hinged Jaw*, in which he calls sf to order in more mathematical and metaphysical terms than is usually the case. Of course, that was during the New Wave when it appeared that sf was about to inherit the mantles of a collection of floating "isms" which have now floated else-where, But we shall get into more of these matters later in the Sixties.

The year 1964 was drawing to a close for *Galaxy* in a quite spectacular way. Gordon R. Dickson, who had first appeared in *Galaxy* under the Gold regime, is in the October issue with a short novel, *Soldier, Ask Not*, which was to win a Hugo award in 1965. It deals with the Dorsai mer-cenaries fighting against the Friendlies, who are crusading religious fanat-ics who think nothing of winning campaigns with suicide attacks, tactics which are currently noteworthy in our daily papers.

Dickson predicates numerous future human worlds which contain "splinter" cultures: all the warlike types tend toward one world, all the philosophers on another, and so on. There are mediators to prevent any one special type from prevailing, and there remain "full-spectrum" humans from Old Earth who still partake of all human tendencies. They have a special role—as the tale will reveal. It is also an adventure, in addition to bearing successfully some heavy psychological freight.

December brought the short novel "The Starsloggers," by Harry Harrison, who was back again doubtless by popular demand and sound editorial judgment. This short novel, like many *Galaxy* items, was eventually expanded into full novel length, as *Bill, the Galactic Hero.* It has something of an ideological message, and has been generally seen as a satirical reply to Robert Heinlein's famous (or infamous) *Starship Troopers.* The Heinlein work was in one of his more militaristic veins and struck many as being rather more suited to Rudyard Kipling than to an sf author of the later 20th Century. Earthmen grit their teeth and rocket forth to conquer or die, that sort of thing.

That sort of thing was wearing rather thin in the Sixties, and Harrison's delightful spoof of military hype and the aggressive psychosexual emotions it plays upon became justly famous as a grand put-down. Poor Bill is bedazzled and dragooned into space force service as a mere replaceable part in a grand Imperial war fleet where he is haplessly drawn into one futile battle after another. The *Galaxy* segment is excellent, and the whole book is highly recommended reading. It is also a good antidote to the *Star Wars* epics where everyone cheerfully throws on uniforms and piles into death-dealing spacecraft of all sorts.

Casher O'Neill, Cordwainer Smith's star-roaming hero, reappears in the February, 1965 short novel "On the Storm Planet." Here on the planet Henriada the weather is so ferocious that machines would have to be used to control it for human colonization—and the planet isn't worth that much expense. The Administrator is an old drunken ex-Lord of the Instrumentality who has an odd plan. Casher wants to reconquer the planet once ruled by his family, but to destroy Colonel Wedder, the dictator who had exiled him, he needs a war cruiser. Henriada's Administrator promises him one, but only on condition he kill a little girl who lives at Beauregard, a manor house owned by a former Norstrilian called Mister and Owner Madigan.

Nothing would seem easier. Casher is desperate and the girl is only an underperson and her master a very frail and ancient man. But why have eighty previous assassins failed and never been heard of again? And why won't the Administrator explain why the girl must die? Through howling storms O'Neill goes to Beauregard, in an isolated part of Henriada which is still protected by weather machines, and soon begins to learn part of the truth. Then T'ruth, the underperson, sets him a task, and it all ends in his gaining unexpected new powers. So much of the story stems from mood and powers more hinted at than described or explained that the reader is best advised to go to the actual work itself. The sum of Casher's adventures, I will mention again, is *Quest of the Three Worlds*, which one may have to locate in the used-book market.

The February issue also brings us the first book review column by Algis Budrys. He begins by saying:

> Book reviewing, like writing, editing or driving a nitroglycerine truck, is one of those occupations for which no one feels need of much previous training. So it must also turn out to be one of those occupations as full of ground rules as a Zen tea ceremonial and as little susceptible to perfect success.

On this cautious and dubious note, Budrys began quite an auspicious career as the *Galaxy* book reviewer. His enthusiasms for works he liked were so infectious that, after re-reading his first review, I sought out the Poul Anderson short story collections he had praised so highly. It is obvious the man knew his stuff.

Keith Laumer reappears in April, 1965 with a novelette, "War Against the Yukks." This turns out to be something of a potboiler in which the "Yukks" against whom an interstellar war had been fought were men, and their foes were women. And this was even before the more effective feminists had been heard from in the U.S.! The remaining women are in competitive groupings which need new seed to increase their numbers. They are so regressed that they have forgotten they only need sperm cells for artificial insemination. They do not actually need the two men they have captured, but the men (who of course find the women all young and gorgeous—at least those of child-bearing age) do not bother to enlighten them. I'm not sure if this sort of story could have been printed very much later than it was, at least not in a science-fictional context.

April does, however, have "Slow Tuesday Night," an excellent R. A. Lafferty short story about the speeding up of life to the point that people make huge fortunes and lose them over and over, marry several times, and write great learned books only to have them dismissed as old hat, all in the space of a single night. And the frantic night he describes is considered slow by these residents of a fast-paced Earth. It is satirical, but even more, it is ingenious, and so all the more worth reading, as indeed are all of Lafferty's works, in my estimation. He contributed much to Pohl's *Galaxy*.

In the June issue Robert Guinn resumes his place on the masthead as official publisher of *Galaxy*, displacing Sol Cohen, who had been working as a sort of "hired gun."

Frank Herbert, who was doing the much more famous *Dune* stories for *Analog* at the same time, has a long novel, "Do I Wake or Dream?" in the August issue. This is not very easy reading and gets a mite tedious. It generously employs much more than the usual *Galaxy* quota of scientific terminology—specifically, neurobiological and cybernetic—per paragraph. The crew of the interstellar exploratory ship *Earthling*, all highly skilled and specialized, confront a crisis. The guiding brains, detached from embryos, which coordinate the ship's automatic functions burn out with severe damage. The crew must then somehow integrate their own human capacities into an augmented computer network. They finally end up where Fred Brown did in "Answer," a famous short story of years before: they get an all-powerful machine which saves them and even creates a favorable atmosphere on one of the planets of the Tau Ceti system. But there is one hitch. The super-conscious computer demands— and of course will get—worship. Fred Brown got there a lot faster but without so much interesting state-of-the-art detail. Here sf readers have at least started hearing about random access memory and other such details hitherto known mainly among the IBM or Univac elite of the period. Now such knowledge, like the restricted drugs, has moved far down into the grades.

October, 1965 was *Galaxy*'s 15th birthday, and the fact was duly noted. The magazine had come through some killer times, and this was indeed a significant accomplishment when even such major *non-sf* magazines as *Collier's* and *Coronet* had been discarded by history. Fred Pohl was optimistic that *Galaxy* would continue and in many directions at once. In his editorial he says, "We don't know which will be the 'true' future—so we might as well imagine as many as we can."

In the anniversary issue the great names of the Fifties are all back with stories—even H. L. Gold contributes one, along with Pangborn, Sheckley, Simak, and Asimov. They are all fine, but I especially like Simak's short story "Small Deer," which gives a new and chilling twist on the disasters that befell the dinosaurs and then the great mammals when each had reached maximum size and population. He shows this through the

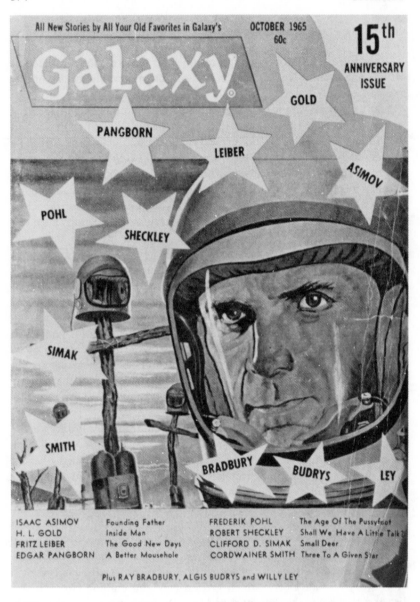

Founding Father. Illustrator: Pederson.

eyes of a time-traveller who arrives at the precise moment to see what does happen to them. The implications are somewhat grim, to put it mildly. This was one story I did not need to re-read, so well had it impressed itself upon my memory.

Another I liked was the Robert Sheckley novelette, "Shall We Have a Little Talk?" This shows Sheckley at his most inventive and humorous. Human civilization, in the form of Jackson, a lone explorer, reaches a humanoid society which looks good. Possibly trade concessions can be had, and diplomatic alliances—but there is one basic problem. Jackson can master some of the native speech patterns and idioms and grammar one day, only to be completely baffled the next.

Jackson finds he has stumbled into an ancient problem originally formulated by the ancient Ionian Greek philosopher Heraclitus, who said that one could not step into the same river twice. Sheckley says, "Concerning the language of Na, this was strictly and literally true." The language changes far too rapidly for any outsider to make sense of it, and any attempt to understand merely muddies the waters, so to speak, and makes matters worse. After all sorts of frustration, Jackson finally packs up and leaves, to the vast amusement of the Na people. This I consider a good idea story, an extrapolation of a vintage bit of philosophy which in itself made the tale of interest to me. Would that more sf writers were as eclectic as Robert Sheckley!

Beginning in this October, 1965 issue Frederik Pohl has a three-part serial, *The Age of the Pussyfoot.* Charles Forrester is frozen in liquid helium after a car accident that would have been fatal. Six centuries later he is revived in a dystopic Earth. He is soon killed, only to be revived again. Mankind is practically immortal, but is not happy. This seems, by the way, to be a familiar theme in sf—the musing unhappy immortals. Of course the immortal gods of Nordic mythology were not exactly Milton Berles, but still the theme in sf is transmuted somehow, divested of grandeur.

Forrester inadvertently spills the beans about an Earth defensive outpost to a Sirian, a race Earth fears may invade. He then expects to be justly arrested as a traitor, but so demoralized are the Earthmen of his not-so-brave new world that they nearly all go into the permafreeze. Forrester and a remaining cadre, despite some obstacles, rally the Earth men and women, and all is just ducky once more.

Harlan Ellison makes an unforgettable entrance (unacknowledged on

Under Old Earth. Illustrator: Finlay.

the cover) in the December, 1965 issue with his Hugo award winning short story, "'Repent Harlequin!' Said the Ticktockman." This is the famous encounter between Everett C. Marm, aka the Harlequin, and the Ticktockman, an all-powerful figure who, in a wildly regimented future Earth, can literally decide when your time is up and end you with the flip of a switch. The Harlequin enters to disrupt the insanely tight schedules and time-structure existence of the whole society. It should have been dedicated to all those who have ever felt like throwing, or have *thrown*, an alarm clock at a wall or out a window. Thus *Galaxy* ends 1965 on another triumphant note.

Pohl, in his fascinating autobiography, spends a little time describing his relationship to this formidable new talent:

> Harlan is an exciting, talented, fun person to be around, a brilliant writer and capable of great exertions as a friend. He is also one of the twentieth century's greatest sources of *tsoris*. For most of that decade I published nearly all the sf that Harlan wrote, and I would estimate that, taking everything together, Harlan was as much pain and trouble as all the next ten troublesome writers combined. If I tried to change a title, the calls started . . . . Usually he won those arguments and maybe he should have; the case *for* is that an author should have control over what he is represented as saying, the case *against* is that a magazine should have some sort of consistent personality of its own, and any time you want to debate, I'll take either side. But he was not always reasonable.

But, to our gain, *Galaxy* kept him among its actives. And *Galaxy* would need a good list of first-string authors. In October, 1965, Pohl's editorial mentioned that Cordwainer Smith was away on an anthropological expedition to the South Seas. Alas, Smith's absence was to be very long indeed. He died in August of 1966; in a eulogistic editorial in the December, 1966 issue, Pohl revealed that Smith was actually Dr. Paul Linebarger of Johns Hopkins and the State Department. It is uncommon for the latter institution to include great prose writers. True, there have been a few Dean Achesons and George Kennans, but they did not write sf. Perhaps other miraculous writers lurk around Foggy Bottom, but I have strong doubts, especially in these times when law grads have trouble with sentences very much more complex than the simple declarative, outside their own jargon.

Smith's February, 1966 novelette "Under Old Earth" was his last appearance in Galaxy until the posthumous publication of a story in April of 1978. In this 1966 piece, fittingly well-illustrated by Virgil Finlay,

Lord Sto Odin, who has a very short time to live unless he chooses rejuvenation, decides to die. He is very ancient and has long since lost all his friends and his wife. He takes two faithful robots down into the Gebiet, a forbidden region of Earth, and there discovers a new cult of dancing to the spell of "congohelium." This supremely dangerous substance is one of the basic building blocks of the universe, and Lord Odin decides to end the menacing practice. However, he perceives some of the reasons for the cult's popularity. The people of Old·Earth need some vitality, since all the old passions have been more or less exterminated. He lets a beautiful young woman cultist escape before he takes steps to end the dangerous use of congohelium. How he does this and what the long-term results are prove fascinating, and also fit right into Smith's history of future man and undermankind. Cordwainer Smith would be sorely missed, and thus Pohl was ever impelled to seek out authors of the same caliber.

Smith was not the only loss to *Galaxy* at that time. Jack Vance, still very much with us, ceased contributing to the magazine after his April, 1966 novelette "The Last Castle" and his 1966-67 novel *The Palace of Love*. "The Last Castle" won him both a Hugo and a Nebula award, and deservedly so. (The *Galaxy* table of contents calls it a novelette, though it is long enough to be a short novel. It has also appeared in five paperback editions, one of them Dutch, and a sumptuous limited hardbound edition from Underwood/Miller in 1980.) The Meks, hitherto a servant warrior class, revolt against their human masters, who are divided into genteel aristocratic clans. One by one the castles of the humans fall—all except for Castle Hagedorn and its Lord, who shows some of the Old Earth backbone and decides to fight it out long and hard and unyieldingly. Yet the grim Meks prove very dread foes indeed. A riveting tale!

As an example of Pohl's successful search for talent, a new writer by the name of Thomas M. Disch appeared in February, 1966 with the short story "The Echo of Wrath." It is a mood piece told from the point of view of a young girl, a Martian colonist. The humans on Mars maintain a successful colony, but we soon detect a note of nostalgia when the girl watches a family heirloom, an old color film of a trip to Earth. The various beautiful sights are mentioned and the old members of her family appear in the film as happy young tourists, although there is mention of the fact that the people on Earth are not entirely happy to see off-planet tourists. In one scene a policeman must protect the Martian (but human) visitors. The Martian colony is powered by a "converter." This must be a fusion device, it would seem, since we find at the end that the very same power that allows humanity to live on other planets has ended all of Earth after a very short war, leaving only a bit of floating interplanetary dust. The girl's grandmother scans the sky now and then waiting for the old green Earth to appear, and the child has the sad task of telling her Earth just isn't there any more. This could have been a very hackneyed story indeed, but Disch writes well enough that it is not. Instead, it is haunting, and far better than a 1940's story I read once where all that remained of Earth culture was a Donald Duck cartoon (unless, of course, the latter story, whose title I can't recall, was meant to be morbidly funny).

All this time Pohl was assembling the author-components of the major sf movement of the later 1960's, the New Wave, which as I have mentioned had already sprung into being. He had published Aldiss, Disch, Zelazny, and various others. True, he never did publish J. G. Ballard or S. R. Delany, but Pohl was very discerning at seeing what was afoot and who was an interesting and fresh writer. He took chances, but was finally justified in his choices.

Frank Herbert has an excellent two-part serial beginning in June, 1966: *Heisenberg's Eyes.* The future Earth is ruled by Optimen who have life spans of up to 80,000 years or more and who treat the Folk—ordinary *homo sapiens*—as serfs and vermin. The Folk are severely limited in regard to reproduction—their embryos are grown outside the womb so they can be checked and altered to ensure genetic conformity. The Optimen are afraid ordinary humans will develop viable long-living breeds, and have an extensive spy service to prevent this. Nothing is permitted to disturb the complete, and so far tranquil, rule of the Optimen.

These near-immortals reward their human servitors and agents by pharmaceutical means that prevent their aging for a few hundred years, and thus buy their loyalty. But to the horror of a medical staff of normal humans an embryo appears that looks as though it could have Optiman capability. It is supposed to be destroyed at once, but an underground of Cyborgs (partly artificial humans) saves it and re-implants it in the womb of its natural mother. Thus there is loose on Earth a potential for indigenous humankind to equal the Optimen in longevity.

Attempting to thwart this development, the Optimen kill the entire Folk city of Seatac with sonics and poison gas. Too late—the Cyborgs have smuggled the embryo out in time. Eventually the efficient Optimen capture the human parents and Cyborgs for interrogation and extermination. But the shock of the sudden violence begins to have a disastrous effect on the Optimen who have too long been precariously perched on their tranquil thrones of power.

The story is a real nail-biter despite Herbert's heavy use of genetic terminology, which nonetheless fascinates though at the expense of any deep characterization of the humans or the Optimen triumvirate.

As previously mentioned, Jack Vance makes his final bow in *Galaxy* with a three-part serial beginning in the October issue. This is the second novel of the Demon Princes series, *The Palace of Love*. Out to avenge the murder of his parents, Kirth Gersen has already disposed of one Prince. Now he is on the trail of Viole Falushe. Gersen befriends a half-mad alcoholic poet named Navarth, who gets him into the stronghold of Falushe, the sinister Palace of Love. Falushe, a notorious sybarite, had evaded Gersen's earlier attempts to trap him by using beautiful women as bait. Now Gersen is inside the palace and in easy reach of Falushe, but is it not possible that Gersen has gotten himself into an untenable, even fatal, position? He plays on Falushe's vanity by posing as a journalist, a course made very difficult in the baroque Vance manner of disguises and courtly mannerisms. Once again, Gersen must use all his intelligence and training to ferret out this Demon Prince. This Vance novel was brought out in a Berkley Medallion paperback in 1967, with some changes from the *Galaxy* version. It also appeared as a British hardcover book in 1968 and showed up in a German translation the following year. The French got to it in 1977, calling it, of course, *Le Palais de L'Amour*, which sounds even more appropriate to the tale than the more prosaic English title.

Galaxy went on, but no more would Vance's magical rococo prose, his dragons, elegant villains, poets, and wondrous ceremony grace its pages, nor would the great Lords of Cordwainer Smith's Instrumentality nor the gallant underpeople nor the near-mythic Norstrilians appear before its readers so proudly and in prose so majestic and yet so near the heart. But Vance would continue his series elsewhere, and Pohl still had new talents to unleash.

One of these was Anne McCaffrey, who wrote for her first appearance in *Galaxy* the novelette "The Ship Who Killed" in the October, 1966 issue. Unlike many of Pohl's new discoveries, notice of her story appeared on the front cover. Helva is an interstellar ship controlled by a woman's brain encased in a shell. She has an unorthodox young woman, Kira, aboard as her "brawn," her human partner. Kira is a "Dylanist," a morbid folk-singing type with suicidal tendencies. The mission they get is a mission of life: delivering embryos to a distant planet whose inhabitants have been sterilized by a burst of radiation from their own sun. On the way they stop at Alioth, where Helva and Kira are entrapped by another brain ship dominating a death-worshipping culture. This is not an ideal place for anyone, but Helva, the intelligent metal space-roamer, comes up with a solution. This novelette, like so many others I've mentioned, became part of an extended series later issued in book form. Anne McCaffrey is more famous for her very popular Dragonrider stories, which by now constitute a substantial series. These tend more toward fantasy, but are also sf because of the extraterrestrial setting. Pohl continued prescient about the talent of new writers, an ability he shared with Gold and for which neither has been given sufficient credit.

Back in the April, 1965 issue there had appeared "Death and Birth of the Angakok," an unusual, to say the least, novelette by the otherwise barely known and mysterious Hayden Howard. This was the first part of an unheralded serial, just one novelette appearing after the other until the April, 1967 issue, when the tale was completely told. This was unlike *Galaxy*'s usual policy, and the series was quite unlike anything else in *Galaxy*.

The series picks up speed with "The Eskimo Invasion" in June, 1966. Dr. Joe West, a former population control researcher for the U.S. Government, becomes concerned when he comes across a new tribe of Eskimos who are growing, and maturing, with unusual rapidity. He goes among them and learns they don't want any government to control their breeding. To his horror, he finds that the women have a gestation period of one month. The series continues through "Who Is Human?" in the August issue, "Too Many Esks" (October), "The Modern Penitentiary" (December), "Our Man in Peking" (February, 1967), and "The Purpose of Life" (April). West tries bacteriological warfare against the Esks, but only harms the remaining tribes of true human Eskimos. He is not understood, and is charged with attempted genocide and has to flee, while all the time the Esk population burgeons. They are, he realizes, induced by extraterrestrial means. He escapes to Red China and is held prisoner by Mao III (well, we can't expect sf to anticipate every meandering of Asian Communist policy). West comes to a final realization of the significance of the many lives brought forth by the Esks, the many additional units of human or humanoid consciousness—the story does not focus but instead winds up on a grand universal scale which I did not expect.

The scale harks back to the work of Olaf Stapledon, a much earlier writer and one not usually thought to have much influence on American magazine sf. Hayden Howard appeared in *Galaxy* only in the Sixties and in 1970. The rest is by now a very long silence. I could not find him to be a pseudonym of any other writer. I'm certain than any further work by this author, or information about him, would be welcomed by the sf world, but all we can do now is wonder.

The December, 1966 *Galaxy* contains the editorial eulogizing Paul Linebarger, headlined with his fictional name Cordwainer Smith enclosed in a black rectangle of mourning.

I have mentioned the New Wave and the fact that one of its chief British practitioners, J. G. Ballard, never got published in *Galaxy*. Algis Budrys, in his regular Galaxy Bookshelf column for December, 1966, perhaps gives some clues as to why that should have been the case:

> A story by J. G. Ballard, as you know, calls for people who don't think. One begins with characters who regard the physical universe as a mysterious and arbitrary place, and who would not dream of trying to understand its actual laws. Furthermore, in order to be the protagonist of a J. G. Ballard novel, or anything more than a very minor character therein, you must have cut yourself off from the entire body of scientific education. In this way, when the world disaster—be it wind or water— comes upon you, you are under absolutely no obligation to do anything about it but sit and worship it. Even more further, some force has acted to remove from the face of the world all people who might impose good sense or rational behavior on you, so that the disaster proceeds unchecked and unopposed except by the inevitable thumb-rule engineer type who for his individual comfort builds a huge pyramid (without huge footings) to resist high winds, or trains a herd of alligators and renegade divers to help him out in dealing with deep water.
>
> This precondition is at the root of every important J. G. Ballard creation and is so fundamental to it that it does not need to be put into words. Being buried as it is, it both does not call attention to itself and permits the author's characters to produce the most amazing self-destructive reactions while making reasonably intelligent and somewhat intellectual mouth-noises.

Thus one of the great Fifties writers and the New Wave collide at nearly full speed. That Ballard, like so many of us, does find the world deficient in order and reason is not significant here. He was operating with rules from the surrealist canon of literature, rules hitherto alien to sf and obviously annoying to the fine writer and critic, Budrys.

The late Philip K. Dick (d. 1982) had a fine and characteristically chilling and rather off-the-wall short story in the February, 1967 issue. "Return Match" has Superior Los Angeles police raid an outworlder gambling casino, only to see it all but destroyed by the jets of the outworlder space ship making its getaway. However, a gambling device is salvaged, an odd pinball machine which fascinates Inspector Tinbane when he plays it. The metal spheres thunder down on a miniature village which responds in a way to protect itself. Some of the village walls are breached and the pinball machine (5 shots for a quarter) begins to defend itself. Tinbane plays game after game despite the increasing nervousness of the other police; it is after all an alien device and they now suspect it of being a booby trap. Finally the machine completes construction of a catapult and fires a steel ball at Tinbane himself. He gives up and goes home, realizing it will not be safer. It is not safer. The machine has as many shots to go as he played, and the steel balls are huge and begin to batter at the walls of his apartment. This story leaves the reader suspended but with nerves appropriately tingling.

C. C. MacApp, a pseudonym for Carroll M. Capps (d. 1971), has the novelette "Spare That Tree" in the June, 1967 issue. It is an example of the continuing humorous vein of *Galaxy*. Another hapless police inspector, Judson Kruger, has to retrieve a stolen rare tree, but it is in an enclosed compound and various protective robots won't let him get near it. When he disguises himself inside a robotic shell, he reaches the tree, only to find further complications. The tree is actually a princess on her own planet and Kruger is then involved in dynastic hassles.

A two-part serial by Poul Anderson, "To Outlive Eternity" (later known in book form as *Tau Zero*), begins in the June issue. This story is truly extragalactic in scope. The interstellar colonizing craft *Leonora Christine* is on her way to Beta Virginis when she collides with a cosmic gas cloud and wrecks her decelerator unit. To repair it requires turning off the external force fields, which would mean certain death for all from hard radiation if the ship hits any further gas clouds. So *Leonora Christine* has to keep going, approaching the speed of light closer and closer, while seeking a place where there is no chance of encountering any menacing gas or particles. As the ship continuously accelerates, relativity requires that only moments of ship time pass during millions of years of time in the outside universe. But this means that the ship has practically removed itself from time and the whole process of galactic collapse and rebirth. This is a novel on a very grand scale. The main interest aside from the relativistic physics and details of ship construction is the way the crew deals with the mind-boggling phenomenon of being necessarily the first intelligent species in a whole new universe. I was interested in this fine cosmological novel throughout, and it ranks as one of *Galaxy*'s better ones for the decade of the Sixties.

Larry Niven, a writer like one or two others in our history who doesn't need the money (Anne Morrow Lindbergh being another), begins to appear in *Galaxy* with some regularity. His June novelette "The Adults," well-illustrated by Virgil Finlay, deals with an intruder into our solar system, a leathery bony creature seeking its own kind. It is actually a representative of the original species that mutated into mankind half a million years past. How he reacts to his godchildren, and the results, make this well worth reading, like most Niven stories. It was later expanded into the book *Protector*.

I have hitherto neglected the very prolific writer and contributor to *Galaxy*, Robert Silverberg. His work had been getting better and better, and his novelette "Hawksbill Station" was recognized as a very superior work. It tells of a future state of affairs in terms of a very ancient state of affairs, for the entire story takes place in the Cambrian period of Earth's geological history, when there is no life on the land and trilobites and nautiloids rule the sea. A totalitarian 21st Century society has decided not to execute its political opponents. Instead they are sent back by a one-way time machine to the Cambrian. The male offenders are in a colony by themselves, for the obvious reason that if they were allowed to mate with female exiles, their descendants would evolve so far that the benignly sinister future totalitarianism would never have come into being. So they are isolated in the past in a very dull world only enlivened briefly by the arrival of new exiles, whose politics they immediately seek to discover, this being their only way of knowing what was happening back in their own time. Lew Hahn, a youngish new arrival, arouses their curiosity and puzzles Barrett, the leader, more or less, of the exile colony. When they question Hahn about his political views he is disconcertingly vague. It turns out that he is no political exile at all and that a major change has occurred in the far future. This will force a decision on Barrett, a decision he had never realistically anticipated. This is one of the *Galaxy* stories likely to remain in the reader's memory, not least for its very intriguing description of what human survival in the Cambrian Age would be like.

"Hawksbill Station" was published in the August, 1967 issue. In the same issue Isaac Asimov was given the editorial page, which he used as a "bully pulpit" (to use a political cliché) to genteelly horsewhip the New Wave. He somehow equates unscientific science fiction (and we know what *that* means by now) with mental pollution and the possible "asphyxiation of technology in the waste of its own over-supply of information." The trend worries him. He says in conclusion:

> So, I hope that science does not go entirely out of science fiction. I hope that when the New Wave has deposited its froth and receded, the vast and solid shore of *science* fiction will appear once more and continue to serve the good of humanity.

This is doubtless why a decade later Asimov began to put out his own digest-sized sf magazine, which from all reports is still going strong. We will in that way be assured of *science* fiction. But of course *Galaxy* was not averse to it, especially considering the Frank Herbert and Mack Reynolds pieces it had been doing in the Sixties. Apparently some other magazines were letting the side down, or the paperback anthologies such as *New Worlds* were beginning to make some inroads into the realm of hard science fiction.

The October issue celebrated Galaxy's seventeenth year of existence! It also celebrated the editor's thirtieth year in sf, and that too was an accomplishment. Pohl had started off in the days of running boards, nickel beers, and wild and lurid pulp magazine covers with largely less-than-completely intelligible pulp fiction inside. His editorial is informative, but I even more heartily recommend his full-length autobiography *The Way the Future Was*, which I hope will still be available in paperback.

This issue is particularly distinguished by the novelettes. One of them, "Damnation Alley," by prime New Wave writer Roger Zelazny, later became a movie (with changes)—once again *Galaxy* made it to the big screen. Zelazny had won a Nebula for a piece in *Amazing Stories*, and Pohl's success in getting "Damnation Alley" is to be commended.

The novelette deals with a post-World War III world. Hell Tanner, a renegade California biker and a criminal many times over, is promised a full pardon from the nation of California if he will deliver some life-saving vaccine to the East Coast. The nuclear holocaust had totally ruined the atmosphere for air travel, with immensely high winds and rock storms, so overland is the only way to go. Tanner faces all sorts of obstacles—giant mutated bats, piratical bike gangs, and spots of high radiation where cities used to be, among other things. He is given a partner, a super-weaponed super car, and the vaccine, and is sent on his way. I wish I had seen the movie. If it is anything like the *Galaxy* story, it must be terrifically exciting.

Former editor H. L. Gold also has a novelette, "The Transmogrification of Wamba's Revenge," which is also interesting though less full of action. Professor Todd, who has being doing research on Pigmy endocrinology, hits upon a marvelous plan to end Earth's wars and population pressures. I won't give away his solution except to say that ordinary domestic pets might become a trifle unwieldy in Dr. Todd's ideal world. It's well worth reading and is also a humorous antidote to Zelazny's excellent but ominous work.

We now end this phase of Pohl's editorship. Some of the greats were gone, and also the American public was starting not to like what was going on in Viet Nam. In addition, the Counterculture was moving in.

11. Frederik Pohl (III)

THE DECEMBER 1967 *GALAXY* HAS AN EDITO-
rial on the Hugo Awards, but basically about
Hugo Gernsback himself. Pohl writes:

A little while ago (as this is written) we got word that the Father of
Science Fiction would be with us no more. He died on the 19th of August,
of a kidney ailment; because he was the kind of man he was, he donated
his body to science. . . .

Not very many people have done as much with their lives as Hugo
Gernsback did with his. Although he was seriously ill in recent years and
past the time for taking an active part in science fiction, he still read the
magazines now and then. And it was good to know he was out there.

We'll miss him.

. . . . Winning a Hugo [for Jack Vance's "The Last Castle" and another
for Jack Gaughan, Vance's illustrator, as "best artist"] is always an
honor. This year maybe a little more so than ever.

At the same sf convention *Galaxy*'s companion magazine *If* won a
Hugo for "best magazine." *If* under Pohl's editorship was to win a total
of three of the prestigious trophies. *Galaxy* didn't win a Hugo all its

The Planet Slummers. Illustrator: Bodé.

own (Gold and Campbell tied one year in the Fifties). It well deserved one all to itself. Pohl was at one point editing four sf magazines: *Galaxy*, *If*, *Worlds of Tomorrow*, and *International Science Fiction*. This diffusion of efforts may have contributed in some measure to *Galaxy*'s lack of Hugos in the Sixties. Yet it was sufficiently recognized in other ways, and the continued founding of new sf magazines by Pohl (whether they lasted or not) was very positive because new magazines always let in new writers who can then make their various ways up to the top-line magazines, which always included *Galaxy*.

Robert Sheckley appears in the February, 1968 *Galaxy* with a humorous (just like the old days) novelette called "Street of Dreams, Feet of Clay"; it was good enough to be anthologized later on in *Wandering Stars*. Sheckley had not contributed much except *Mindswap* to the 1960's *Galaxy*, so it was good to have him back. He writes of an ideal city named Bellwether which takes out ads for people to come live in it. One of Sheckley's gullible characters, Mr. Carmody, occupation unspecified but weary of the increasingly deadly life in a New York plagued with snipers, decides to try out Bellwether. The city is oddly but comfortably designed. Various sections reflect different architectual styles and it has excellent restaurants. But it has no inhabitants, even though it pathetically tries its hardest to please. It also admonishes Carmody for unhealthy habits such as not bathing enough, definitely like someone's idea of a Supermom. The premise is acceptable. In the 1980's Coke machines have begun to chat with their customers. If an entire city does so—and there is no reason now why one could not, in the form of a talking central computer—then would not the average person be somewhat overwhelmed? The dialogue is hilarious and I do urge the reader to seek this one out.

The cover is by the notable Vaughn Bodé, of whom more later. It illustrates "The Planet Slummers," a short piece by Terry Carr and Alexei Panshin (the latter of whom I quoted in Part I as an sf critic, and a good one). The story deals with an encounter between a young Earth husband and wife and a pair of aliens who block the road in something that looks "like a fantastic cross between a World War I airplane and a basketball." The aliens are maddening, giggling collectors of unusual life forms, and they make off with the man's wife. They are pure energy and ungraspable, but the utter frustration of the man *is*. The couple's car, by the way, is stopped electrically dead in the road much like the pickup in the later movie *Close Encounters of the Third Kind*.

I have mentioned something about the New Wave and how it had picked up some of its ideas from surrealism. It might be appropriate to quote the central surrealist, André Breton, who wrote in 1929:

> Everything suggests that there exists a certain point of the mind at which life and death, the real and the imaginary, the past and the future, the communicable and the incommunicable, the heights and the depths cease to be perceived contradictorily. Now it is in vain that one would seek any other motive for surrealist activity than the hope of determining this point . . .

This point of the mind which Breton mentions is also a focus for so-called absurdist sf where an inner space can be described as inclusive of events which have no exact objective hard scientific reality but are nonetheless strongly determinative of much modern sf (later Sixties to the present), particularly in the works of such writers as J. G. Ballard (discussed earlier), Harlan Ellison, Philip José Farmer, and Stanislaw Lem. Mainstream writers such as Donald Barthelme and Jorge Luis Borges also use the methods and ideals of surreality in their work.

Cory and Alexei Panshin in the "SF in Dimension" series (*Fantastic*, July 1973) find a problem in this tendency of the New Wave:

> The problem is a subjective problem. It is not the sense of the symbols of science fiction that is in question. It is the meanings these symbols are used to produce, the emotional action at the heart of a speculative fantasy story. . . . The solution of the problem of the renewal of speculative fantasy is to turn the devices, conventions and symbols of modern sf to truly adult ends.
>
> But this is not an intellectual problem amenable to intellectual solution.

This was a problem dealt with much earlier by the surrealists who relied on dreams, chance, automatic writing and so on to overcome the intellectual block keeping us from marvelous beauty, a beauty also sought by sf and fantasy writers, with much success in the cases of Ellison, Ballard and the others. In fact even very, very mainstream authors such as Evelyn Waugh, to Edmund Wilson's amusement, could write entire novels (*The Ordeal of Gilbert Pinfold*) as the product of a single long hallucination. In Waugh's case it was a combination of barbiturates and alcohol (unintentional) that did the trick. Edmund Wilson (the late beloved American literary critic laureate) said *Pinfold* was "the greatest Protestant allegory ever written."

To sum up, the old sf task of bringing out the blasters whenever the ET's showed up, or teaching astronautics within the flimsy structure of a plot filled with nebulous characters, was no longer going to be enough. It was going to take some really thorough comprehension, or apprehension, of deep human psychology, metaphysics and true poetry and its roots to bring off a good New Wave story, and by Godfrey, a lot of writers managed it. But, of course, there always did remain that subjectivity problem which to the Unconverted would make the fictions of Ballard or Farmer come off like a garbled telex message. It was not a rebellion, as a duke once explained to his unbright monarch, it was a revolution.

Revolution—the title of a Beatles' song of 1968—Top 40, of course—and it well matched the mood. By 1968, in this country, the writers of the new movement were picking up headway, in *Galaxy* and in other magazines, even as the mood faded back in England from whence had come the innovators. Revolution, and the hapless mood of the time. I mentioned ominous 1963 before. Had JFK lived on, perhaps 1968 would have been less grim. Perhaps we would not have seen so many memorial flags in the papers next to the names of those killed in Viet Nam, battling a revolution.

It was strange how all coalesced in that year, the New Rock became widespread, sf changed in the way I've described, and politics and live rounds of History shattered the glass walls of whatever tranquility we had left and sundered the Valhalla of the highest ranks of science fiction. Pete Seeger used to sing the old coal mining union men's song "Which Side Are You On?" In June of 1968, the sf authors answered the question—see the advertisements reproduced on the next two pages.

The announcement on page 194, also out of the June, 1968 *Galaxy*, seems somewhat pathetic now, in the light of later experience. But most of us *were* confused. It was an unprecedented war, and we had not fought an ideological war since Appomatox ended the "unpleasantness between the states." Oddly, Pohl's effort here was reminiscent of some of the Fifties editorials of H. L. Gold asking the readers' advice on various topics. The results were to be tallied and reported on in *Galaxy* later in the year. The results of the war too would be known in not too many years, and years after that there would be another list of names carved into memorial stone in Washington, D.C. History often seems to be too cruel a playmate for both science fiction writers and readers.

Paid Advertisement

5

What Would YOU Do About Vietnam?

Assume you are being asked for advice. Assume the people who ask you are the President of the United States, the Congress, the State Department, the Joint Chiefs of Staff — anyone and/or everyone who has any decision-making authority concerning American involvement in Vietnam. Assume they want one suggestion from you . . . and assume they will follow it.

What would you tell them to do?

Don't tell them. Tell us. We will take the most provocative and seemingly productive suggestions received, submit them to problem-solving analysis, and present the results in a forthcoming issue of *Galaxy.*

The Rules

1. Anyone is eligible to enter, and may submit as many entries as he likes. Each entry must be on a separate sheet of paper, one side only, and include your name and address. All entries will become the property of Galaxy Publishing Corporation. Please limit yourself to a maximum of 100 words for each entry, preferably in the form of (a) your suggestion, (b) followed, if you wish, by a statement of why you think it worth doing.

2. Suggestions may be on any area of American involvement in Vietnam —ways of winning the war, ways of bringing about a peaceful settlement, whatever you think would be of value.

3. Five prizes of $100 each will be awarded to those entries which, in the opinion of the judges, best deserve them. In the event of duplicate suggestions, the first entries received will get the prize. Judges will consist of, or be appointed by, the Editors of Galaxy Publishing Corporation. Winners will be notified by mail, and their names will be published in a forthcoming issue of this magazine.

4. Send your entries to: "What Would You Do About Vietnam?", Galaxy Publishing Corporation, 421 Hudson Street, New York, N.Y. 10014. Entries must be received by July 4th, 1968, to be eligible for prizes.

11

An interesting two-part serial begins in the April, 1968 issue. It's *Goblin Reservation*, by Clifford D. Simak (who did *Galaxy*'s first-ever serial in the long ago first issue). Peter Maxwell returns to Earth shortly after a double of his has come back and been killed. The real Maxwell has travelled to a mysterious crystalline planet with a great repository of lore and legend, all of which can be at the disposal of humanity if certain conditions are met. One of these is the return of a mysterious Artifact. Maxwell has to deal with traitors who are trying to deliver the Artifact to a very odd race called Wheelers, who are not to be trusted.

Maxwell is on good terms with goblins and ghosts and a banshee, and eventually some trolls, as he is a professor of the Supernatural. With their aid the Artifact is secured, though not without some interesting twists and turns in the plot. As in Simak's first *Galaxy* serial, one finds the intervention of the mysterious planet in one man's life which will ultimately be of benefit to all of Earth. This serial is obviously more on the fantasy side, but also rates as sf because of the interesting aliens.

Harlan Ellison has a novelette in the June issue, the noted Hugo-winning "The Beast That Shouted Love" (reprinted as "The Beast That Shouted Love at the Heart of the World"—and people thought that *Raise High the Roof Beam, Carpenters* was a long title!). This work by Ellison reminds one of Bradbury in its plotlessness and in its sheer emotional power, though Ellison has an edge in sheer decibels. It deals with a sort of astro-psych-ecology: if someone is getting rid of a lot of hate and other psychic garbage somewhere in the galaxy, it's going to just turn up someplace else to cause a lot of problems. The premise here is that the absence of evil is good, which is very dubious. St. Augustine was more on the mark when he said that evil is the absence of good. Hugo Gernsback might not have been too interested in all the metaphysics, but Harlan rightly earned his Hugo.

Galaxy went monthly again! Pohl's efforts finally succeeded, and the July issue was the first such in a decade (and an unimaginably long decade it was). Fritz Leiber began a three-part serial entitled *A Specter Is Haunting Texas*. The plot is rather outrageous, but I shall try to summarize it. Christopher Crockett La Cruz, who prefers to be called "Scully," comes down to Earth from an exotic Lunar colony which had been neutral when nuclear war swept the Earth. In the post-nuke era, the Texans—grown to impossibly great heights, eight feet or more—dominate most of North and Central America. They are constantly at odds with the Mex people,

Latinos who continue to rebel against Texan overlordship, and are on tenuous terms with the remaining Russians and black-dominated Southern California.

Scully ends up doing propaganda plays for the Latino group, while all the time looking for his family's long-lost radium mine, which, it turns out, has already been found by the tall Tex people. Scully also finds himself with two jealous girlfriends. His task is made all the harder by the fact that he has to wear a battery-powered exoskeleton to counter Earth's gravity, since he is weak even for one raised in the light gravity of the Lunar colony. I recommend the novel for all his adventures and his romantic solution and the future history of Texan America. It came out in book form in 1969. Leiber's best work lies in the realm of fantasy, as in his Lankhmar series, but he has long been recognized as an sf star too. It was gratifying that Pohl could bring in a new generation while keeping on the good old *Galaxy* pros.

In the July issue Brian Aldiss has a short story, "Dreamer, Schemer." In a definitely decadent future Earth (the Sixties seem to have been quite productive of dystopias) people spend much of their time doing "play-outs," a sort of combination of high drama and mental therapy. The point in this piece is what happens when a loser and a winner of this future time meet in a play-out.

Since the early Sixties I had not bought a copy of *Galaxy*. The summer of 1968 found me hanging in a limbo where I suppose most lost philosophers go, though I hadn't expected to get there so soon. The War of course was very much upon my mind. While I brooded at home once more in Iowa, I noticed a once-familiar logo on a newsstand. But the cover was what made me buy the magazine. I had long admired surrealist art, and this August, 1968 cover by Vaughn Bodé attracted me enough to resume purchasing *Galaxy*. It was an illustration of "Going Down Smooth," a Robert Silverberg short story about a crazy computer (and I hadn't met HAL in *2001* yet). The description of the cover comes from Silverberg's text:

> I see the blue-green ocean with all its living things within. I see a ship, olive drab, bright carmine at the Plimsoll line, the decks a ruddy brown, two tall non-nuclear smokestacks. And from the water rise periscopes, silvery, with face plates of pure white, each with intersecting horizontal and vertical lines, curved so that the plate appears convex. It is an unreal scene. Nothing in the sea can send such mighty periscopes above the

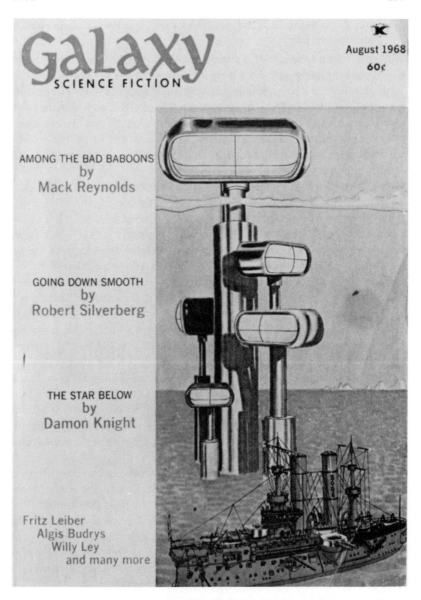

Galaxy
SCIENCE FICTION

August 1968
60¢

AMONG THE BAD BABOONS
by
Mack Reynolds

GOING DOWN SMOOTH
by
Robert Silverberg

THE STAR BELOW
by
Damon Knight

Fritz Leiber
Algis Budrys
Willy Ley
and many more

Going Down Smooth. Illustrator: Bodé.

water. I have imagined it, and that gives me fear, if I am at all capable of understanding fear.

This is a fine example of a surrealistic inner vision, a radiating point which unfortunately conveys a deeper madness to the patients which this computer, for it is a psychoanalyzing diagnostic machine, has in its charge. It cannot, oddly like HAL, admit it is capable of error, so it is withdrawn and overhauled. After that it continues to send digitally coded obscenities at humans—but not so they can hear them and not so that it will be withdrawn from use again. I found this story much more entertaining and poetic in the surrealist sense than I did disturbing.

The other story that interested me in the August issue was a novelette, "Among the Bad Baboons." In a future New York almost totally devastated by riots, a few people still continue to live in a ruined Greenwich Village. Arthur Halleck still hopes to sell his paintings. There is a functioning government "on the mainland," but Arthur refuses to go to live on its welfare dole and insists on his Bohemian existence, shared by his live-in girlfriend Pamela, who helps him forage for food among ruined delis and apartments. Their lives are always threatened by "baboons": skulkers and pillagers with no esthetic pretensions whatsoever. They are also menaced by licensed Hunters, usually bourgeois and jaded businessmen or government bureaucrats who can legally visit ruined New York and hunt any human they see. But Arthur continues to paint until one day the menace becomes real in both its manifestations. This work is by Mack Reynolds, a frequent *Galaxy* contributor. It reflects the fear widely held in the Sixties of bigger and bigger urban riots. From our vantage-point later in the century, we can see that these fears were not well-grounded. Exactly why massive urban riots seemed to come to a dead halt is a matter, I suppose, for the sociologists to explain.

In the October issue H. L. Gold and his son Eugene contribute a novelette, "The Villains From Vega IV." It deals with the mishaps encountered by an android detective who tries to help the President of Vega IV, a human colonial, find his wife. She had come to Earth to track down suitable actors to take back to Vega. The detective does the Vegans a valuable service and is promoted to the desirable rank of android philosopher, an "andyphilo" or, perhaps, android philosophical detective, in a word play on S. S. Van Dine's famous Philo Vance!

Mack Reynolds appears again in the October issue with "Criminal in Utopia," an intriguing novelette showing how a criminal can get away with major thefts in a highly computerized society where everyone has personalized thumb-printed ID cards. The protagonist is quite ingenious and thinks of some things that might even used in a regimented future like the one described, if the police of the future have not bothered to read sf back numbers.

There is also a "non-fact article" on war robots in this issue, "The Warbots," by Larry S. Todd ("the history of armored war from 1975 to 17,500 A.D."). These are all highly ingenious devices and would be a good match for anything *Star Wars* has to offer. Ironically, the warbots evolve back into being more or less human in appearance but with unprecedented and fearsome abilities. This sort of really imaginative future projection was one of the specialties of *Galaxy.*

Galaxy's second Hugo winner of 1968 (awarded in 1969) had come in the previous issue, September. I refer to Robert Silverberg's famous "Nightwings," a novelette of a ruined future Earth which is populated by true humans and such elegant mutants as the slim Fliers who are so delicate they can only fly at night. A female Flier, Avluela, is accompanied by an older man, a Watcher whose job it is to periodically scan the skies for invading alien fleets. With them is Gormon, a big person of a type known as a Changeling, normally neutered and enslaved, though Gormon is neither. The three make their way to Roum, a holy city reconstructed on the ruins of a former holy city which had been destroyed in the "Sweeping," presumably a global catastrophe in a much earlier period. Roum also has a few Pilgrims bound for a second sacred city, Jorslem. It is an often grim and sometimes quite poignant tale and one well worthy of its award.

In the November, 1968 issue Robert Silverberg's novelette "Perris Way" continues the story of the Watcher, now an ex-Watcher, who accompanies the former Prince of Roum to Perris where the aliens have taken possession. The two are disguised as pilgrims and the former Watcher seeks to join the cult of the Rememberers, who have all the files and memories of human history. At one time mankind stretched out to the stars as conquerors, but they over-reached themselves. Geological calamities engulfed whole continents and other-worlders had to come in and help. Then Earth began a precarious rise again which was halted by the new invasion. The ex-Prince of Roum and the head Rememberer's wife are having an affair. It becomes quite a grim situation. Tomis, for now we know the former Watcher's name, and Olmayne, the ex-wife of the Rememberer guildmaster, set off on a pilgrimage to Jorslem. This story is another of those that was actually a section of a serial novel, but, oddly, was not advertised as such, perhaps because the sections did not all follow each other in chronological order as one would think they should.

This issue also had some of the results of the "What Would YOU Do About Vietnam?" contest. Responses came from all over the U.S., from at least eight foreign countries including El Salvador, and from servicemen actually in Nam. The ideas ranged all the way from Gandhi-style non-violence to nuking them back to the Stone Age. Frederik Pohl decided to have a panel of experts deal with a few dozen of the better suggestions. However, he reminds the reader that peace talks are under way in Paris and a new President may have ideas of his own. Nixon and Kissinger would soon be in power, although at the time of Pohl's writing he could not predict the election results and the events that prolonged the unsettling aspects of the Sixties rather than immediately end them.

"Building on the Line," a novelette by now-veteran writer Gordon R. Dickson, also appeared in the November issue. This was a good workmanlike piece on the hazards of constructing an interstellar matter transmitter station. John Clancy shows a great deal of heroism and common sense in rescuing Plotchin, his co-worker who is injured by falling rocks from what seems to be a construction explosion. Actually, indigenous life forms called "hobgoblins" are responsible, and they also cause Clancy such bad hallucinations that it is doubtful if he can get Plotchin and himself back to their ship. I considered this a good sf tale, if not exactly a milestone.

Galaxy had its third Hugo award-winning work in the December, 1968 issue, a novelette called "The Sharing of the Flesh," by Poul Anderson. This one mixes a revenge plot with xenobiology. Evalyth Sairn's explorer husband has an audiovisual transmitter with him, and she is watching when he is killed by Moru, a native of the slave class. Evalyth is a tall proud woman determined to track down Moru and make him pay. But she is also a scientist who wants to know why he removed certain portions of her husband's anatomy and why a certain type of cannibalism exists on the planet, and how it can be extirpated. The natives are a degenerated human type, and study of their cell structure gives her the clues she needs. With stories such as this, *Galaxy* was keeping up its eminence.

British author John Wyndham, who was to die the next year, also had a novelette in December, "A Life Postponed." Willie Trevinnick knows that his attractive young girlfriend Cyra wants children, but he is not sure the world is safe enough. So he has himself frozen for a century. The puzzled but determined Cyra does the same, to Willie's great surprise when he awakes. The marriage bureau people can't forebear from remarks about elderly couples. Births are strictly regulated and licensed, but they qualify, which is just as well when twins result.

I cannot leave 1968 behind without another note on changing times. In the August issue Pohl's editorial was a eulogistic biography of William Anthony Parker White, whose *nom de plume* was Anthony Boucher. (He didn't use his own name because there were already "no fewer than 75 writers named William White in some variation or another.") He wrote mysteries and was one of the charter members of the noted Baker Street Irregulars. Then he wrote stories for the old *Unknown* magazine. His greatest accomplishment was the founding, with J. Francis McComas, of the magazine now known as *Fantasy and Science Fiction*, which became one of the big three of the Fifties through the Seventies. At last report *F&SF* is still going strong. Tony Boucher died on April 30, 1968, six weeks after being master of ceremonies at a California sf convention. He was only 56. He was, and is, sorely missed, for sf needs more of his sort of urbane wit. With Boucher's death an era had begun to pass. Gold was in semi-retirement and Campbell's clock over at *Analog* was slowly winding down.

Interestingly enough, Campbell's future successor at *Analog*, Ben Bova, appeared in *Galaxy* in January, 1969. (This was his second *GSF* appearance—the first had been the short "Men of Good Will" in June 1964, but that was with a co-author, Myron R. Lewis.) In the 1969 novelette, "Foeman, Where Do You Flee?" Bova is more successful with a longer form. He tells the tale of a scared humanoid tribe discovered on the planet Sirius A-2. He describes the great care taken by the xenobiologists and sociologists in studying this tribe of seaside dwellers who have somehow survived the explosion of their own sun, which appeared to have been induced by enemy action. They discover that the tribe is in fact a former human colony, and that humanity has not come off too well in an ancient encounter with an interstellar enemy. Bova concludes with some disturbing thoughts and implications for the future.

A novelette from the January issue which has long remained in my memory (one of my tests for a good story) is "Parimutuel Planet," by James Tiptree, Jr. There was a great deal of mystery about the identity of this author until 1977, when the truth came out that Tiptree was actually Alice Sheldon, a behavioral psychologist, a former employee (like her husband) of the CIA, and thus one of those Washington *apparatchiki* we were so apprehensive of in the Sixties. But she has turned out to be an excellent sf writer, a winner of Hugos and Nebulas, and sympathetic to decent humanitarian worldviews. There is a fine interview with her in Vol. II of Charles Platt's *Dream Makers*.

In her story, Earth has been destroyed but Earthfolk survive by being hucksters and interstellar entrepreneurs. They run a racetrack world where all species from all planets can enter strictly fair contests to satisfy a universal quest for supremacy and an equally universal desire to bet on races. The story is comic in the descriptions of the myriad beings and customs the hard-pressed Mr. Christmas, manager of Raceworld, has to be acquainted with and work with, just to keep the games going. This, incidentally, is the first of four Tiptree/Sheldon appearances in *Galaxy*.

Also in January, Harlan Ellison and Keith Laumer have an amusing novelette called "Dunderbird." A gigantic pteranodon with a heavy gold chain around its neck crashes down dead onto a New York intersection, crushing many people and causing a great deal of confusion. The police try to restore order. Rabbinical students coming out of a nearby deli try to decide if the flying reptile is kosher. One determined man tries to steal the big gold medallion and chain. Suddenly the time warp is reversed, to the misfortune of the thief but the relief of the police and the clean-up crews.

The Robert Silverberg series concludes in the February, 1969 issue of *Galaxy*, with the novelette "To Jorslem." Tomis, the Watcher, finally reaches the holy city of Jorslem with the adultress Olmayne and some mysterious and precious star-stones. He is renewed into a young man again, and regains the love of Avluela, the lithe and lovely Flier. As for the alien rulers of Earth, the ex-Watcher in Jorslem and other humans have definite plans for them, but they are not the revengeful sort one would imagine. There is a gentle, contemplative note through this series which is indicative of the mature strains in sf (which are now more obvious) and the sadness which is unfortunately endemic to maturity.

The enigmatic Hayden Howard is back with an enigmatic novelette, "Kendy's World," which tells of a future barracks U.S.A. governed under a permanent National Emergency which has caused the death of the doves and liberal elements. The best of the country's youth are being deviously recruited into sinister counterespionage organizations. But one of the young would-be recruits fortunately seems to have a mind of his own.

Algis Budrys, *Galaxy*'s book reviewer, has a thought-provoking short story in the same issue. "Now Hear the Word of the Lord" tells how a future group of human survivors is trying to save the world from a grimmer fate, and even to avoid a nuclear disaster after all by sending back robot surrogates to serve in key positions. A group of real humans, who happen to be rather lunatic militants, discovers and threatens the survival plan, and things become rather tense. I found the story well worth re-reading.

In the March *Galaxy*, Keith Laumer begins an interesting three-part serial called "And Now They Wake," dealing with mythology interwoven with a computerized starship that crashed on Earth long ago. A new Earth power station somehow taps the energy of this ancient interstellar craft, and its former inhabitants, immortals who seem as gods to Earth-people, re-appear. So do vast Earth-destroying seastorms. The Pasmaquoddie generator must be put out of action. How a handful of heroes deal with a situation seemingly beyond their powers makes up much of the tension in this novel-length feature. Old veteran *Galaxy* artist Gaughan is on hand for some excellent interior art.

Anne McCaffrey was still in the beginning of her formidable sf-fantasy career. Here she makes her second appearance in *Galaxy* with the novelette "The Weather on Welladay." She tells of the great whales on the stormy planet Welladay and how they are severely menaced by pirates seeking the precious radioactive iodine produced in the whales' thyroid glands. An outer-world vessel arriving to pick up a load of the iodine for mercy purposes is mistaken for a pirate and shot down. Its pilot, a young woman named Shahanna, is saved. A native accidentally gives her a valuable supply of the iodine, but a pirate realizes this mistake and comes after her. In the meantime the planetary authorities are trying to stop the whale extermination and also to save Shahanna. McCaffrey always writes good work, and it's a pity her career with *Galaxy* was so short. Fred Pohl found good writers, but the gravitational pull of the paperback worlds was too great for any editor to have a magazine monopoly of a writer as Campbell had done in the long-ago days of the halcyon 1939-41 *Astounding* (before my time).

March also has an amusing pseudo-fact article by Larry Niven on "The Theory and Practice of Teleportation," showing that some of the ideas taken for granted in sf are rather nonsensical. He does it tongue in cheek, for one cannot imagine a writer of sf insisting on strict logic and unchallengeable scientific proof for every extant sf convention. Then what we would have would be not science fiction but, instead, The Future!

The Laumer serial continues, of course, in the April, 1969 issue. The cover is by Reese and is amusingly in the manner of the former *Galaxy* artist Ed Emshwiller. The story it illustrates is the novelette "How Like a God," by Robert Bloch. A super-being who is something of an insubstantial immortal plasma is to be punished for an offense barely conceivable to us. He has to assume corporeal shape and live for countless cycles of a planet's culture. Guess which planet and which cruel people he is settled among and must hide from, though their weapons can't hurt him? It's an interesting concept. This was one of Bloch's six appearances in *Galaxy*. He was much better known for his fantasy horror stuff such as *Psycho*.

One of the *Galaxy* writers from the very beginning re-appeared in the April issue. This was Clifford D. Simak, with the novelette "Buckets of Diamonds." His stories usually feature a local setting encountering alien phenomena. In this case, it's the little rural town of Cottonwood in the Midwest. (There actually *is* a Cottonwood, Iowa.) There's one of his usual eccentric characters, too. In this case, it is good old Uncle George who somehow gets hold of some future stuff thrown away after some future revival meetings—another time warp sort of thing. What about time warps, Larry Niven? Anyway, Uncle George does find some buckets of diamonds and even a future vehicle, but in the end the warp reverses itself. One should not, the thoughtful reader will conclude, stand too close to any time warp. I guess that for me the good old Simak formula wasn't quite doing its old stuff. Or perhaps his vision of the rural Midwestern town needed revision—by 1969 the Old Iowa of the East Coast or tourist imagination had mostly vanished. This is certainly true of Simak's Wisconsin or Minnesota also. The quaint red barns, putt-putt tractors, chickens in the farmyard, *and* eccentric Uncle Georges living at the town's edge have long since vanished.

There is one more story, a short, in the April, 1969 issue that cannot be passed over. At this time *Star Trek* was fading fast as a TV series, though it already had its hard-core following (me too, I suppose). But the only *Galaxy* story to make some use of its themes was the classic, rather ironic "Beam Us Home," by Tiptree/Sheldon. None of us imagined then that the Trekkies would grow mightily in strength and that Kirk, Spock, McCoy

Star Dream. Illustrator: Bodé.

and Co. would become a major growth industry. In a way, I'm glad—if only because I think many of its TV plots were clever and also because the show introduced a lot of people to sf who might otherwise have not gotten above the level of the usual TV cops and crooks and chase sequences. (The only chase sequence I was ever much fond of was the classic in *The French Connection* and the parody chase done by Bob Elliot and Ray Goulding showing a couple of middle-aged men trying to get to their cars and chase each other in normal urban traffic conditions.) Sorry, I got side-tracked there a bit. Anyway, I heartily recommend the Tiptree. I'm sure it is in one of the collections of her shorter works.

And now we are to the May, 1969 issue and the end of the *Galaxy* editorship of Frederik Pohl. He had been traveling overseas to various sf symposia. When he came back from one in Brazil, he was told that Bob Guinn had sold all his magazines to another publisher. Pohl might have stayed on with *Galaxy* except that, as Pohl says, the new publisher, Arnold Abramson, wanted his editors to keep to a nine to five schedule. Pohl declined so fixed a routine but agreed to be "editor emeritus" for a while (so he would not sign up right away with a competing sf magazine). Ejler Jakobsson succeeded Pohl at *Galaxy*, as he had succeeded him at *Super Science Stories* a quarter of a century before!

Pohl's last issue was a fairly good one. The Bodé cover is spectacular, more so than the story it illustates: "Star Dream," by Terry Carr and Alexei Panshin. This is more of a mood piece than a straight-out sf work, dealing with the contradictions and conflicts of two men from different generations of space engineers, and the first interstellar ship both men are responsible for, the *Gaea* bound for the Centauri system.

There is "Little Blue Hawk," an odd novelette by Sydney Van Scyoc about humans and human-animal hybrids. One of them—half human and half hawk, but wingless—was the oddest and saddest of all the experimentally-bred creatures until he realized he had some quite unusual powers and was brave, free, and unique. There are some elements of the New Wave about this tale which may account for its standing out a little among the others.

The last story of the Pohl years I will mention is the short by Dean R. Koontz in his one and only appearance in *GSF*. It's called "Killerbot" and tells how the warring nations, eschewing nuclear weapons, will use massive mutual terror by turning people into murderous androids who can fire either bullets or poisoned or explosive darts. They are very hard to detect, and the attrition rate among police is high, especially when ordinary human psychos start arming themselves like killerbots and following their example of random mayhem!

Interviewed by Charles Platt (in *Dream Makers*), Pohl said:

> There is no editor in the science-fiction field now who has any real control over what happens. . . . There just is not a place or publisher who defines the field or even defines his part in it. It has become big business, where books are merchandised and promoted and distributed and placed on sale like slabs of bacon or cans of soup.

But it was not so during Pohl's years with *Galaxy*, and we can thank God for that!

12. Ejler Jakobsson (I)

THE NEW EDITOR WAS A FINNISH-AMERICAN, born in 1911, and a pulp magazine writer since the 1930's. He worked briefly with *Astonishing Stories* and (as mentioned earlier) *Super Science Stories*, both of which fell victim to paper shortages in World War II. Now Jakobsson took over both *Galaxy* and *If* magazines. He believed in innovations and was aware of the spirit of the times, and his tenure at *Galaxy* was to reflect this. In my opinion his work in editing *Galaxy* was quite competent. It was in fact while he was in charge of the magazine that I once more became a regular purchaser. I lived in Minneapolis most of that time and *Galaxy* was easily obtainable. I think some of the magazine's real difficulties were caused by distribution problems in smaller areas, the rural towns, and so on. The reader will remember from Part I how H. L. Gold's *Galaxy* very nearly fell prey to distribution problems.

There was a hiatus in *Galaxy*'s publication as Abramson (Universal Publishing & Distributing Corporation) took over. There was no June,

1969 issue. The July issue appeared, Jakobsson's first, with one of a continued series by Willy Ley on the history of the early German rocketeers he had known. But Ley himself died in June of 1969. He had won two Hugos for his distinguished writing on science, and was a particularly strong backer of our space program. On July 16th, 1969, Apollo 11 lifted from the Kennedy Space Center in Florida. On July 20th at 4:17 p.m. EDT, the Earth heard the words, "The Eagle has landed." Men were on the moon. John Kennedy had said we would have men on the moon within the decade and he had been proved right, but, like Willy Ley, he never lived to see this triumph of technology as what had once been science fiction became actuality, and with no small drama.

Galaxy would retain its continuity for a while. There were the emeritus editorials by Pohl, the as yet unpublished articles by Ley which lasted through November of 1969, and Algis Budrys continued valiantly on as *Galaxy*'s book reviewer.

By this time, as the Panshins pointed out in the April, 1973 issue of *Fantastic Stories*, the New Wave which had once caused such a stir had come to something of a halt. What had occurred was that its best writers and more workable progressive techniques had been absorbed into the mainstream of sf, and the inept writers (like the inept pulp writers before them) had been consigned to oblivion and were doubtless now performing more useful functions for society, such as managing fast food restaurants or running for the state legislature.

The good new breed of writer was welcomed into the ranks and wrote on. The Panshins despaired of Zelazny in 1973 but he was to come back in a big way, and in *Galaxy* too! Ellison, Le Guin, Tiptree and the others are still with us. In fact, the New Wave, by means of its rousing approach to new styles, had rejuvenated some of the older writers like Sturgeon and book reviewer Budrys.

Budrys' continued dedication to sf is clear in his interview with Charles Platt in *Dream Makers*:

> I think that all forms of fiction and art are actually survival mechanisms. Far from being frills and decorations on the face of some kind of practical world, they are just about the most practical thing there is. They consist of a series of affirmations or denials of conventional reality, and of tests of various facets of reality. Science fiction has unique capabilities in that respect. I can talk seriously in science fiction about otherwise-unattainable aspects of very important situations.

One of the triumphs for *Galaxy* in 1969 was the publication within its pages of *Dune Messiah*, by Frank Herbert. The original *Dune* had been published in the "bedsheet" *Analog* of the middle Sixties with the size and interesting covers that had caught my eye. I thought that any magazine that had to go to such lengths to be noticed had to be doomed. I was quite wrong. But now Herbert was on *Galaxy*'s team with the second of what, of course, was one of the campus classics of the Sixties.

The fact that no one remembers much about the Sixties except that a lot of unfortunate things happened and that the Beatles (Paul McCartney's old band, one young girl described them) were rather big forces me to not presume that the other two cult books of the time will spring readily to mind. One of them was not a single book at all, but a series: *The Hobbit* and *The Lord of the Rings*—not to be confused with the Ring Cycle (a mistake which I've heard). The Ring Cycle is by Richard Wagner and is strictly musical drama, and requires the major portion of a week to listen to. *The Lord of the Rings* is strictly literary, almost too literary, and can be read rather briskly, though here too a bit of endurance is required. There was an ingenious cinematic version, sophisticated high-tech graphics stuff, but it didn't make it.

The second major cult book was Robert A. Heinlein's *Stranger in a Strange Land*, which received mixed reviews but became tremendously popular. I recall times where there would be at least two or three young people reading the paperback in a bus terminal. This novel, also a lengthy work (and American youths are supposed to have such short attention spans) had an odd history. It had actually been published in 1961, but the time then was somehow not suitable for cult popularity, perhaps because the Kennedy presidency held out some hope for a better world here, and so the interest in otherworldly mysticism or the actual *need* for an ET-based cult book was not yet present.

The cult book *Dune* was succeeded by *Dune Messiah* in *Galaxy*, in a five-part serial beginning in the July issue. One can't understand the second novel without knowing a bit about the first. To quote the Nicholls *Science Fiction Encyclopedia*:

> *Dune* is a novel of extraordinary complexity. It encompasses inter-galactic politics of a decidedly feudal nature; the development of psi powers; religion, specifically the reluctant but inevitable evolution of its protagonist into a messiah; and war. Its primary impact, however, lay in its treatment of ecology, a theme which it brought into the forefront of

modern sf readers' and writers' awareness. The desert planet Arrakis, with its giant sandworms and its Bedouin-like human inhabitants, the Fremen, clinging to the most precarious of ecological niches through fanatical scrupulousness in water conservation, is possibly the most convincing alien environment created by any sf writer.

Dune Messiah deals with very Byzantine politics. The *Dune* hero Paul Atreides is now the Emperor Muad'dib and rules many worlds, but also has many enemies. There is the inevitable plotting about the succession to the Empire, and of such plotting and counterplotting is this novel made. It is only the second novel in the Dune series. It was followed in the Seventies by *Children of Dune* and in the early Eighties by *God Emperor of Dune*. Neither of these appeared in *Galaxy*. It has always been the consensus of those who have read all four that the first is the superior book, but the series is of course quite an awesome undertaking; for anyone who wants to find out the ultimate fate of all the characters, I suppose reading all four is necessary. The large Dune sandworms, by the way, make a skeletal appearance in *Star Wars*, on the home world of Luke Skywalker.

In the July issue, we also find a good novelette by James Blish, "The City That Was the World." His story, in fact, has the cover (by Adkins). Blish tells of John Hillary Dane, a billionaire who is equipping an agent and building fantastically expensive time-travelling equipment in order to do something to the central computer of a future Earth society. Toby Walker is hired for a million dollars to go into the future and help fix this computer which, Dane informs him, will otherwise go zonkers and wreck the future world which relies so much upon it. But then Walker, the clever volunteer, begins to suspect that Dane's plans are not all that they seem. And that is where we begin to have complications. Blish is always worth reading.

The August, 1969 *Galaxy* features a distinct change in the cover. The red "Galaxy" seemed to grow to three times its former size, thus compressing the cover illustration somewhat. And the authors' names are given a bit more emphasis on the spine.

In August there is a very good novelette by Poul Anderson, "The White King's War," in which Lt. (j.g.) Flandry of the Imperial Terrestrial Navy is bribed by cash and a professionally sensual blonde to investigate a moon of a large planet to see if heavy metals really can be mined there. If so, Flandry's employer stands to make a good deal of money and

Flandry himself a good bonus. The problem is that the mining company's computer has been left alone too long and has evolved a chess-like defense for itself which Flandry must somehow penetrate.

The second August novelette, "Star Hunger," by Jack Wodhams, is a more prosaic tale of an interstellar crew seeking an inhabitable Earth-type planet, and the Lord knows how few of those there are (which does not seem to prevent us from scheming ways to utterly wreck this one). The brave captain leads the despairing explorers onward and onward.

In August of 1969, *Galaxy* also bids farewell to Clifford D. Simak, who had been with the magazine since it began in October of 1950. He was growing older and writing less, and he wrote no more for *Galaxy*. His last work for it is a short story, "I Am Crying All Inside." It tells how a work robot feels when it discovers that all the higher type of humans have decamped from its planet and moved on, pioneering as befits superior breeds of men, etc. The robots now have as masters just the 'ignernt pore white trash' who drink corn likker immoderately. No hint of grandeur is left to the robot, who is sensitive enough to realize this. It is a saddening story and well done. I might suggest, however, that the poor white might be a bit underrated in sf as he is in real life. In actual fact, out of his ranks came such Presidents as Andrew Jackson and Abraham Lincoln, and on the other side of the Mason-Dixon line, out of the ranks of the poor whites came the gallant and legendary Army of Northern Virginia.

I seem to have gotten on to the Civil War somehow. At this point in my history of *Galaxy* I feel something like Douglas Southall Freeman must have felt when writing *Lee's Lieutenants* (a massive three-volume work). The South was reeling in 1863, at the midpoint of the war. Many of her leading generals were dead, others were wounded and forced to retire, and some were captured. The main writers of *Galaxy* somewhat corresponded to the Confederate generals. They led on small but gallant bands amongst an unhelpful populace against a powerfully fortified enemy: complacency and simple lack of imagination, or religious fundamentalism. And now Cyril Kornbluth lay dead who was Jackson to Frederik Pohl's Lee. And the older writers of the Fifties such as Mark Clifton were dead or disabled. And great ones fell in the midst of action, such as Cordwainer Smith in the manner of Albert Sidney Johnston at Shiloh. This attrition had as serious an effect on *Galaxy* as it had on the Confederacy.

The comedians who worked in burlesque and vaudeville simply had a lot more style, better timing, and more real humor, because of their extensive experience, than do the current force-fed brand who work night clubs or are blown into too-sudden prominence by TV (which sometimes is fatal). The old vaudevillians like Bert Lahr, to take one of my favorite examples and heroes, slogged from decade to decade from one tank town to another until their sheer persistence, plus the talent they knew they had, finally got them onto radio and into the movies and onto Broadway and into the very heart of America. The sf old-timers did their soft-shoe routines for decades in ill-paying and crumbling pulp magazines with lurid covers people used to disguise, often did mystery stories or even westerns, and made a few bucks from shaping up some trite radio script or screenplay, until finally a few of them, all too few, started to make it big: Bradbury, Asimov, Heinlein. They came up the hard way in sf. But now the pulps are gone, the sf writers have no equivalent of the tank towns to tour in, and the stage (with a few exceptions such as Niven and Pournelle and Ellison) is still occupied by the old-time greats, like former Confederate generals being senators and governors after their really effective days were long gone.

The chief problem for *Galaxy* and sfdom as a whole was the same as that which faced Lee. How were the gallant ranks of the officers, especially the higher ranks, to be filled when the talented survivors of the pulp system began to vanish? There was no effective way to train and properly test replacements because the training academies, the myriad lesser sf magazines, no longer existed, and the fanzines were basically one-person affairs which may or may not have produced more new talents, but certainly no more than a very few.

Long-time sf writer A. E. van Vogt turns up in the September, 1969 issue with a novelette, "Humans, Go Home!" Dav and Miliss are two human immortals on the planet of the Jana people. Over the centuries they have been bringing this people forward from barbarism. Now the leaders of the Jana have developed near-Machiavellian cunning and the planetary tutors from Earth are menaced by their former pupils. But with a few interesting intrigues Dav and Miliss are reprieved. Van Vogt was not really a *Galaxy* regular. This was his first of only two appearances.

Joe Haldeman, who was to be one of the rare new young authors to win into the higher ranks of sfdom and fill in his way one of the open positions, makes his first of seven *Galaxy* appearances in September. "Out of Phase" is a good and chilling short story about Braxn the G'drellian, who is inadvertently landed on Earth by a group of really advanced galactic races. They worry briefly about Earth but dismiss whatever is about to happen to it as merely the result of Braxn going through one of his adolescent phases.

With the September issue the cover format is further changed. The huge *Galaxy* logo remains as large but the old inverted-L design on the cover (which served as a border to the cover art and contained names of stories and authors) was gone now, and the magazine had lost a bit of its old-time character. It had been unmistakable for just that very cover design, over which a small verbal war had raged between Gold and Campbell back in the early 1950's. Now all that distinguished the magazine's appearance was the futuristic logo lettering. As a sort of benchmark, the price of *Galaxy* was 60 cents. It had gone from 50 cents to 60 in December of 1964, and would become 75 cents in August of 1970.

The October, 1969 issue has another piece by the mysterious Hayden Howard. "Tomorrow Cum Laude" takes place mostly on the campus of the University of Southern California. In this sequel to "Kendy's World," Kendy has been recruited to be a government spy, but he isn't too good at the job. The story presupposes a future society where a sort of permanent martial law is in effect and where most of the black population lives walled away from the white society. Based on some of the latter 1960's moods, this might have seemed feasible but certainly has failed as a prediction. Some of our worst fears have not come true and that is some comfort for us.

Damon Knight, another of *Galaxy*'s stars of the Fifties, returns in this issue with "Truly Human," a short story which involves a simple test a group of aliens give three randomly chosen Earthmen to determine whether the place should be assisted into galactic maturity, or possibly sterilized as a menace and nuisance. One can only become frustrated with these superior beings for judging Earth or toying with it all the time in sf, but in this story their test does have a point, a very simple, but for us in the past (and I hope permanently in the past), a deadly one.

Ernest Taves, one of *Galaxy*'s newer recruits, has a funny novelette in the fine old *Galaxy* manner. It could be a story from an earlier period but that isn't the point. It is a good dilemma story based upon an almost incomprehensible gadget. "Take the B Train" involves invoking variants of the same woman, Professor Amos Appleby's wife, who is accompanying him on a European jaunt. I suppose Jakobsson thought a little break from the heavy metaphysical trips of the time would be a relief. He was correct.

In the November issue, Robert Silverberg begins a four-part serial, *Downward to the Earth*. Edmund Gundersen, a former sector chief of colonizing Earth, comes back to Holman's World because he feels he has treated badly the intelligent elephantine creatures who form the dominant culture. There are the truly elephantine nildoror and the more human-like sulidoror; they have been treated as two separate groups. The nildoror have a rebirth rite and don't want humans to discover their secret. But some humans have, and have then undergone Rebirth along with the nildoror and become something new and strange, and immortal. Gundersen uses stealth to get near the holy place of the nildoror, and he too undergoes remarkable experiences. Gundersen ends by finding the local version of religion and immortality and becoming a Messianic figure. The novel actually concludes with some phrases from the New Testament.

Here, however, I must quote from Samuel R. Delany's interesting collection of philosophic and esthetic criticism of sf, *The Jewel-Hinged Jaw*, for a timely word of caution on all-too-tempting Messiah-making in sf (and not sf alone). He says, "Any attempt to be totally rational about such a basically mystical subject as man's ultimate place in the universe tends to squeeze all the mysticism into one bright chunk that blurs all resolutions at the end."

This is well said. If you approach such sf stories as Silverberg's with an analytic philosophic approach, you will be distressed at the often inherent incoherence and plotlessness and what could be construed as a lot of not particularly good prose poetry at the end (excluding Biblical quotations). One wishes for either a rattling good adventure yarn or else a serious work of theology—although James Blish at his best could meld the melange quite well, as in *A Case of Conscience*, unfortunately not a *Galaxy* work.

The last issue of 1969 adopted a new size, about a quarter inch taller than its predecessors. The *Galaxy* logo, red from the very first, now turned a medium shade of purple which did not really do an awful lot for the cover. Jakobsson was doing some external changes. On the inside he was counting on winning over some of the Counterculture (then still not so utterly invisible as now) by getting a monthly comic-strip feature done by Vaughn Bodé, to start in the January 1970 issue. Bodé, who appears in a self-sketch in this December issue, was quoted in Jakobsson's editorial as saying:

> The monolithic awareness of youth stirs and rises up greatly and powerfully. I am awash on a new shore and I am at home with the New People. My acceptance is running like a fast tide . . . I want to do many things with my life but mostly I want to share the places deep in my head with readers everywhere.

The main feature of the December issue was "Half Past Human," a novel by T. J. Bass about the remnants of the true humans versus the Nebishes. True five-toed humans are on an Earth where they are vastly outnumbered and even hunted down by the Nebishes, four-toed hive-culture humans. The Nebishes are so enervated by their hive-city lives that they need strong uppers just to be able to go out and hunt. But they are often killed by their intended prey, for original homo sapiens remain more adaptable and clever. In the end, true humans depart the crowded hive-world of old Earth for new fields of adventure and development.

Also in December, David Gerrold, one of the high-caliber new authors *Galaxy* needed, made one of only four appearances in the magazine with "Oracle for a White Rabbit," a short piece concerning a metaphysical computer named Harlie, who ponders the illogicality of Man's being. Any of these computer tales are timely, for exactly now the machines are beginning to write poetry, although they haven't reached the stage of literary critic yet, thank heavens. With this we end the *Galaxy* Sixties.

Jakobsson had said Bodé's strip was to begin in the January 1970 issue. But there was no January issue; this was an omen, and not a good one. In the February issue Bodé did begin his promised feature, "Sunpot," starring a large-breasted topless space girl named Belinda Bump. It is actually rather amusing. Flying a futuristic spaceship, Ms. Bump and a reptilian ally encounter an Apollo mission with strange results. The space-craft look like advance sketches for some of the craft in *Star Wars*.

There is a novelette in the February issue by Gerald Jonas, who made only this one *Galaxy* appearance. "The Shaker Revival" is about a counter-cultural religion, and was a vision nearer the mark than any of the equally enigmatic Hayden Howard's had been. It tells of a new electronic-rock-enhanced religious order which espouses all the old Shaker monastic virtues: no sex, no booze, communal ownership, etc. It is winning con-verts at a vast rate and is viewed askance, needless to say, by the Estab-lishment whose sons and daughters are joining the New Shakers as new

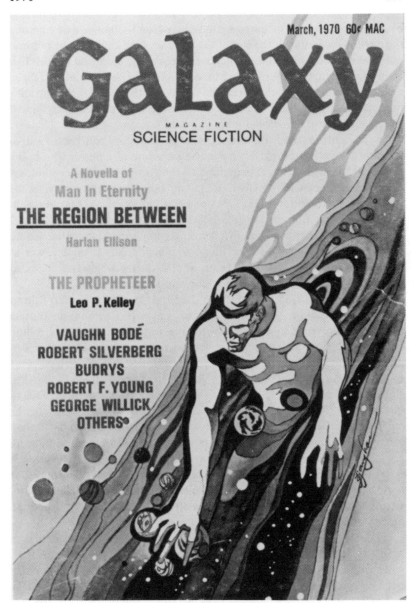

The Region Between. Illustrator: Gaughan.

brothers and sisters. There was a good deal of semi-religious desire among the disaffected young at the end of the Sixties which could not be put into political channels since the left had been wrecked and the best liberals had been shot down. Groups like the Moonies actually filled the cultural niche delineated in the story about the New Shakers, though without the anti-nationalist element both Old and New Shakers shared. They just wanted to make a blissful little kingdom of spiritual peace.

The second novelette I'll comment on is Theodore Sturgeon's Hugo-winning "Slow Sculpture," a very moving account of a healer who in the end is also healed by his patient. The story involves much microbiology, electrical charges within cells, and so on, but this is secondary to the work's great strength: insight into our great vulnerability. Another well-earned Hugo for *Galaxy*—so Jakobsson wasn't doing so badly at that!

Galaxy in March began to display on its spine the Jakobsson slogan, "The Best in Pertinent Science Fiction." This defiant statement was to remain on the spine through March of 1972, after which the policy of listing the better writers included within was resumed.

In March, 1970 *Galaxy* featured a dazzling novella by Harlan Ellison called "The Region Between." A future Earth has euthanasia centers which are allowed it by the great galactic entities who are busily rolling dice with Destiny and transporting souls into bodies of many kinds of different entities in order to win local contests, and some not so local. One of the galactic soul traders obtains the essence of one William Bailey (Bill Bailey, as in the song?). This galactic super-force is known as the Succubus and has gained great repute among his peers by the quality of the souls he can deliver. But Bailey turns out to be less easily managed than the other souls, causing near-mutinies in wars he is supposed to fight in, and so on. He is finally drawn into a memorable encounter with the Succubus himself. This particular novella so preoccupied me during a bus trip that the driver had to remind me that I'd reached my destination. At this point I began buying *Galaxy* with more serious intent. I became quite sure it would be worth my effort to seek it out.

"Sunpot" continues in this issue with some mayhem aboard Belinda's craft—a berserk robot shoots her, but luckily only in her falsies, so she will recover. However, the characters continue to talk in an obnoxiously cutesy way.

The April, 1970 issue has the first installment of Robert Silverberg's three-part novel *The Tower of Glass*. Silverberg was going to make this one of his biggest *Galaxy* years. This novel tells of a society dominated by industrialist and scientist Simeon Krug, who has created a subculture of androids by combining chromosomes. Krug's son Manuel falls in love with a beautiful android woman of the alpha class (gamma being the lowest) who has all the human characteristics except fertility, and also discovers that the androids worship his father as a god.

While all this is going on, Simeon Krug is constructing a giant tower in the Arctic tundra to communicate via tachyon beams with nearby stellar civilizations. He has also built a starship. When his attention is called to the android religion, of which he previously knew nothing, the results are unfortunate for many concerned. The novel does have a certain vast scope, but one is not sure how many changes can be rung on the oppressed android theme. Clifford D. Simak, after all, started *Galaxy* off in its first issue with a novel using man vs. android as a central theme.

In the April issue, Ray Bradbury has a pleasant medium-length poem called "Darwin in the Fields." A lot of people always said that Bradbury was really a poet at heart, and here he seems to be confirming their suspicions. It's fine, but not precisely sf.

Bradbury would do one more poetic piece for *Galaxy*, and then his name too blinks out as another of the old sf leaders retires with honor from the field of battle. But there is no more *Weird Tales* magazine for a future Bradbury to come from, even though Sam Moskowitz made a gallant attempt to revive *WT* in the early Seventies. This is another instance of the attrition I spoke of earlier.

James Blish has the lead novelette, "A Style in Treason," in the May issue. Old Earth is in a colonial struggle with the Green Exarchy and both have agents on certain worlds to influence policy. Simon de Kuyl, High Earth's chief agent of treason and deception, is sent to Boadicea. He has a series of grim encounters with the local treason guild and with creatures of the Exarchy, some of whom have insinuated themselves into high places. Simon has too many tricks and drugs for them, and ends by bringing Valkol the Polite, ruler of Boadicea, over to his side and frustrating the Exarchy. This story, though somewhat Vance-like, is not at all playful and a deep pessimism runs through it. The reader is left in doubt as to what will finally become of Simon. It is known that Blish, the great sf master and critic, was himself in doubt over his own personal fate at this time. He was battling cancer, the disease which had already carried off Groff Conklin, *Galaxy*'s first book reviewer.

There is another Harlie the Computer story in the May *Galaxy*, "The God Machine." David Gerrold is using the computer theme to bring up some more metaphysical questions. This time the company behind Harlie wants the machine to quit fooling around and start making money to justify its existence. That leads Harlie to contemplate its termination—its death—and this, in turn, leads to even more speculation between the computer and its philosophically-minded operator. It makes intriguing reading if you are not familiar with some of the arguments, but otherwise you might like a bit more plot and the old formula of someone coming through the wall with a blaster!

May has the last episode of "Sunpot." It must not have caught on with readers. I found it hard to get much information on the rather sudden eclipse of Bodé. He died in 1971, strangled accidentally by a yoga-breathing device. Curiously, he died the same year as Virgil Finlay, who lived to age 57. Bodé, in comparison, had hardly even gotten started, and now *Galaxy* was deprived of both their talents.

June, 1970 was the last time Frederik Pohl's name appeared on the *Galaxy* masthead as Editor Emeritus.

Carl Jacobi, in his only *Galaxy* appearance, has the lead short story, "The Player at Yellow Silence." The Yansis have invaded the Earth and dire war is expected between them and the Earthmen who still inhabit Europe and the Western Hemisphere. Just when things are looking quite bleak, a mysterious super-golfer named Joseph Forbes appears and builds a mysterious course called Tranquillity Heights. He invites the leading Yansis and humans to play a tournament. Forbes is more than he appears, and some surprising things occur during the games. The tournament seems at first most fateful, and indeed it is, but it ends on a note of peace and accord. Some of the plot may seem a bit facile, but it is a novel idea. Golf is a much better game for traps and surprises than chess, as it turns out.

The mysterious Hayden Howard makes his final bow in *Galaxy* in June with his short story, "Oil-Mad Bug-Eyed Monsters." A pleasant young man is buying up Pacific Coast property fouled by a spill from rich offshore oil deposits. He finds most of the people eager to sell and get out to a less-polluted environment. He only has real trouble with one couple and nearly gets himself killed. Still, he gets the final lease to clear the shore for his kind. Now he has to wait another twenty years before the breeding fleet of his true oil-eating alien kind appears. Twenty years to secure the oil supply. This type of story might not have been done after the first Oil Embargo when we proved ourselves to be the real oil-eating monsters and began to mend our ways.

Duncan Lunan, who was to make five contributions to *Galaxy*, has his first one in June, a short story called "The Moon of Thin Reality." I enjoyed this because it shows what might happen if one crashed too precipitately into an alien interface transfer point. You end up way, way out there, and wonder if you will ever get back. This is a properly tense adventure yarn.

Ejler Jakobsson got the legendary Robert A. Heinlein to come aboard *Galaxy* in July for the four-part serial *I Will Fear No Evil*. Johann Sebastian Bach Smith, an elderly tycoon—a centenarian, in fact—has his mind transferred to the body of his young secretary, who has been murdered, somewhat opportunely for the plot, just as the old man's body is about to give out. The *Science Fiction Encyclopedia* refers to this novel as a bloated and interminable tract. I did not find it so when reading it. Toward the end, when problems arise with organ rejection, in this case rejection of Smith's brain and personality, I felt a genuine sense of sadness and empathy. But the reader must judge on his or her own behalf. It is another big book to add to the already impressive Heinlein shelf. It *is* undoubtedly true that he has since written better ones. This was his second novel-length contribution to *Galaxy*, the first, of course, being *The Puppet Masters* in 1951. And with this novel, Heinlein too takes his departure from *Galaxy*, depriving it of another of the grand old sf masters. Of course, no one knew that at the time. The losses kept on accumulating in a quiet and deadly way.

R. A. Lafferty has a novelette, "The All-At-Once-Man," which is quite odd and disjointed, even for a Lafferty piece. It contains the idea that a man could learn from the legendary magician Prester John how to be immortal by being all ages at once. The story is rather a mess and never seems to resolve itself—but then perhaps that is the point when the main character is also incapable of resolving himself.

"Sittik," by Anne McCaffrey in *her* last *Galaxy* appearance, is a short short in which she shows somewhat ominously that, like sticks and stones, names really *can* hurt you, even an odd nonsensical one.

The next *Galaxy* was for August-September, 1970—back to the bimonthly system. *Galaxy* had been going along fairly smoothly as a monthly, but now it was starting to falter again. The price went up to 75 cents (all the prices of everything started jumping with the advent of the 1970's), and the issue was also larger in length, not just in height, by 32 pages. (However, as of the May-June 1971 issue, 16 of those pages were taken away, cutting *Galaxy* back to 176 pages.)

The Heinlein serial continued, but the cover-featured novel was *The Day After Judgment*, by James Blish (the sequel to his *Black Easter*, which had been serialized as "Faust Aleph-Null" in *If* in 1967). This is one I have always liked, one of the more interesting of the post-nuke-attack stories. A select group is underground in a SAC headquarters protected from the nuclear weapons which destroyed Denver, but the war isn't over yet. It is in fact only in the middle of the scale which would mean complete planetary destruction. The surviving characters are scattered around the world and witness odd things. The Antichrist and other demons start showing up, and soon even Satan, the fallen archangel, puts in an appearance. The U.S. forces try to attack the City of Dis (from Dante's *Inferno*), which materializes in Death Valley, but the tanks and paratroopers are no match for the demons. The U.S. determines to use other weapons, but at that point there is a rather surprising plot twist, with Satan doing a whole page of dialogue which reads as if John Milton had written it in *Paradise Lost*. It was quite an effective device, though what he says I will not here divulge. Blish was back in really good form when he did this one.

R. A. Lafferty has a clever short story in this issue called "About a Secret Crocodile," which reminds us of all the times that we've thought there must be a tiny group of people who think up all the funny jokes in the world or invent all the current slang words, etc. It turns out that there is, and there are other elite secret groups like them. But they find themselves menaced by a yet smaller group which is, unfortunately, not as united as the others. Lafferty humorously puts into story form what we now and then suspect.

In the October-November issue there is a rather startling innovation for *Galaxy*. In place of an editorial, Jakobsson has printed some letters from readers. His predecessors had never done so. Some of the readers praise the cover and interior art. One seems convinced that Jakobsson is cutting down Budrys' column, but is reassured by the editor that this is not the case. There were four reactions printed about the disappearance of "Sunpot." Two readers were very glad it was gone, and two missed it.

One reader sent a letter from Viet Nam and protested against the spine slogan, "The Best in Pertinent Science Fiction." Ejler Jakobsson replied,

"I think some science fiction published is not particularly pertinent—while science fiction as a whole is probably the most pertinent writing being done today. And I want the best for *Galaxy*."

Robert Silverberg continues his distinguished year at *Galaxy* with his novella "The World Outside." This is one in a series of stories about a future in which enormous Urbmons (urban monads), each practically a whole nation contained in one gigantic building, dominate Earth except for the primitive communal agricultural settlements. Different sections of the urbmons are named for previous entire cities—the Warsaw section, or the Edinburgh section. The rulers dwell on the upper floors, of course. It is a very static and tyrannical way of life inside the urbmons, and a working class person by the name of Michael Statler feels rebellious and wants to see what's outside his tightly-controlled environment. He will have reason to regret these urges. Overpopulation was another constant theme of stories during this time period, along with pollution, repression, and militarism. As a result, some quite dystopian works appeared, and some were quite well written, including Silverberg's.

There *was* a December, 1970 issue—*Galaxy* was temporarily back on a monthly schedule. Jakobsson's editorial praises Willy Ley and tells how Judy-Lynn Benjamin, *Galaxy*'s managing editor, suggested to astronomer Dr. Donald H. Menzel that a hitherto unnamed lunar crater be named for Ley. Menzel proposed it at an international commission meeting in Moscow and his proposal was accepted. Willy Ley's crater is at 43 degrees North and 154 degrees East on the Far Side of the Moon. Thus it is that one of *Galaxy*'s people and a pioneer rocketeer has a fixed place in the heavens, and a well-deserved one.

Silverberg has another urbmon novelette in this issue, "We Are Well Organized" (subtitled "An Episode—Urban Monad 116"). In this one, Siegmund Kluver is a consultant manager and on his way to the top floors of his urbmon. But the contradictions he experiences in the lifestyles of the rulers and those of the less advantaged on the lower floors proves to be more than he can handle. It is a worthy sequel to the earlier urbmon story.

Stephen Tall, in one of his six *Galaxy* appearances, has a short story, "The Mad Scientist and the FBI." This is an amusing piece about a batch of very odd zinnias that turn out not to be harmless zinnias at all. Very brightly colored, they are huge and dangerous—a swat of a leaf can cut through a hoe handle. The geneticist Dr. Jameson finds himself quite by accident raising these remarkable plants. As rumors about them spread, he and the plants fall under FBI surveillance—there is a ridiculous sequence of FBI agents sitting on a fence watching the plants at a time when they are not acting unusually. The scientist and his friend keep the seeds and wonder what the next year will bring.

13. Ejler Jakobsson (II)

BEN BOVA BEGAN A TWO-PART NOVEL, *EXILED
From Earth*, in the January, 1971 *Galaxy*.
This was to be his last appearance in the
magazine, for in July of 1971 John W. Campbell, H. L. Gold's old rival
and editor since 1937 of *Astounding/Analog Science Fiction*, passed
away, and Bova succeeded him as editor of *Analog*. Bova would also
continue to write. His novel in *Galaxy* became the first of the "Exiles"
trilogy.

The World Government has exiled a number of brilliant scientists to a
satellite because their work on genetics and astrophysics threatens world
stability. Lou Christopher, his girlfriend Bonnie Sterne, and several other
experts are saved from exile in space and set to work, but they are still in
exile on an uncharted island. They are working for a rebellious faction of
the World Government headed by the sinister Mr. Marcus, who has
designs of his own for control of the Earth.

Biochemical engineering experiments on a friendly gorilla, Georgy,
raise him to near-human intelligence. Then Lou discovers that Mr. Mar-

cus is also having nuclear weapons made, and that the seemingly benign experiments on the gorilla are only being done so a reverse procedure can be developed to lower the level of much of Earth's population while Marcus and his elite group take complete charge of them. Of course, certain sections of the existing population must be destroyed. Lou begins to sabotage these plans, at extreme risk to himself and his friends. Finally Marcus and his group are defeated, but it is, as the Duke of Wellington said of Waterloo, "A damned close-run thing."

In this same issue, Jakobsson takes a stand against the theories some scientists had then about IQ being linked to race. He comes out strongly on the side of IQ determinance being based largely on environment and motivation, and against any genetic bias. He had also taken issue with this in a previous editorial. The renewed clamor for quality education for all which we now hear resoundingly supports Jakobsson in his antiracist position.

Cold January was an appropriate time for the novelette by Michael G. Coney, who contributed seven pieces to *Galaxy* in the early Seventies. "Snow Princess" seems to anticipate the "nuclear winter" we are now being warned about. We join a band of human survivors who scavenge food and alcohol and other supplies through sheets of near-glacial ice while contending with mutant bear-like creatures they call "pads." They go from scrape to scrape but are still surviving at the end, and even linking up with more human survivors. They frustrate the pads and other predators by sailing on top of the ice in snowboats which can skim along very briskly in the Arctically cold winds.

Still shivering from that story, we are scared by the short story "Lot 22A," by David J. Rogoff. This one tells of the results of a pact in which the superpowers agree to destroy their biological weapons. Lot 22A is a blood disease which can mutate dangerously under radiation, but heavy doses of radiation are needed to destroy it. While the irradiation is going on, a janitor notices an electrical fire beginning. He sounds the alarm and the scientists are alerted. All seems well—except for the fact that one of the last vials being irradiated got a hairline crack during the excitement, a crack so tiny no one notices it. And there is no cure for what's in Lot 22A.

There are two novelettes of interest in the February 1971 issue, by old-timer A. E. van Vogt and comparative newcomer Stephen Tall. Tall's is the cover story, "This Is My Country." In a future U.S.A. where the red, white and blue still is waving, robots plan resistance to their rulers.

The robots self-destruct when their plans at disruption are frustrated. Lord Ferron and the other leaders frantically use loyal unreprogrammed robots to foil the revolt—but it turns out to be a revolution, with an unexpected ringleader. After it is all over the old flag is still, ironically, flying.

I had some problems with the van Vogt, "The Reflected Men." For one, the title is misleading, for it is a woman who is reflected into different copies of herself by a miraculous crystal from the far future which can simultaneously produce the best and the worst of each human individual. This somewhat defies logic, but we are not come to sneer at A. E. van Vogt, whose powers were at their height in the 1940's with *Slan* and *The Weapon Makers*. One *can* puzzle through the story and even applaud as this great sf writer makes his next-to-last *Galaxy* bow. It is as though Jakobsson was dashing around to the weary troops and saying, "Come on lads, one last time! You can do it!" And surprisingly many rose to the occasion.

This issue also has a short story by Michael G. Coney, a British writer residing in Canada, whose work finally does import into *Galaxy* some of the influence of J. G. Ballard. "The Sharks of Pentreath" tells of an English seaside resort as plastic as all-get-out. But this doesn't matter to the tourists, who are people stored away in the Shelflife Center but experiencing life through remotors, small robots that let them "travel," however old and frail they are, and cheaply too, sensing everything through the robotic link. An interesting tale, with even a pathetic love theme!

In March, Robert Silverberg is back with another serial, in three parts, "A Time of Changes." Here is Silverberg at his most Sturgeonlike, and, of course, Messianistic as well. Kinnall Darival, Prince of Salla, is an exile on the planet Borthan, an exile from his own strict province where a puritanical religion is in force which forbids "self-baring" or even use of the word "I." He escapes to more sophisticated Manneran and stays with some of his relatives, fellow aristocrats. (Someone in *Harper's* recently commented that sf has more dukes, lords, and counts than any fiction since the days of *The Prisoner of Zenda*.) He encounters the tempter Schweiz, who introduces him to the Sumaran drug which causes ultimate self-baring. Used "with love"—with another or with a whole group—all can achieve utter, loving oneness. This is a road it seems we have been up before (which is why I mentioned Theodore Sturgeon). However, it is not universally helpful, and even causes a suicide. Nonetheless, Kinnall sets out to change his puritanical society by inducing ultimate openness. He sees himself as a foredoomed Saviour figure. And who said the 1960's were over!?

Ernest Taves has a fine short in March, "Pegasus Two." A U.S. space mission is on the Moon, doing experiments and sampling Lunar rocks, when one crewman comes across a wrecked Soviet LEM with one surviving astronaut aboard, a pretty Russian woman. The word "astronette" is used; thank heavens they didn't think of that one for Sally Ride. The problem can be easily resolved and international tensions eased, one would think. Not so. The U.S. LEM pilot turns out to be more than a little right wing, and therefore there are Problems.

Also in March, Greg Benford, a fine sf writer, checks in with a cheerful first *Galaxy* appearance. In "But the Secret Sits," Dr. Fredrick Black and an assistant have made some very significant discoveries in the theory of matter vibration and disintegration which could have military uses. The fun part of the story is how Dr. Black plays off various corporations and bureaucracies to keep his discoveries to himself and become more or less independent of such big sinister entities.

Chelsea Quinn Yarbro also checks in, with the first of her three *Galaxy* stories. The basic topic of "Frog Pond" is pollution and the mutations it causes. It's told from the viewpoint of a young girl who is out catching frogs for her family in a rather strange pond. A stranger talks to her, but is scared away when she shows how she sees the frogs underwater: she has a nictitating membrane.

Yarbro and Benford would seem like inspiring new recruits for *Galaxy*, to help keep it in action. Unfortunately, their contributions were to be too few for the magazine's health. And "James Tiptree, Jr." makes *her* final appearance in *Galaxy* with a razzle-dazzle novelette, "Mother in the Sky With Diamonds." This one tells of the life of a wandering trader/explorer/ rocketeer in the great asteroid belt, a crazed old woman space pioneer who is the last inhabitant of the huge derelict ship *Ragnarok*, and nuisances such as the smugglers of "phage," a sinister and illegal narcotic. This is the sort of story I would have liked to have seen more of in *Galaxy*, but now "Tiptree" would not provide them anymore.

The April, 1971 issue opens on an amusing note. Jakobsson has thrown open his editorial column to letters again. These largely concern Heinlein's *I Will Fear No Evil*, and vary widely in reaction. My favorite is the following:

Dear Sir:

Galaxy was one of my favorite sf magazines and Robert Heinlein one of my favorite authors.

Now Heinlein has descended to subtle pornography in *I Will Fear No Evil*, as well as becoming endlessly boring—couldn't stomach finishing his serial. Many of your stories now seem selected with an eye to socialistic and left radical slants. You have both lost me for good.

M. K. Johnson
Omaha, Nebraska

The very idea of the former naval officer and libertarian Robert Anson Heinlein being accused of smut and socialism must have caused many a chuckle in the *Galaxy* offices. That would make Heinlein one of the few SF writers accused of following an "ism"; moreover, it would make him the only one to have been called a fascist and a socialist in more or less the same decade. Political ideologies are really fairly alien to sf except for a certain rather widespread *laissez faire* individualism which seems endemic to all "romantic" adventure fiction. By definition, science is neutral—the Nazis could never construct a *Deutsche Mathematik*—and fiction is, well, fiction, and only the worst totalitarian systems try to make fiction writers and poets toe a strict pseudoscientific party line. Some of the other writers admired Heinlein's novel, so, mixed reviews!

Joe W. Haldeman has a fine novelette, "To Fit the Crime," in the April issue. Interplanetary investigator Otto McGavin is sent to the planet Bruuch to find out why the already short-lived natives, who mostly work as miners for a human company, are dying more quickly than they should. He goes disguised as xenobiologist Dr. Isaac Crowell, a much older man who had written a book on the planet. McGavin is hemmed in between traitorous humans and natural dustpits which swallow up the unwary. He also has a good deal of difficulty with the Bruuchian gravity. Then he makes a quite startling discovery about the *real* Bruuchian life cycle.

The May-June issue followed. *Galaxy* had once again fallen back to a bimonthly schedule, to which it would adhere until October of 1973. This on-again off-again rate of publication could hardly have done much for it. In any case, the magazine's readers were clever enough to adjust to it. Jakobsson has another column devoted to reader response to a poll initiated in the December, 1970 issue. More than two-thirds of the readers responding were in the age group 18-39, and three-quarters of this group had an educational level of college or better. Nearly 80% didn't mind four-letter words in their SF at all. So perhaps the Omaha reader was well-advised (self-advised in his case) to seek his sf elsewhere!

A novelette in this issue called "Tip of the Iceberg," by Ernest Hill, was another J. G. Ballard-influenced piece. An experimental laboratory in the English countryside has somehow liberated a universal antihuman intelligence merely by experimenting with a gorilla's brain. The somewhat improbable ending has the scientists and various constables and government ministers besieged by an army of brown rats who have suddenly materialized. I found this . . . illogical.

The May-June issue also has a novelette by James E. Gunn, "The Message." To jump forward a bit, this would be followed in January of 1972 by a sequel, "The Answer." Briefly, these are two events in radio communication between Earth and planets in the Capellan system. The message to Earth is interpreted variously by different groups. A religious leader wants it to be seen as a picture of an angel with an uplifting message of blessing for all mankind. The leading radio astronomers and the U.S. President, a black man, carefully and thoughtfully analyze the message and assess its dolorous true meaning. One of the Capellan suns is going nova, and already the beings calling from 45 light years away must wear protective suits on their own planet. The President eventually decides on an appropriate response: we send a radio picture of a human arm in arm with a Capellan. These are really quite moving novelettes. I try to avoid excessive generalization, but I find that very many of the sf stories of the Seventies are very serious and melancholy, like the thoughts of an adult who realizes how much has already gone past him and how much is irretrievably out of his control—a star going nova is one particularly striking example of the images encountered. Computers going crazy are not quite so serious, unless they are hooked into a planetary defense system. There have been stories on that topic also.

Going back to the May-June issue of 1971, Budrys has a lengthy column in which he takes particular pains to demolish Stanislaw Lem's *Solaris*. This was something of a surprise to me when I reread it, for Lem has since been praised high and low (although not quite to the point of getting a Nobel prize like his gallant fellow Pole, Lech Walesa, for a work in a not necessarily unrelated field, human freedom). The Polish authorities, thank heavens, have let Lem write whatever he pleases in the sf field.

Budrys, of course, attacks on esthetic grounds:

Lem's unique gift to the kind of science fiction written by classicists, then, apparently is no more than an infusion of the same lack of logical rigor as that which distinguishes much "New Wave" commercial sf of the 'sixties, in which illusions of profundity are generated by imprecise reference, paradoxic exposition and a ruthless unwillingness to let the characters act as smart as they say they are.

I might comment here that the earlier translations of Lem were not really very good. They have since been properly Englished. I've found a lot of his stories to be as interesting or well-plotted as anything by, say, Poul Anderson or "James Tiptree, Jr." Apparently the translator of the book Budrys reviewed was the same person who accompanied President Carter on his famous trip to Poland during which he was misrepresented as saying he would like to make carnal love to the Polish people, in addition to such other unhelpful references as "the duchy of Ohio." Still there would remain some irreconcilable differences between a writer like Budrys and one like Lem who genuinely did incorporate some New Wave ideas, among many other things, in his fiction.

Jack Sharkey has a memorable short story in this issue, "Rate of Exchange." We come to the gradual discovery that the lost continents of Atlantis and Lemuria were lost to interstellar attack, and they had retaliated. A clay shard message from their time turns out to be a warning to us. But as we awake to the horror that is implied, the story comes to an even more abrupt and spectacular ending than any in the *Galaxy* of the previous years, and that's saying something.

The July, 1971 *Galaxy* begins a three-part serial by Jack Williamson, illustrated by Gaughan. Williamson is a real sf old-timer. He is honored in the magazine not only by the usual biographical sketch, but also by a photo, an unprecedented distinction for *Galaxy* to give one of its writers. His novel, *The Moon Children*, deals with the fortunes and misfortunes of three children born to the wives of three lunar explorers who were contaminated by "moon grit" when they responded to mysterious light phenomena on the lunar surface. These children turn out to be forerunners of an ET confederacy which wishes to help Earth, which is now plagued by sinister "biocosms," deadly fogs and weird metal ants, among other things. It was not exactly clear to me whether the biocosms are more part of the disease, or part of the cure, in the sense that they galvanize some Earthmen to seek help through the tachyon communicating tower built by the Moon Children. Nevertheless, the novel ends on a note of hope and Earth is helped to "adjust to the culture of the stars."

Larry Eisenberg, who contributed a lot to *Galaxy* and whom I have unforgiveably slighted, has a good and amusing short story in the July magazine, "Duckworth and the Sound Probe." Duckworth, a bearded and newly-wed computer expert, is off on a tangent of his own. He has invented a probe which can make sense of old imbedded sounds in walls, crockery, or almost anything. He is set upon at once by various ominous agencies who seek to use his work for their own purposes. In the end, everyone realizes the Probe would be universally embarrassing. The UN draws up a protocol in which all the signers agree not to use the Probe, and Duckworth and his friend, none the worse for the publicity, cheerfully toast marshmallows over a slow fire fed with the drawings of the Probe.

Gaughan also does the cover for the September, 1971 *Galaxy*. Gordon Eklund has a fine novelette, "The Edge and the Mist," a tale in the fine old space pioneer tradition which the sf reader was seeing less and less often. Eklund takes us to the Edge—the planet numbered 3D7698 at the very end of the galaxy. He starts off with a bar room scene complete with ominous aliens, anticipating the scene in *Star Wars* by more than half a decade. Some of the scruffy crew of a ship that is going out from the Edge are involved in a fight in the bar, but come out victorious. These two old spacers are joined soon by a young chap named Alpha and a woman whom they rescue from an abandoned spacecraft. Their ship enters the great barrier Mist, which is extremely sinister and can drive humans mad with its vivid visions unless self-control is really deeply learned. The crew successfully penetrate the Mist, and to their amazement see a giant alien ship. They receive a mental message to the effect that you've done OK so far, humans, now get ready for our next test. This turns out to be another (to borrow a phrase from Eric Frank Russell) "sinister barrier," the Wall. That they have gotten through the Mist is cause for immediate celebration, and only old Hawkins, the captain, broods on the Wall. There is apparently enough civilization among the stars that any new sign of it is a somewhat tired topic; in order to get into the Club, you have to show that you've "got the right stuff." That is the premise of an awful lot of sf works —good, bad, or indifferent—and is arguable on various grounds. It's a lot better than the older premise that humanity is a great conquering force and would go through the alien natives either with contemptuous ease or

Starcult. Illustrator: Claude Newkirk.

else with grand space battles like Jules Verne crossed with C. S. Forester
and biographies of Admiral Lord Nelson of Trafalgar.

Speaking of naval matters, there is a first class nautical yarn in the same
issue, "Sister Ships," by A. Bertram Chandler (subtitled "A Commodore
Grimes Novelette"). The difference is that this takes place on the water
world Aquarius. Grimes is customarily a space commodore of immense
experience, but he also enjoys being the captain of an ocean-going vessel.
It turns out that the *Sonya Winneck*, which is supposed to be on a
relaxing cruise, is victim to all sorts of sabotage. Captain Grimes finally
figures it out when he gets into the psychology of some of the sophisticated computerized navigational equipment on board.

The November, 1971 *Galaxy* is simply outstanding. It has three excellent novelettes. The first is "Birds Fly South in Winter," by Stephen Tall.
It is a gentle tale of a xenobiological expedition to a planet that has a
diversity of life, the dominants being large bear-like telepaths who are
quite civilized and unaggressive. Tall makes much here of interspecies
cooperation and sympathy, and the story leaves one with a warm-hearted
outlook about some of the Good Guys out there.

"Rammer," by Larry Niven, is the second novelette. A future Earth
society is reviving the people frozen in this century because of incurable
diseases. But it is not only healing them, it is *using* them, either as cheap
labor or else as "rammers," highly trained human components of star-
ships. Niven's hero, Corbett, is initially servile but later on his handlers
are given a well-deserved shock!

Eileen Kernaghan's novelette "Starcult" is the most memorable of them
all. It deals with the confrontation of a mesmeric cult leader with a sinister
telepathic colonizing alien crew. The confrontation is memorable, but its
results are ironic to the narrator, who had known the Cult Saviour from
school days.

In the November *Galaxy*, book reviewer Algis Budrys writes a column
that is more questions than answers, mostly concerning the nature of
writing, the real value of a serious story versus a less serious but entertaining story, and the relationship, very tenuous if existent at all, between the
writer and the reader. He seems to take the quite valid esthetic point that
the reader should consider the song, so to speak, and not the singer. This
is basically the sort of position held by such an author as the distinguished
poet T. S. Eliot. This is all quite stimulating—and then in the last paragraph comes what Jakobsson referred to as Ajay's bombshell:

> And with that, we close. . . . your faithful reviewer has no further grounds for believing himself even marginally competent. It has been about five years, I thank you for your kind attention and I am hanging it up.

Many years later, Budrys' reviews have been collected as *Benchmarks: Galaxy Bookshelf* (Southern Illinois University Press, 1985). Budrys' sudden departure startled me. I well remember reading the issue, for at that time I was working at a rather dreary job in a Minneapolis hospital and found my life much aided and enlivened by sf, and most especially *Galaxy*. Whenever I changed environments—and I did so more often in those years—I could always count on running across my old companion, *Galaxy*, on some newstand or other.

January, 1972 has the first of a fine two-part novel by James White, *Dark Inferno*. We are with Mercer, a doctor who is seeking space medicine experience aboard the passenger-carrying ship *Eurydice*. Mercer is looked down on by most of the crew, and is expected only to aid the space-sick passengers, get them to go through survival drills, and so on, much like a glorified steward. However, before the ship has gotten very far on its trip to Ganymede, but far enough, the survival drills become the real thing as a major accident makes casualties of the captain and some other officers. Mercer effectively takes charge and has to "talk people down" from fear and horror feelings. He fails in one signal instance but is successful in all other cases; he also aids in guiding in the rescue attempt and keeping the ship's survivors close together. Mercer thus gains the respect of the veteran space officers, but it was touch and go all the way, a real "gripper" which I recommend.

Bob Shaw returns to *Galaxy* (he appeared twice in 1969) in this January issue with a rather strange short story. Shaw was not a frequent contributor to *Galaxy* and is better remembered for his famous "slow glass" series for *Fantasy and Science Fiction* during the early Seventies. Here, in "Stormseeker," he writes about a post-holocaust Earth where a mutant wanders the sky hunting the lightning. Waiting beneath the surface is physicist Archbold, who needs electrical power to continue his experiments. The problem is that when the stormseeker diverts great bolts of electricity to the energy cells of the underground laboratory, he is preventing that same electrical energy from transforming atmospheric nitrogen into soil-nourishing nitric acids—so he is hindering the Earth from regrowing its diversity of vegetation and animals. His erstwhile mate senses what he is doing and leaves him, saying she will have no children by him. The stormseeker doesn't care; he is excited at the prospect of a new storm coming and new lightning bolts to be sped down to the physicist for his experiments on the nature of matter. It all seems very much of a parable, in a New Wave manner.

Isaac Asimov, one of the leading generals of sf, to use military terms again, returned to *Galaxy* with a full-length novel—a Nebula and Hugo winner, no less! I should say he made a *Galaxy/If* appearance, for the first installment was in the March, 1972 *Galaxy*, the second ran in the March-April *If*, and it concluded in the May *Galaxy*. This is a brilliant work, as one could have expected from Asimov, and is also his goodbye to *Galaxy* (save for one article later on). I am reminded of how all the great comics abandoned radio in the early 1950's and went on TV—even a reluctant Fred Allen, whose real *métier* was always radio. But the sf top bananas had nowhere else to go but into the paperback and hardbound book market (of which more later), *except* Isaac Asimov, whose prestige was so great that he began his own magazine.

His novel *The Gods Themselves* takes place in 2070. Dr. Frederick Hallam discovers a curious conversion of tungsten to a plutonium isotope. This is a result of a leak between two universes, and the process can be harnessed in electron pumps to produce free and limitless energy. Hallam is greatly honored and revered, though a few other physicists have doubts. One of them, Peter Lamont, has a very large doubt indeed. The pumps create an electron drain to the other universe. While most scientists are sanguine about the process, Lamont and another scientist, Benjamin Denison, realize that the electron drain could very shortly result in a massive catastrophe for our segment of the galaxy. Beings in the para-universe are also concerned, for they too could suffer a catastrophe, though of a different sort. The difficulty is that Hallam has all the political power, and Earth loves the new "free" energy source. The problem is finally solved by another scientific breakthrough, with the aid of some Lunar colonists. Good science and good prose here combine for a novel worthy of its recognition, another credit for *Galaxy* (and *If*).

The May issue is also noteworthy for the fact that the slogan "The Best in Pertinent Science Fiction" has been dropped and the older scheme of putting the names of the leading contributors on the spine is restored. This practice would continue until the June/July 1979 issue.

Larry Eisenberg is back with "The Grand Illusions." His character

The Gods Themselves. Illustrator: Gaughan.

Duckworth has come up with a system of multiple holograms for study-
ing molecular structures. The device comes in quite handy when there is a
student protest on Duckworth's college campus. (There were still student
protests in 1972, lest we forget.) Duckworth projects multiple images of
the same protestor, to the utter frustration and bafflement of the police
who wish to physically subdue the "crowd." He then concludes a truce
with the school's president, who agrees to drop military research projects
in exchange for no more high-tech high jinks from the formidable Duckworth. This is an enjoyable little story.

Also in May, David Gerrold has "Trouble With G.O.D.," another Harlie episode. The computer is still busy ascertaining the meaning of God
and existence, while the owners are getting more frustrated all the time
because of the machine's expense. We get some more good human/
super-computer dialogue, and at the end Harlie has reached the point
where he can write quite a creditable love poem. Auberson, the researcher
working with Harlie, wonders if the computer is not straying from the
point. Harlie replies that he is not, and then counter-queries whether
men really *want* to know the objective truth about the metaphysical and
theological problems he has been set to work on. The story ends there.
Obviously, Auberson has to do some thinking about that.

Jakobsson had begun a policy of paying for good *letters* to the editor,
which he published in a section called "Directions." This was a mostly
serious continued discussion of what sf was and where it was going. It is
worthwhile to quote part of one letter in the July, 1972 issue, from Ronald
Archer of Falls Church, Virginia:

> Most authors of 1940 space operas used characters who were card-
> board cutouts in black and white—good guys and bad guys. And the
> plots were often resolved by luck, coincidence or a fortuitous invention
> ("I just whipped up a new space drive out of this six-pack of used beer
> cans, Commander!" "Good going, Sparks!"). This was insulting to most
> readers over the age of ten.
>
> What's happening now is that sf writers are setting their sights on
> better stories, ones in which melodrama is replaced with more genuine
> insight into human conditions.

As if to reinforce Mr. Archer's point, the July issue has the first half of
the novel *Dying Inside*, by Robert Silverberg. This is an unsurpassed
story of David Selig, who has the ability to read minds, most minds. He
knows of only a few other people in the country with the same power and

they are all isolated. He is now beginning to lose his power as he goes into the nebulously-defined segment of life called middle age. During the course of the novel we are moved at his plight and how little he has really done with his power. He is reduced to faking term papers for students at Columbia University to make a little money. There are passages and insights that are unforgettable as he has a few brief glimpses of his old ability. Yet, as he becomes a quite normal human, we feel he gains as much as he loses. This one was well worth a Hugo, but unfortunately it came out just as Asimov and Clarke came back onto the field. Anyway, this is another "must-read."

The July *Galaxy* has a humorous short story by Sandy Fisher (last of two *GSF* appearances, both in 1972) called "Farewell to the Artifacts." All the household appliances in a suburb of Los Angeles start to act oddly. One worried family even tries an exorcist, but nothing works. All their neighbors are having similar problems. Eventually the the electrical and gasoline-powered devices trundle away to immolate themselves in the Pacific Ocean. The people are left to their own natural devices, and seem rather cheerful about it. It is certainly better to have the machines simply depart rather than turn ominously upon their owners as in some of the stories in the Gold Era of *Galaxy*.

Philip José Farmer has a novella in the same issue, "Seventy Years of Decpop." This is a story relating to the problems of overpopulation, which was then (as I've mentioned) very much a matter of sf concern. A certain Dr. Clabb has perfected and released an aerosol which renders most of humanity sterile. Entire countries have only a few hundred people who can reproduce. It will be up to them and their descendants what sort of new human society will appear. Jackson Canute watches the changes over the years as entire towns and cities are removed from the map. Canute is delighted at the end to witness evidence that though there are fewer (and, of course, newer) people, they are still people, with all their historic faults and good points. This novella is good reading, but is unfortunately also Farmer's last *GSF* appearance. Another light winks out for *Galaxy*, though of course Farmer would have many major works in his future.

Joe Haldeman is back in the September, 1972 *Galaxy* with "Power Complex," a novelette following up his 1969 "Out of Phase," about the maturing of Braxn the G'drellian on Planet Earth. He has now entered his power phase, one of his adolescent cycles. Braxn makes himself into Ross

Harriman, and becomes President of the U.S. after causing the previous President to die of heart failure. He soon discovers he has plenty to handle in the job, especially when his "father" tells him that if he is destroyed in the Harriman body, he will also die as a G'drellian entity. He finds himself often leaving the Harriman body to save certain injured humans from death, and he is growing a sense of compassion. But some of his forward-looking work as President causes a man named Harry Doyle to begin stalking him for assassination. Braxn has caused, not quite directly, the death of Doyle's old boss, a rather obstructionist senator. Despite Braxn's great powers, Doyle cleverly closes in, and the story gains a good deal of tension as it goes on.

There is a strange short story in this issue called "Changing Woman," by W. Macfarlane, who had five *Galaxy* appearances in the early Seventies. This one is representative. An American Indian woman, Girl Cloud-Walking, finds employment with the Mundy Foundation, a strange California high-tech organization that concerns itself with very advanced map-making. It is headed by a sinister woman, Arlis Mundy. It becomes apparent that Ms. Mundy is more than a little deranged and that her organization has very great and ominous, literally Earth-shaking, powers which Girl Cloud-Walking eventually has to counter. The descriptions of the workings of the Foundation are rather interesting and intricate.

Also in the issue is "True School of Modesty," by Ernest Taves. This is basically a follow-up to the ill-fated mission in "Pegasus Two" (March 1971). Succeeding lunar explorers make more discoveries and also find the sad and touching evidence of the American and Soviet astronauts that Pegasus Two had abandoned so hard-heartedly.

In the November issue, Frank Herbert, of *Dune* fame, begins a major three-part novel called "Project 40." (As a paperback it is known as *Hellstrom's Hive*, being loosely connected with a 1973 film of that name.) To quote from the *Science Fiction Encyclopedia*:

> It describes in persuasive detail an underground colony of humans selectively bred on insect-hive principles into various specializations. It is a society in which the individual's existence is of minor importance; the continuation of the hive as a functioning entity is paramount. The novel points up the contradictions of a society which in its own terms is a successful Utopia, but which from an outside human viewpoint is horrific.

Herbert's novel makes *1984* seem like *The Bobbsey Twins on Grand-*

father's Farm. It ends in a virtual stand-off between the outside human societies and the fast-growing hive society with its powerful secret weapons. This is a dystopia with a vengeance.

On a more cheerful note, Commodore Grimes is back in a novelette by A. Bertram Chandler called "The Dutchman." Space travelers in the new contraterrene-powered ships report an odd craft which seems to suddenly appear and disappear. The phenomenon seems menacing enough to call for the services of Commodore Grimes, who ships aboard the light-jammer *Pamir*. He encounters a legend who has shifted his operations, sixteenth century ship and all, into the reaches of outer space—another space-nautical yarn!

November also has a somewhat puzzling short story, "Journey," by Sonya Dorman, concerning the ascent of an awesome peak on an alien planet. Despite fatalities, the humans climb on, to be met with a somewhat surrealistic party when they have reached the peak. What is the point of this ascent? What are they trying to prove? This is more New Wave influence, doubtless.

In the "Directions" section of *Galaxy* for January, 1973, Brent Higginbotham of Brockton, Massachusetts makes a wise contribution to the debate about sf. Higginbotham writes:

> We are in another Age of Reason. If something appeals to our sense of beauty and not to our intellect we mistrust it. If it gives us pleasure without purpose we fear it. And if it somehow manages to hang on despite these obstacles we feel obliged at least to pump it full of "meaning." Give it a cold, concrete handle.
>
> Let's keep a touch of poetry in this prosaic Age of Reason.

This is a refreshing point of view for *Galaxy*. The magazine throughout its career had always, but not really notoriously, been on the somber, didactic side even though it made much use of humor and satire to achieve these ends. It often struck a happy balance, but recent issues had been a bit on the ominous side, so a whiff of the same spirit that animated James Branch Cabell and Jack Vance (no longer appearing in the magazine) was a good thing.

In the January issue is a good novella by Theodore Sturgeon, "Case and the Dreamer." It is about a space rescue and the revival of a lost couple on a lost planet far from Earth, and is not a lightsome piece. The tale is more effective because it makes use of flashbacks, a common enough literary device, one would think, but all too rare in sf where the

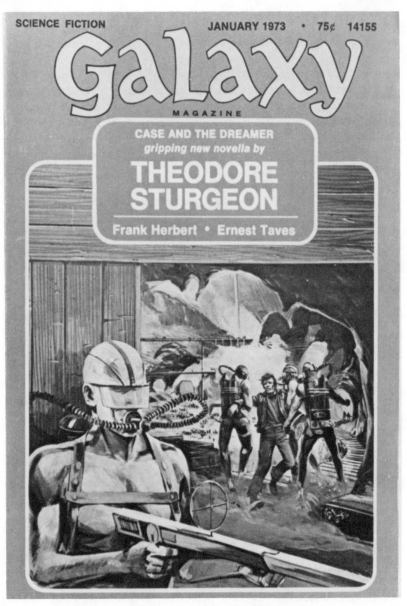

Project 40. Illustrator: Brian Boyle.

single or multiple person narrative tends to plow right on from moment to inexorable moment even in the most alien of settings.

"La Befana," a short story by Gene Wolfe, also appears in the January issue. It's an interesting combination of the Christmas and Wandering Jew legends combined on a world far distant from Earth. This story was later anthologized in *The Best From Galaxy: Volume II*. Under the editorship of Jakobsson, *Galaxy* had been continuing with anthologies in the paperback market. They were issued by Award House, a subsidiary of *Galaxy*'s publishers, Universal Publishing and Distributing Corporation, and emphasized the fact that the anthologized stories were by *bona fide* Hugo-winning authors!

Colin Kapp has an interesting short story in the March, 1973 issue. "Crimescan" deals with a very powerful law-enforcement device of the future which can jump backward and forward in time and discover what really happened at the scene of a crime. There are some rather graphic scenes. As the inventors realize the awesome power the device could have, they decide to rather drastically terminate its use before it can be put to any possible serious misuse. This vaguely seems to echo a quite archaic mode of sf, the type of H. G. Wellsian story which generally concludes, "Thank heavens, we are rid of it, Professor. The world is not now ready for such an invention." However, I don't mean to ridicule the Kapp story. He's a good writer.

There is also an interesting technologically-oriented short story in the same issue: "Interference," by William Walling, a not very prolific author, apparently. Scientist Richard Dallin is on a doomed expedition on the far side of the Moon, the sort where everyone goes crazy and dies one way or another due to unfortunate psychological complications. However, an alien technology fulfills Dallin's fervent wish to be back with his family. He gets back—fixed in an acrylic resin photosculpt only eight inches high. He is in some way alive, and back where he wants to be until the scientists can figure some way to bring him out of the photosculpt safely.

The May, 1973 *Galaxy* has the first segment of a two-part serial by John Boyd, *The Doomsday Gene*. Amal Severn is a young and brilliant seismologist; he is also an AE 7, a product of human genetic engineering. This is where the story loses me, because he is supposed to be an ideal type of human, one who will contribute much to mankind and then self-destruct, possibly killing thousands of people. This strikes me as a definitely hare-brained scheme. In any case, lovely psychologist Lyn Oberlin finds out about this AE 7 business and tries to save him from disaster. His seismological activities are brilliant, but when will the disaster be? And will she save him from self-programmed destruction? I'll spare the reader some trouble on this one. He does inadvertently cause a quite major quake in the L.A. region and then gets killed by a laser beam. In the story his death is accidental, but on the cover it looks suspiciously deliberate.

In May, "Parthen," a short story by reliable R. A. Lafferty, tells rather sardonically of a take-over of Earth by beautiful young ladies. They are all gorgeous and give the men pleasure, but soon take over all the companies, bear only female children, and eventually refuse to hire men, who are sent out to starve on the garbage heap of history, which at this date must be growing to great proportions. The displaced men still are grateful to the gloriously lovely young ladies.

A longer story in May is "Girl Saturday," by Robert F. Young. It tells the adventures of Robinson Feeney, who finds himself on an ISLE, a sort of temporal distortion from which he must rescue the daughter of King Croesus, no less, from a gang of kidnappers. There are some charming touches—a used-car lot and a fast-food hamburger joint are set next to King Arthur's realm and Yasnaya Polyana, Leo Tolstoy's estate (though, to my disappointment, Tolstoy does not make an appearance). Still, the tale contains some amusing premises and ends happily enough.

In the July issue there is an amusing novelette by Ward Moore, the author of the famous sf novel *Bring the Jubilee*, which tells of a world in which the Confederacy did win the Civil War and how different modern history was as a result. His *Galaxy* piece, "Frank Merriwell in the White House," is almost as anachronistic, except that it involves a robot. This robot takes the name Frank Merriwell and is elected to high offices, and finally to the Presidency, by taking a firm stand against progress. Everyone then enthusiastically gives up all modern appliances (hmmm) and all the world's nations agree to scrap all weapons of war, "stimulated by Frank's honest antagonism to any weapon more lethal than a rock." Then the robot President resigns and decides to do what he was designed for in the first place, play baseball! Ah, if wishes were horses . . .

The other story in the July magazine I'll mention is "A Voice and Bitter Weeping," by Buddy Saunders and Howard Waldrop. It was later anthologized and still later became a full-sized novel called *The Texas-Israeli War: 1999*, which some readers might recall. Most of world civilization has gone up in nuclear exchanges. Part of the U.S. is left and it needs the

SCIENCE FICTION

OCTOBER 1973 • 75¢   14155   s•m

GaLaxy

23rd Anniversary All-Star Issue!

ARTHUR C. CLARKE
Rendezvous with Rama

URSULA K. LeGUIN
Field of Vision

RAY BRADBURY
Ode to Electric Ben

THEODORE STURGEON
Agness, Accent and Access

HARLAN ELLISON
Cold Friend

JAMES WHITE
The Dream Millennium

Rendezvous With Rama. Illustrator: Brian Boyle.

aid of its ally, Israel, in bringing Texas back into the Union. And so the Israeli tank columns boldly head down toward Dallas where the main Texas resistance is to be found. There is a lot of combat, and the premise of the story is quite intriguing.

The September *Galaxy* has a real "scoop": the well-known and long-time sf writer Arthur C. Clarke contributes a two-part novel. This is the famous *Rendezvous With Rama*, which won the Hugo, Nebula, British SF, and Jupiter awards—in short, nearly every sf award of any consequence!

At this point I have to take note of an essay quite hostile to sf, Arnold Klein's "Destination: Void" in the December, 1982 *Harper's Magazine* (shame on it!). In a few wildly swinging pages he tries to dismiss as stupid and juvenile the entire body of science fiction and fantasy literature. Coming to Clarke's *Rama*, Klein says:

> . . . Sci-fi novels are more inane in practice than they have to be. Plots are stereotyped: the hyperprolific wordsmiths naturally repeat classic tales, quests, odysseys, *Tempests*, *Vies de Jésus*, and so on. That is, when they bother to produce plots at all. In Arthur C. Clarke's *Rendezvous With Rama*, which won sci-fi's three [sic] highest awards, a giant thing floats into the universe, is investigated, unfolds various technological marvels, and departs. *That's it.*

Mr. Klein is quite easy to demolish. In fact, I sometimes suspect the essay is a spoof of the sort sf writers have themselves been notorious for. To begin with, the Rama object floats into the Solar System, quite a different proposition from floating "into the universe," which is nonsensical. There is genuine concern about whether or not it might be a menace to Earth, and the story holds a charm that anyone who is in the least curious about exploring lost or alien worlds will not easily avoid. And Clarke does write very well indeed, so the novel is worth one's time to read.

Klein also says that in sf there is no death. Now, not even Robert Silverberg has written anything *that* Messianic (in the strict Christian sense of that word). Entire planets get blown up, for grief's sake, and people get stranded on the Moon, to cite an example in *Galaxy*, and hurt and loss *are* reckoned with. To the back of the class, Mr. Klein!

With the September, 1973 *Galaxy* the monthly schedule resumes. The magazine had started using a fine Kromekote cover stock again in March of 1972. It was genuinely still in the top category of sf magazines.

October was the 23rd anniversary issue and it featured numerous fine offerings. For the first time (of three) Ursula Kroeber Le Guin made a *GSF* appearance in a quite unforgettable short story called "Field of Vision." This was one of those that remained with me even in somewhat confused times. (My wife and I moved from a rural community into Minneapolis. She attended graduate school and I was doing urban research for a history project.)

Le Guin's story tells of what happened to the Psyche XIV mission to Mars. It becomes an emotionally impressive story of man and the Vision of God which is revealed to three astronauts. They enter a center for conversion which had been constructed 600 million years ago by interstellar missionaries. One suffers a cortical overload and dies. One is overcome by the vision and can see nothing but God, though he would rather be a plain man again and see simple things on a scale less grand; he takes his own life. The third astronaut becomes a prophet of the True Religion. Hughes, the man who does not wish the intensity of the Vision, is a very sympathetic and understandable character. Le Guin also quotes the 17th Century English poet Henry Vaughan to good effect. Sf should interlink with poetry more often than it does. In this case, the combination is very effective.

In this issue James White begins an equally effective three-part serial, *The Dream Millennium*, about the first interstellar colonizing expedition carrying several hundred passengers in cold sleep. They are seeking a new world, for old Earth has become far too crowded and violent. Devlin, more or less in charge, is periodically awakened to make crucial decisions on whether the ship should land on a planet or go on to the next one. Things grow tense because soon they are running out of fuel and options on their thousand year search.

In the book *Galaxy: Thirty Years of Innovative Science Fiction* (ed. by Pohl, Greenberg and Olander), Harlan Ellison comments on this issue:

> Jake was editing *Galaxy* at that time, and I hadn't seen him in years. He saw me, came over, we shook hands, and the first thing he said was, "I'm putting together an all-star 23rd anniversary issue of *Galaxy*. It wouldn't be an issue without you in it."
>
> I blushed prettily and said I didn't have anything available at the moment. . . . And I knew I wouldn't have any time to write a new story . . . But Jake was insistent. So, since I was bored anyway, I said, "What's a good length for you, Jake?"

He said about three to five thousand words would fit because he already had stories from Arthur C. Clarke and Ted Sturgeon and Ursula Le Guin and James White, and he even had a new poem by Ray Bradbury. I nodded sagely at the auspicious company I'd be keeping if I could write something, and said, "Wait here; I'll be right back."

Then I went to the room in which I'd been working for a week, sat down, and three hours later came out with "Cold Friend."

Jake was socializing with the other writers and editors who had come down for the wrap-up party, and I came to him and dangled "Cold Friend" in front of his face, and I said, "Two conditions if you want to buy it. . . . First, no tampering. You leave it as it is. Not one word altered. Second, you copyright it in my name."

Jakobsson read it and agreed to take it from Ellison, and though he did try to change the title and altered a word or two in the text, what appeared was basically what Ellison wrote. In the 1980 anthology quoted above, the story appears *exactly* as it had been written. And a strange and eerie and solipsistic tale it is, about a postal clerk who died but is still alive in the mental world of a girl whom he barely remembered from school days. Highly recommended!

In this October issue *Galaxy* sees the last work it will ever have from Ray Bradbury, "Ode to Electric Ben," a pleasant poem in *rhyme* about the electrical experimentation of Benjamin Franklin. And it also saw the last story it ever ran by Theodore Sturgeon, "Agnes, Accent and Access," an amusing tale of the Voice InPut system which controls a computer so powerful it shouldn't make errors but nevertheless does. A clever chap named Merrihew meets Agnes, the VIP machine's operator, and finds her to be a lovely young lady who has a West Bronx accent that appears when she is under stress, causing the machine to misinterpret her commands. Agnes is pleased at the solution to her problem and accepts a dinner date with the astute trouble-shooter.

October also saw the last of Arthur C. Clarke in *Galaxy*, the conclusion of *Rendezvous With Rama*. It was a glorious issue, but something of a Pyrrhic victory. So many old friends left at once—and without really telling us. We felt the loss later on.

In the November issue there is a novelette by Michael Kurland, "Think Only This of Me." Diana Seven is a real but genetically manipulated woman who is spending some time in an artificially constructed Seventeenth Century Earth. She is on both a recreational mission—a series of pleasant liasons—and a training mission, as her escort, Christopher

Charles Mar d'Earth, finds out. They must eventually part, and the scientists explain that she must leave for her true mission, but perhaps she will see him again. He has grown to love her, and he weeps. Weeping puzzles her, for it is not part of her genetic structure.

A novelette by Robert Sheckley, "A Suppliant in Space," brings back that old-time writer's satirical sense. He tells of an exiled alien who could not fully comply with all of his planet's complicated social norms (which sound worse than anything Jack Vance could think up), and now must survive on an alien world. There is a problem. A colonizing vessel from Earth is landing on that world, and one of the Terran officers is a paranoid militarist. How Detringer, the alien, outwits the Earthmen is as amusing as the Fifties Sheckley at his best.

The November issue's masthead showed for the first time the name of James Baen as Managing Editor, replacing Albert Dytch, though of course Jakobsson continued as Editor.

The December, 1973 *Galaxy* was significant for two reasons. It was the last time the letter column would appear until July of 1974. And it had the first installment of an outstanding four-part serial, *Inverted World*, by British author Christopher Priest. This work shows definite New Wave influence, as did many of the best British imports. To quote from a footnote in Charles Platt's interview with Priest in *Dream Makers: Volume Two*:

> *Inverted World* (1974) is a surreal parable in which the earth has been transformed from a sphere to a saddle-shaped surface of negative curvature, on which a giant city must be hauled across the landscape in order to stay in a zone of normal space-time. Remembered mainly for its totally original central concept, this novel is also notable for its concern with solipsism and the creative process . . .

We shall return to Mr. Priest in a later section. At this moment, sf was still in a period when such influences as the New Wave were still operative and certain other sociopolitical influences were also having an effect. What eventually happened and the direction sf took will cause us to come back to this most inventive author.

I have been paying insufficient attention to the excellent book review columns of Theodore Sturgeon, who takes a somewhat different line to sf's definition than his predecessor, Algis Budrys. Exercising the common sf book reviewers' delightful penchant for cheerfully interjecting their own piques and esthetic criteria at any old time, Sturgeon remarks, "Personally, I have always felt uneasy with the hardline, stonewall definitions of sf, a field toward which I was drawn originally because it seemed to have no horizons, no limits at all, like poetry."

The January, 1974 issue has an excellent if somewhat violent novella, "The Only War We've Got," by Joe Haldeman. Once more we meet special agent Otto McGavin, who is being sent under assumed identity to the planet Selva, which is plotting a quite illegal little war against the comparatively nearby and prosperous planet Grunwelt. He is to impersonate Ramos Guajana, a deadly duelist and killer who is already wanted on a murder charge, but whose actions are explainable in terms of the harsh Selvan ecology and the weird evolution of the governing of the colony, originally founded by Uruguayan Maoists(!). Unfortunately McGavin/Guajana is detected, and his confederates as well. The reader really begins to wonder how he's going to get out of this one.

There is a pleasant little piece by Joanna Russ, "Passages," the first of her several contributions to *Galaxy*. It is a rather surreal meditation on what it would be like to assume a doll's place and be stared at by Christmas shoppers. But of course it is more than that—it deals on a serious poetic level with simple communication.

Fred Saberhagen has a short story in the January issue called "Calendars." (They seemed to be favoring short titles that month.) In a future Earth where immortality is common and people all live quite well, some eventually get bored with the whole thing and decide to opt out. This is the decision of Michael Pandareus, who finally manages to get "Termination" put on his crowded schedule, for he and his wife are very busy people indeed. But, just as the day draws near, he has to cancel because his wife suddenly remembers that they have never had a child. He withdraws from his planned termination and realizes that now he and his wife will be very busy indeed.

The February issue has an interesting novella by Phil Higgins, "Created Equal." The courtroom format is used to debate whether or not a highly sophisticated computer named HOPE was a person and therefore it was "murder" when it was destroyed by a man who felt he had been slighted by the HOPE project. Sam Beneke, an eminent Perry Mason-type trial lawyer, is given the job of defending the human computer wrecker, and he gives it his best! It's an intriguing story when you think how widespread computers have come to be and how many human characteristics they may take on. These sf stories show that almost all such possibilities have been dealt with by the creative imagination. That is why, in fact, some of the news items an sf reader comes across are such big yawns. It's more than likely something that he came across in *Galaxy* or *Analog* a decade or so before, if not even earlier.

Sydney Van Scyoc has a strange novella called "Deathsong." This deals with the weird flutes left in temples by a race of superior beings who have somehow died off. It's always hard for me to grasp the concept of super-beings that simply die off—unless, of course, it happens because of pure boredom, a topic *Galaxy* writers have touched upon more than once. Verrons, one of the exploration party, realizes that the flutes draw upon the energies of the explorers and weaken them while re-animating the spirits (ghosts) of the ancient race. He finds the remains of an earlier nonhuman expedition who had been fatally crippled by the flutes. This is such a perfect story for late Nineteenth Century decadent artists to picture or put in rhyme that it seems just a bit odd in science fiction—but that, of course, is what is great about sf. Many things may seem odd in the genre, but they can all be included somehow. Sturgeon was quite right.

John Brunner, an infrequent *Galaxy* contributor, comes forth in the March, 1974 issue with a two-part serial. *Web of Everywhere* is about the social problems caused by the skelter, a sort of matter-transmitter (beam us down!) that has proliferated on the Earth. Humans being the conniving and worthless wretches that they are, the skelter proves to be socially disintegrative until Chaim Aleuker invents the privateer, a device to prevent unauthorized and especially criminal use of the skelter. Aleuker becomes the world's richest man and gathers around himself other men of genius, who quietly rule the world.

Hans Dykstra, however, wants to keep away from such elitism and even to illegally salvage and restore what he can of the old world. He solves an intellectual treasure hunt sponsored by Aleuker and is invited to the latter's villa. No sooner is he there than a Maori attack kills nearly everyone, including Aleuker. Dykstra escapes with a beautiful seventeen-year-old girl who seems a total innocent in the modern world. Dykstra knows many skelter codes (quite illegally), and the world government, such as it is, follows him relentlessly as he jumps all over the Earth. He eventually takes "the longest of all journeys." It's not quite as much fun as jaunting was in Alfred Bester's *The Stars My Destination*, and the conclusion isn't

quite so grand. However, it is touching and poetical—one of the central
characters is Mustapha Sharif, a blind but wealthy Arab poet who shares
some of Dykstra's interest in preserving the best of past Earth culture.
The novel is made more expressive of human emotion by including passages of Mustapha's poetry.

Michael G. Coney has his last *GSF* appearance with a peculiar
novelette in the March issue, "The Hook, the Eye and the Whip." In a
strange future Earth convicts can be bonded out to help sportsmen in a
game where they use the tension in a coiled "whip" to dash their craft out
to a metal "eye" mounted on a pedestal in hopes of inserting a hook into it
and whipping safely back. It seems like a dangerous enough sport, and it
is no fun for the bondsman, since he must replace his sportsman-master's
body parts with his own should an accident occur. Of course, if the
accident is fatal, then the bonded man is freed. It sounds like one hell of a
way to run a railroad, if I may be excused the durable cliché. To me the
story is notable mostly because of its odd mutated semi-domesticated
creatures. One of these is a "landshark," which inescapably calls to mind
the Chevy Chase routine on the original *Saturday Night Live* in which he
mocks the movie *Jaws* by showing up as a "landshark." This story is also
notable because it was indirectly referred to as one of a typical bunch
of silly stories that have appeared recently in *Galaxy*, so the reader says,
with dumb characters and plots and dumb things like landsharks roving
around the landscape.

A writer named Cynthia Bunn makes her only *Galaxy* contribution, the
novelette "Infidel of Five Temples." It's another one of those exploration
party things where some of the Terrans fall under the spell of the odd
alien temples, some don't, and some are otherwise occupied. I rather liked
the temple design in the illustration, but as for the story itself, one's time
could have been better occupied otherwise.

The April issue, however, brings us quite a different proposition. The
magazine begins a three-part serial called "The Org's Egg," by former
GSF editor Fred Pohl and the old luminary, Jack Williamson. Their
collaboration produced a novel of great old-fashioned adventure and
tension. The gigantic intergalactic body called Cuckoo is the object of
interest and colonization by humans and nonhumans alike. Its ecology
includes human tribes, some of whom have tamed huge insects like
dragonflies and ride them through the wide skies. Their peaceable existence is threatened by some genuinely despicable insectoids, and adven-

turers from human planets have come to aid them. One interesting feature is that the human rescuers are teleported to the Org realm, and the same person can be sent repeatedly to create multiple copies of himself. This creates the side plot of how these duplicates are going to get along with each other. There are a few logical problems with the plot, but here we mainly want adventure and that is what we get. The last installment came during what was known as the 'Jakobsson-Baen Interface,' in June of 1974.

I missed this serial and some of the other stories at the time because I was rather preoccupied with the interesting events then unfolding in Washington, D.C. which led to Richard Nixon's downfall and departure from the scene.

"Mindhunt" is a novelette by Robert Wells telling of a unique mental clash between two genius telepaths, one a space explorer called Grigor Cernik and one on the Earthbound control team named Alan Durain. Grigor makes the mistake of getting one of Alan's team fired, a woman Alan has grown to love and rely on. He takes out his rage and frustration on Cernik's next space mission. They effectively cancel out each other's powers and the tragic consequence is that Cernik's ship crashes—but Alan will never get him out of his mind.

Also in the April issue, Jerry Pournelle begins his science fact column, "A Step Further Out," a worthy addition to the magazine and very welcome to those fans who had missed the old hard science columns by Willy Ley.

So now we come to the May, 1974 issue. It was Ejler Jakobsson's last one as editor. In June he was listed as Editor Emeritus, but by July the 'interface' has snapped and his name was seen no more on the masthead. Jakobsson went without fuss, fanfare, or farewell. He had guided the magazine through a very difficult period in our nation's history, and aspects of this history were naturally enough reflected in *Galaxy*. Nonetheless, Jakobsson brought in some fine new talent and gave them their starts, got some good novels out of some of the old-timers and recognized "names," and chose many stories that will always stay in my memory. In my personal opinion, he was a much under-rated editor at *Galaxy*, and richly deserves our belated thanks and congratulations!

Ironically, Jakobsson's last issue has a Robert Sheckley short story, "End City." A traveler on Fat Cat Spacelines unexpectedly gets put off the ship at End City and there is nothing he can do about it. It's a place where no one is really happy, a limbo with addresses like Minus Boulevard and Null Park. It concludes:

> You come hesitantly forward at last, clear your throat, say, "Excuse me but this is all some kind of mistake, isn't it? I mean, I shouldn't be here at all."
>
> "You're in the right place," Bernstein [a frustrated professor] says. "Welcome to End City." He doesn't even bother to laugh at you.

14. James Baen (I)

J IM BAEN IS NOW IN COMMAND OF *GALAXY*. In the June, 1974 issue there is an article by Alexei and Cory Panshin called "Farewell to Yesterday's Tomorrow." They make some really unwarranted predictions. They think that sf is about to enter a new and bright period (it seemed to them that the grim spectre of Richard Nixon has been banished). They also say:

> We are likewise entering a period of radical international readjustments. The bases of world finance and of world trade will be redefined. The arms race will be abandoned as an anachronism. World controls on population growth will be established. It will be demonstrated that the United Nations is no longer an instrument of American foreign policy. The UN will grow in effectiveness and change in function.

They conclude by saying "A new tomorrow is waiting." Unfortunately, to use a very mild adverb under the circumstances, this roseate post-Nixon afterglow did not last, and now we are even hauling the old-time battleships back into commission.

The Frontliners. Illustrator: Wendy Pini.

In June, Bob Shaw begins *Orbitsville*, a fine three-part novel. Vance Garamond is an interstellar explorer employed by the vast Starflight Corporation, which is headed by the psychotic Elizabeth Lindstrom, the richest and most powerful human ever. She kills her employees for minor transgressions, so great is her power. Her son dies accidentally while in Garamond's care. Certain that she will take reprisals against him and his family, he flies them off to a new corner of space. They find a sun completely enclosed by a gigantic "Dyson sphere" more than 300 million kilometers in diameter. The vast inner surface is the site of ancient civilizations and battles and is now comparatively empty except for a minor and harmless race called "clowns" who stay near the few entry portals. Elizabeth Lindstrom and a big fleet soon follow, intending to settle and exploit this enormous and rich new region for mankind. Garamond is sent on an exploration mission way around the sphere while his wife and child are, sinisterly, put under Lindstrom's supervision. Sabotage downs his spaceship, and he has to devise a flying craft to get back some millions of kilometers to the growing Terran settlement at the entry portal, so he can rescue his family. It is a tense and very interesting novel.

Joe Haldeman has a fine short story, "The Private War of Private Duckworth," which is sort of a preliminary study to his excellent anti-war sf novel *The Forever War*. He goes to some lengths to point out the deadly futility of space warfare and the reason why good old Sergeant Melford was able to keep from being killed in combat for so long.

James Blish, the great old *Galaxy* veteran, has his last piece in the June issue, in collaboration with L. Jerome Stanton. "The Glitch" is a short story about how ULTIMAC, a computer that is running the world, is ruined by one Ivor Harrigan, who prefers a little more human freedom of action. It is not Blish's best, but is mildly amusing. Blish was then quite ill. He died in 1975 after a long fight with cancer, and sf was deprived of one of its better writers and certainly one of its very best critics.

In July there's a lively novella by Verge Foray (who only appeared twice in *GSF*, both times in 1974). "The Frontliners" tells of the adventures of a new species of woman (and of man, too, eventually). The one we first meet is Gweanvin Oster, who has a rival in Marvis Jans, another superwoman. They represent two rival worlds fighting an econo-war, and both are also seeking a superior male with whom to mate and produce children of the new breed. They have enviable superpowers, but are not dislikeable individuals.

Bob Shaw also has a good novelette in the July *Galaxy*, "A Full Member of the Club." Philip Connor is in love with Angie, who is very wealthy. He finds out why: she is dealing in merchandise from the future which is immeasurably superior to anything of this age. Angie is becoming too prosperous for the likes of Philip, but he resolves to win her and also make contact with the suppliers of the advanced merchandise. And that takes much skill and a lot of salesmanship.

In the regular Forum feature, Isaac Asimov makes his final *Galaxy* appearance. His article says the human race may survive, but only if racism, sexism, overpopulation and the arms race are ended. He makes a very sound case, especially on racism, where he shows the illogicality of bigots who condemn some races for being less intelligent while putting down others for being *too* clever. He also says the arms race will prove to be too expensive and that nuclear war will be more clearly seen to be a form of international suicide. His case for that is now even more strongly supported, although the arms race, which must end, has not yet done so. He zeroed in on the exact problems but did not make the error of being too sanguine about our chances.

In the August *Galaxy*'s Forum, Poul Anderson says, after some discussion of the earlier days of sf:

> To hell with jabber about a New Wave. It never existed. The people usually identified with it almost all denied being part of any such thing. . . . What we got was simply a wave of, shall I say, new blood.
>
> . . . during the past few years, science fiction as a whole has again become less interesting than it used to be. The younger writers are no longer exactly young, . . . it's gotten hard to find a story that isn't a variation on a well-known theme. Not impossible, but hard.

Ursula Kroeber Le Guin makes her last *GSF* appearance in the August, 1974 issue. "The Day Before the Revolution" is a short story which is a sort of "prequel" to her major novel *The Dispossessed*. It tells mainly of the past and present travails of Laia, one of the co-founders, with her late husband Taviri, of a soon-to-succeed syndicalist revolutionary movement. It is intriguing and moving, and a worthy overture to the novel (which became an sf classic like her earlier *The Left Hand of Darkness*).

The August issue is also notable for the first installment of *The Company of Glory*, a three-part novel by *Galaxy* old-timer Edgar Pangborn (his final appearance, too; he died in 1976). It takes place in a future semi-feudal America which has been devastated by a nuclear war and various plagues. A storyteller called Demetrios and his companions—Angus Bridgeman and his dog Brand, Mam Estelle, the old Professor (who doesn't speak), some young women, plus a few other dubious characters—set off to find an island where they are determined to set up a democracy which the world now sorely needs. In their picaresque adventures they fall in with a traveling circus and meet some interesting new characters: Wynken, Blynken and Nod are three of them! At tale's end some of the original characters are gone, but the dream of the democracy is not dead, and the remaining band plus some new younger acquisitions are about to set sail for the long-sought island. It is a slightly rambling tale with overtones of Jack Vance, but descriptions of such future societies are usually interesting, and Pangborn had not lost too much of his somewhat subjective, unique writing style.

August also has a newly-discovered novelette by Pohl and Kornbluth(!), called "The Gift of Garigolli." It's typically funny and satirical, involving microbial aliens who try to cheer up their host by giving him financial solvency. They manage, and also accidentally help Earth's ecology. Any Pohl-Kornbluth story always aided *Galaxy* greatly, but this was the last.

Arsen Darnay provides a novelette in the September issue. "The Splendid Freedom" tells of the adventures of Grom Gravok, who is making a pilgrimage to Earth from his distant world of Vizillo. He is a structure guard, keeping always alert for changes in planetary conditions that might imperil a structure. That is an important job, since a "structure" might hold up to five million people. Grom comes from a clan system which requires young men to make an Earth pilgrimage to become tribal elders. While doing so, they must retain an inner sense of *bal*, a sort of mystical equanimity. However, Old Earth is not quite as advertised, and it takes great effort for Grom to fulfill his mission without losing his tribally defined sense of poise. It takes him great effort even to see what the *real* Earth looks like, since for ages all its inhabitants have lived far underground.

Advertised as a tragic farce, J. A. Lawrence's novelette "Family Program" is instead rather confusing. An unfortunate man somehow ends up with two android mothers-in-law whose doings, combined with sinister news of the current oil crisis, do create a genuine crisis atmosphere. His plans to deal with them backfire and he ends up in a mental institution, refusing even to talk much with his wife, doubtless suspecting she might be an android too.

SCIENCE FICTION OCTOBER 1974 75¢ 14155 S•M

Galaxy

David Drake
UNDER THE HAMMER
Arsen Darnay
THE EASTCOAST CONFINEMENT

EDGAR PANGBORN

STURGEON · POURNELLE
Warwick, White, Christopher

Under the Hammer. Illustrator: Jack Gaughan.

"The August Revolution" by Mary Soderstrom is a short story about an underground nuclear test in Alaska and an Andean earthquake triggered for political purposes, originally to try to eliminate the repressive military government in Chile. But Nature lends a hand with the unexpected fall of a large meteorite, and events turn out much worse than the scientific plotters could have imagined. A grim tale, and yet another one in *Galaxy* on earthquakes of ruinous proportions.

Arsen Darnay also stars in the October, 1974 issue with the novella "The Eastcoast Confinement." In a new repressive U.S. all the malcontents and revolutionaries and antisocials of all stripes are confined in the general New York area by a wall of fiery energy held in place by a huge fusion power generator. Karl Schmidt, Berlin Superintendent of Police, is given a tour of the Confinement and is horrified to find that the people packed into it cannot possibly all survive. This does not bother the ruling New Puritans, who feel that the fewer dissenters there are, the better. Schmidt does not reveal his true emotions, but manages to aid a few of the Confinement's leaders so they are strengthened and encouraged rather than being brainwhipped in a manner right out of Orwell. Schmidt feels the confinements might even breed a form of society that will be better for Earth when the energy walls are finally breached.

"Under the Hammer," by David Drake, is a novelette about a typical day in a mercenary military operation by the famous Colonel Hammer's "Slammers." It is mostly fierce battles using advanced ground attack weapons. There is no lack of action in this one!

A short story in October, "The Long Night," by John Christopher, tells of a potentially disastrous mishap to a lunar exploration crew. Their caterpillar vehicle gets hung up in a gully. But the two crewmen have no serious problems until a new form of lunar life is suddenly and unpleasantly brought to their attention. Since they are not conveniently near a base, and sunspot activity is fouling up their communications, it requires some ingenuity for them to get out of the scrape. This is a good old-fashioned nail-biter!

The November, 1974 *Galaxy* begins the three-part novel *Love Conquers All*, by Fred Saberhagen. Here we are in an advanced, so to speak, U.S. where sex and the religion of Eros are officially encouraged, and words like "chastity" are profanities. This is right out of Orwell, too, come to think of it. Art Rodney's wife is pregnant, which means she will go over the legal limit of two children a family can have; because of overpopulation, abortion is compulsory. She runs off into hiding, and Arthur has to find her and dissuade her from having the child. At the very least, he must find her to protect her, for the government is particularly unforgiving and the new society is quite rough and anarchic despite the harsh government. He has recourse to the services of all kinds of interesting and dubious characters before he can see any glimmer of hope, for even though he finds out where his wife is, it would be insanity to go back to their previous life.

Frederik Pohl, *Galaxy*'s editor after Gold, has an interesting Forum article about his adventures with sf fans in Communist countries. It turns out that Yugoslavia has a *Galaksija* (not related to ours), a popular-science magazine which prints a little sf—some by local talent but mostly translations of foreign work. Pohl recommended some new American authors to the Yugoslavs he met, but since those authors tended to be feminists or semi-anarchists or quite sexually liberated, he had strong doubts that any of their work would surface in Yugoslavia. He also visited sf fans in Romania and even the U.S.S.R. and had many good discussions. The Soviets, of course, have their own sf authors. One of the best of them, Biyaelev, died during the Siege of Leningrad in World War II. Pohl politely disagreed with some of his hosts but on the whole got a good feeling from his trip. More such exchanges, I think, would help immensely in mutual understanding.

November also has another David Drake novelette about Hammer's Slammers, "The Butcher's Bill." This one has even more action than the last, but at least one of the mercenaries has a pang of conscience when one of the most fiercely contested battlefields turns out to be a shrine left by a higher culture that has disappeared. Most of the shrine unfortunately is in the way of a clear field of fire. The Slammers, of course, win again!

The December issue has "Cry Wolf!" by Mack Reynolds, a good detective novelette about a citizen who is a volunteer policeman. He manages to kill—always kill—more than his share of social delinquents. An investigating officer finds out a little more about this man who is such an efficient vigilante and decides to take action against him. This leads to some rather tense scenes.

Ursula K. Le Guin has a good Forum article in which she suggests that much of American sf and fantasy has been a little too much on the escapist side. She is therefore all in favor of academic study, teaching and thoughtful criticism of sf. The Forum articles all along are good and thought-provoking.

Robert Silverberg returns to *Galaxy* for one final time with a short story called "The Man Who Came Back." Burkhardt has returned from Novotny IX, a particularly forbidding planet, after an absence from Earth of eighteen years. He intends to marry his old girlfriend. But she has gone from one rich husband to another, all the while getting wealthier and older and crueler. But Burkhardt is a determined man, and he finally visits Lily Leigh, who intends to laugh him off. But he has learned a few things from the Novotny natives—so Lily doesn't have a chance to avoid matrimony, much to the astonishment of the Terran press!

With the January, 1975 issue *Galaxy* incorporated the previously separate *Worlds of If* magazine. *If* had been plugging along valiantly since the Fifties. It had run some classic stories—by Blish and Ellison, among others—but had been in a decline for some time. Some of the *If* columns were transferred to *Galaxy*, notably "The Alien Viewpoint," an sf critical column by Richard Geis, and the SF Calendar.

There was also a frankly fantasy series taken over from *If*, the noted *Amber* novels by Roger Zelazny. The first one serialized in *Galaxy* was *The Sign of the Unicorn*, beginning in January. It is the third of the series, of which *The Science Fiction Encyclopedia* says:

> The land of Amber (like C. S. Lewis's Narnia) exists on a plane of greater fundamental reality than Earth, and provides normal reality with its ontological base; unlike Narnia, however, Amber . . . is ruled by a cabal of squabbling siblings, whose quasi-Olympian feudings have provided a great deal of complicated plotting . . .

The Zelazny series would have two more novels appear in *Galaxy*. The *Amber* stories show an intriguing fantasy world which has attracted its share of fans. However, it is more along the lines of sword and sorcery than sf, and thus does not reflect the mainstream of *Galaxy*'s stories (except of course for the works of Jack Vance, which are a unique combination of sf and quaint fantasy). In any case, the *Amber* series is now complete in six novels, and available in its entirety in a largish hardbound two-volume set. Mine is a book club edition, so it should be fairly inexpensive.

A January short story, "A Horse of a Different Technicolor," by Craig Strete, was well enough regarded by Baen that he later anthologized it in paperback. It tells of a surrealistic future in which we have all turned into a kind of TV programming in which the whole world stops in 2074. Some of the plugged-in sleeping-people-TV programs try suicide, but this is not possible. Their images are reconstructed electronically and their "lives" go on. Strange.

There is, by the way, some quite excellent interior art in the *Galaxy* of this period, by various artists. Some is very reminiscent of the late Virgil Finlay, except the nipples aren't covered by the Sally Rand bubbles any more. Baen did come across some fine artistic talent as his predecessors had done.

The February *Galaxy* begins with a fine short story, "The Annihilation of Angkor Apeiron," by Fred Saberhagen. The berserkers are huge super-sophisticated robotic space warships programmed by their long-dead makers to eliminate all rival life forms in the galaxy (a theme not new to *Galaxy*). A berserker battles the cruiser *Dipavamsa*, and both are badly damaged, the cruiser mortally so. The berserker searches *Dipavamsa* to get her star log to find an Earth colony it can use for refitting (after destroying the humans). One of the civilians aboard, unarmed but shrewd, undoes the alien machine with a plan devised in the human worlds to frustrate quite a different enemy. It is foolproof.

"Allegiances," a novella by new writer Michael Bishop, is actually part of a book to be later issued, *A Little Knowledge*. It tells of a fundamental-ist Christian Southland reconstructed with domed cities with many under-ground levels. The section in this issue deals with an expedition of Urban Nucleus of Atlanta city dwellers traveling out into the hinterlands among the yahoos and the all-smothering kudzu (which war radiation seems to have positively encouraged). The novella is worth reading, for we are introduced to some unique characters and the descriptions of the future South are well done. I have not read the entire novel, but I understand that this new Revivalist South is due to have an encounter with an alien race during which one of them is converted with bizarre results!

In the March *Galaxy*'s Forum, Lester del Rey has his say. He rebuts Ursula Le Guin's claim in the December Forum that sf was basically male chauvinist egotism and escapism during the Golden Age (the late Thirties to late Forties). He says Le Guin is wrong to think that stories "tackling totalitarianism, nationalism, over-population, prejudice, racism, sexism, militarism and so on" have been published only recently. Del Rey tells us (and it is fact) that all these topics were touched on in the Golden Age, if not even earlier. One remembers Jules Verne's Captain Nemo taking on the warships of oppressor imperialist nations with his *Nautilus* (though del Rey does not use that particular example).

He stands for sf of and by itself and does not think it especially needs any nursemaiding from the sachems of the Academy:

> Science fiction has evolved pretty much by itself for nearly fifty years. During that time, it has grown and developed. Now, at a time when most literature is in decline—despite the nostrums of its bedside critics—science fiction is healthily capturing more and more readers. Perhaps there is something to be said for a field that can establish and maintain its own values.

Zelazny's *Sign of the Unicorn* ends in the March issue, leaving the reader in suspense for more of the *Chronicles of Amber*.

Spider Robinson (soon to become regular book reviewer) has a grim novelette, "Nobody Likes To Be Lonely." A man named McGinny is confined in a future prison where the rooms are sterile but comfortable, stereo systems and other luxuries are provided, and there are even guards now and then to talk to. McGinny's guard is very young and rather strung-out. On the outside is a couple named Sol and Barb who are having some sexual difficulties (he seems impotent); they live their lives in an oddly pressed-in atmosphere which is as cruel in its indifferent attentiveness as the guard is to McGinny. His prison stay is not long, but his cell is soon occupied again.

Effective with the April issue, the price goes up from 75 cents to a full dollar.

A rather confused two-part serial called *Helium*, by Arsen Darnay, is featured in the April, 1975 issue. A thousand years after the U.S. was split up and badly hurt in thirteen(!) small(!) nuclear wars, a consortium of East Coast and Southwest giant city-colony structures in coastal areas must deal with a group of the militant Ecofreak tribes who live in the Hinterlands. The high-technology cities depend on helium obtained from the anti-technology Ecofreaks. There is quite a lot of religious mumbo-jumbo mixed in with pig-headed reactionaries and the inevitable packs of young ecofreak rebels. The word "freak" as a term favorable to the counterculture was by then almost universally in disuse. In the end the towers totter and the Saving Remnant treks off in the direction of the Midwest (I hope they remembered their thermal underwear!). All is resolved, mainly because a large proportion of the characters are dead, along with a few million city dwellers whose calamities make a backdrop somewhat like the big Hollywood disaster movies that were then coming into vogue.

In any case, this carries the struggle between city and rural dwellers about as far as it will go. These Seventies stories seem to have eliminated the suburbs which were such a feature of so much Fifties sf.

In the June issue (there was no May issue), John Sladek, a young talent, has "Elephant With Wooden Leg." This is a rather good short story about a cockroach group intelligence plotting to make men subservient to them. The tale was later anthologized by Jim Baen in one or possibly two paperback collections.

Also in the June issue is "The Venging," a really tense novelette by Greg Bear (the first of his two *GSF* pieces). A human colonial ship accidentally runs afoul of the religion of the Aighors, which involves falling into black holes, which seriously menaces the Terrans who are in the way. How the humans escape polluting the Aighor afterlife is a really imaginative exercise for author and reader alike!

It might be said here that the science columns of Jerry Pournelle were quite often very hard science indeed. In July of 1975 he presents a table of distances, times, and delta-v's (velocity changes) showing how far one can travel at one gravity acceleration in a given time, with velocity approaching light speed. Pournelle was proud of this table, explaining how he had worked it out on his Texas Instruments SR-50, but bewailing the fact that it had just been superseded by the SR-51. I find myself in a similar wailing mood as my TRS-80 Model III becomes the equivalent of a Model T —not that I have used it for anything so complicated. The reference to Texas Instruments dates this column by Pournelle, just as does a reference in his story in this issue to space outfitting done by the now-defunct Abercrombie and Fitch. Datedness and obsolescence are no fault of sf writers as change gains ever greater delta-v.

Pournelle also has a fine novella in this issue. "Tinker" tells of the adventures of Roland Kephart, who roams the asteroid belt on the good ship *Slingshot*. On this trip he is bringing his family along to Freedom Station on the asteroid Jefferson, where there is foul play afoot. Some rather large corporations, a big insurance company represented by a prim Mr. Dalquist, and the local miners and owners are not exactly seeing eye to eye on the management policies of the asteroid. And the Hansen Enterprises people have lost a good former field agent, Joe Colella, in a suspicious accident. In the midst of this the huge spaceliner *Agamemnon*, carrying 1700 passengers, drifts into radio range, seriously low on power and in very great danger. Kephart must up ship, rather reluctantly because of the dubious goings-on, and go to help. The rescue procedure is tense and rather complex, while in the back of the reader's mind are questions about what will be resolved on the asteroid, which has no lack of rowdy and scheming characters.

Pournelle strikes again in the August issue, in collaboration with Larry Niven, with a famous novel which appears in *Galaxy* in three installments. This is *Inferno*, a brilliant and sardonic updating of Dante's work. Before I discuss it, I should mention that the *Galaxy* covers were becoming cluttered to the point of tackiness. This one has the one dollar price crossed out and a small circle superimposed on the cover art announcing a "special 79c trial offer." And the covers still have the obligatory small "with *Worlds of If*" logo tucked into the top lefthand corner.

These artistic considerations aside, the magazine and its two succeeding issues did contain the marvelous *Inferno*, in which a lot of contemporary pests and humbugs and monsters are shown getting their just deserts. There are some fine touches. The narrator, Allen Carpentier, is trying a stunt out of *War and Peace*: he is sitting on a window ledge trying to drink a whole bottle of rum without touching the sides. He is a minor sf writer and has his fans clustered around him. Just then Isaac Asimov enters the room (an sf first, surely, when an author in the same *genre* is used, even though in a non-speaking part). Carpentier's fans flock to Asimov, and poor Carpentier gags, loses his balance, and does a header out the window to fall eight floors. *Then*, he finds himself in the outer vestibule of Hell with his guide, Benito, to lead him through, as Virgil once led Dante. He notices real estate developers being eternally chased by bulldozers, a dogooder who worked to ban cyclamates being grotesquely obese, and so on. One of the best touches is that the medieval Wood of Suicides has been largely chopped down and paved over (of course, what else in the Twentieth Century!) and is patrolled by menacing driverless black Corvettes. Carpentier is puzzled; he thinks the cars should be Cadillacs, vehicles which along with their owners richly deserve to be in this circle of Hell!

It would not do to give away any more of this excellent work. It is well worth reading and was a credit to *Galaxy* and to Jim Baen for securing it.

A. Bertram Chandler has another Commodore Grimes novella, "Rim Change," in the August issue. The narrator is George Rule, captain of the *Basset* of the Dog Star Line, now taking his merchant craft out among the worlds of the galactic Rim. Rule lands his ship rather haphazardly on the

Inferno. Illustrator: Ames.

planet Lorn, where he meets his old nemesis Grimes in the *Basset*'s wardroom during a happy landing party. Rule is not overwhelmed with joy to learn that his ship has been chosen to go to Kinsolving's Planet, a very weird and forbidding world which is a mysterious gateway planet—but no one yet has been able to find out what it is a gateway to and where it might lead. A scientific crew goes along, and good, gray Grimes as well. There is a kind of odd extra-dimensional temple on Kinsolving, and needless to say, several of the characters get themselves into some quite extraordinary difficulties. Grimes must use his ingenuity to get them out safely. The late A. Bertram Chandler, by the way, actually was a ship's captain in the Australian merchant marine, which goes far to explain the nautical tendencies and proper shipboard tone of his stories.

The August issue also has a chilly little short story by Swedish writer (and sf critic) Sam Lundwall. In "Nobody Here But Us Shadows" he tells of a scientific institute where people study the probability lines of alternate Earths and futures. A sad displaced person has appeared out of one of the alternate worlds and then cannot get back, as her world has become a nullity. All she can do is hang around the huge Probal Building with about as much hope as any character in Kafka.

In the September, 1975 issue there is a short story by Christopher Irwin called "Evening Song, Night Dancer." It is about a few talented mutants, products of some experiment or other. We almost seem to be back in the heyday of the Mad Scientists in their labs of the Twenties and Thirties, to judge from many of these more recent *Galaxy* stories. In this case, the protagonists are fawn- and centaur-like, and clearly superior to the humans sent to destroy them and their kind. The ordinary mortals are easily disposed of as the godlike duo prepare to join a superior creative tribe. The story is quite short; in the old days a subject like this would have gone on at least two or three times as long. It was perhaps getting to be the case that all one had to do was sound a few notes and everyone else could fill in the melody—including, of course, the final overlapping irony that these godlike mutants are the results of the science of the so easily dispersed and therefore despicable humans!

There is an inspiriting essay in the September issue by Poul Anderson in the Forum feature. He discusses various ways by which we might possibly break the light-speed barrier, which is something of a nuisance to the more scientifically finicky sf writers. Editor Jim Baen had devoted an entire column to the topic and urged us to keep our chins up, we'd find a way. It must be mentioned that Baen and Pournelle, especially in these 1975 issues, take some time explaining to us the necessity or good sense of space-age laser anti-ICBM technology and the possibility of space plat-forms loaded with nukes to intimidate the enemy. It seems as though the Pentagon of today has somehow stumbled across these old columns.

The September *Galaxy* has a good and funny short story by Spider Robinson. "Overdose" is about a soldier tripping out while in the Nam and foiling an interstellar invasion by inadvertently giving the alien Yteic-Os the Voracious what used to be known as a "mindfuck."

October 1975 was, of course, *Galaxy*'s 25th anniversary. In this Silver Anniversary issue is an entertaining Forum article by H. L. Gold, from which I quoted in Part One. I did not mention how emphatic he was on not being a magazine editor again. Gold concludes:

> *Galaxy* is safe in his [Jim Baen's] hands, and solidly established enough, and fresh and refreshing enough, to endure at least another quarter of a century, whoever runs it.
>
> No, I wouldn't take a million cruzeiros for the memories I have of the writers and readers and great stories I encountered in those eleven years I served. That took some doing. And nothing could induce me to do it again. . . .
>
> Meanwhile, happy 25th anniversary, *Galaxy*!
> And long life to you!

October continues the excellent *Inferno*, of course. It also has "Helbent 4," a good novelette by Stephen Robinette about a space-roaming killing machine of Earth origin. It has participated in a huge space battle in which a great Spacething fleet from the direction of Sagittarius was de-stroyed, thus saving Earth. Now Helbent returns to Earth, mission accomplished, and awaits further orders. But it has gotten into a dimen-sional warp, and has come back to a different Earth some centuries behind in technology and hostile to Helbent. Finally the mighty machine takes it upon itself to settle matters and also give this Earth a technologi-cal boost which it apparently much needs.

Spider Robinson, who had permanently replaced Theodore Sturgeon as book reviewer in August, has a good column in the course of which he reviews *The Other Glass Teat*, the TV critique by Harlan Ellison. "The stirring saga of Harlan Ellison's appearance on *The Dating Game* is alone worth the price of admission." He relies on Ellison's account of it, for "they ended up burning the tape."

Sinisterly, there is no *Galaxy* for either November or December of 1975.

January, 1976 has the first installment of a two-part serial, *We Who Are About To . . .*, by Joanna Russ. In the year 2040 a survival pod has crashed onto a planet where humans can survive, but "X" (the narrator) will not cooperate with the others. They are a fairly representative cross-section of humanity except for X, a woman who has a wildly variant personal philosophy and who rebels at the idea of becoming breeding stock for a human colony. She also objects on aesthetic grounds to a society devoid of fine music and musicology. She is forced to defend herself, but she over-reacts. I won't go into the details, but I'm really reminded of the old Walt Kelly dictum, "We have met the enemy and he is us." (Or she is Russ!)

Kevin O'Donnell has a wistful novelette of what might have been, "Shattered Hopes, Broken Dreams." Earth is negotiating with the more advanced members of the Galaxy for partnership; the emissaries are members of the Perspe race, empathic amphibians looking much like huge bullfrogs. Just when a treaty is nearly signed, the narrator makes the mistake of taking two of the Perspe to a football play-off. Disaster happens. Thereafter, the Earth is closely surrounded by blockading alien vessels, and we are treated as scum because we cannot control our rage or keep our minds from broadcasting it.

In the same issue Steven Utley has a short tale that is almost as mournful, since it tells of an ugly, overpopulated, and polluted future. However, the protagonist of "Getting Away" has a peculiar mental power that aids him in overcoming life's huge frustrations. His mind can take him back to ancient geological eras where he can inhabit the bodies of pterosaurs and the like. But he has little or no control over his "chronopathy," so he can use the talent only for hack writing and minor poetry. (Why hack? Think what a Doyle or Wells could have done with such an ability!)

Moving on to the February, 1976 issue, Larry Niven has a novelette, "Down and Out," the rather delayed second part of his "Rammer" series. Jerome Corbell had been brought back to life by the State to serve as the human component on a ramship, an interstellar exploration vessel. He seizes control from Peerssa, the shipboard computer personality, and goes adventuring on his own. But as he approaches the center of the galaxy, Peerssa reminds him that he had best begin planning to return to Earth while still living, since even his ramship has limitations. This involves some technological derring-do, and Corbell must entrust himself to Peerssa and hope for the best, while wondering what Earth must be like after so many tens of thousands of years have gone by.

"Only Outlaws and Women," by Thomas Deiker, is a short story also in this February issue. It is set in a apocalyptic future Earth where the concepts of the importance of education have been radically altered, to say the least, by a brutal tribal society. This is carrying something to a logically absurd conclusion, but I'm not exactly sure what (and I won't go to great pains to find out).

"The Phantom of Kansas," by John Varley, is a fairly interesting novelette set in the next century or so. The central character is a creative artist, using natural forces such as winds and clouds. But she has problems: she keeps being murdered. Her personality is on storage in a memory cube so she can be revived, but no amount of protection has helped her several predecessors. When she decides to seek out and confront the determined killer, she makes some surprising discoveries and even circumvents some of the basic laws of her time.

The March, 1976 issue is a good one with two fine novellas. One is "Plutonium," by Arsen Darnay, dealing with the reincarnated lives of an SS trooper and camp guard and two of his Jewish victims. The SS man has picked up some bad karma, unsurprisingly, and needs some generations to improve it. The novella is sometimes rather confusing because of this combination of an Eastern religious belief mixed in with some Native American beliefs plus a new priesthood of a holy order watching over temples erected to guard radioactive waste after a nuclear war. But we follow the reincarnations of the Nazi and his victims, who nonetheless settle scores with him. Some sections are vaguely evocative of Walter Miller's 1959 *A Canticle for Leibowitz*.

Fred Saberhagen's "Birthdays" I liked even a bit better. This tells of a multi-generational starship, following the lives of an entire generation. They live full-time, while their caretaker is awakened to see them only one day a year. Eventually he becomes their pupil and finally sees the last of them die. Then the ship's computer wakes him up again with a new group of babies whom he will accompany to maturity, waking more often. When this batch is fully adult, the colonizable planets will be in range. I thought this was a quite novel approach to a theme that, frankly, was not altogether new to sf, since it had been done already by Heinlein and others back in the Golden Age of the Late Thirties-Early Forties.

Kevin O'Donnell is back with a novelette with a happier conclusion than his last one. "Hunger on the Homestretch" tells how our Earth is spared an invasion by alternate Earths because the advance agent who was to open the gateway lacked about 76 dollars!

The May, 1976 issue carries the first section of Roger Zelazny's new novel in the *Chronicles of Amber* series which I have described previously. This one is in three parts and is called *The Hand of Oberon*. There is further fantastic byzantine plotting on the world of Amber as the siblings contend fiercely for power over the feudal realm. Eventually, half of the six novels in the series appeared in *Galaxy*.

There is a fine novelette by John Varley which I shall preface with a quotation of his in the book *Galaxy: Thirty Years of Innovative Science Fiction*:

> I made a vow [to write nothing more for *GSF*] when [*Galaxy*] gave me such a hard time over the payment for this story and three others; they still owe me money [as of 1981] . . . and I will not do anything further for the firm until the accounts are balanced. Going into any more detail would be boring and petty, and I retain enough respect for what *Galaxy* was to not want to kick at the thing it's become. So if I tried to write a memoir I'm sure I'd just get angry. I feel saddened by this, as *Galaxy* was my favorite magazine when I was growing up and being introduced to science fiction.

However, John Varley apparently did consent to let the anthology use his novelette. "Overdrawn at the Memory Bank" tells of a man named Fingal who lives in one of the sublunar colonies. His body is being used as a teaching aid for school children, while his personality is being recorded so he can animate a lioness in a nature park. There is a slip-up and he is still discorporated. His mind is stored in a memory cube attached to a computer, but the cube will degrade and cannot store an entire human personality for long. Things get a bit tense despite attempts to raise his morale. The conclusion leaves one with a pleased why-didn't-I-think-of-that feeling, if you know a little about computers.

The May issue also has an amusing short story by Lenny Kleinfeld called "Opening Night." A young and virginal bus boy at a Catskills hotel is about to make it with Barbara from New Jersey, another of the help, in the back seat of a convertible. A UFO descends and takes them aboard. The pair are urged to couple, to be recorded for the edification of the galactic races. Barbara and the young man are promised one fulfillable

The Hand of Oberon. Illustrator: Sternbach.

wish. They manage to have sex under scrutiny, and then make their wishes. Barbara's is *fulfillable* and quite sensible, the young man's is much less so, and he develops an interesting, if predictable, sexual aberration.

On an ominous note, quite as ominous as Varley's preface, there is no June, 1976 issue. The month is something of a nullity in my existence as well, so on to July, in which Varley has another novelette (I hope he got paid for this one as well). "Gotta Sing, Gotta Dance" is about a human/exotic-plant symbiotic being who goes to Janus, innermost satellite of Saturn. Janus is something of a Left Bank or Greenwich Village of the future where artists of all kinds *must* go to do their really best work. In this case the two-in-one persona works with a woman named Tympani, an instructress who helps them create an artistic synthesis of music and dance, all under the beneficent influence of the Ring. This tale is rather more poetry and lyrical depiction than hard science or problem-plot. In short, seek it out and read it if you are a Varley fan, or even if you aren't.

Steven Utley has a short story in July, "Larval Stage." A flawed human tries to kill an alien emissary. Instead of retaliating, the aliens simply cure him by advancing him beyond what they consider to be an arrested larval stage of development. The cure is magnificent, but the curee— well, you read it and decide, for he now has a new kind of misery.

Also in the July issue is another piece dealing with musical creativity, this time of a rather advanced tribal kind. It is a short story called "Wind Music," by Diana King. A young woman and an old woman participate in a music festival on Spindrift under its two moons. Candace, the older, creates a new more-personalized style of performance, dealing with pain and isolation and separation, which leaves all who attend deeply moved. This is another of those descriptive, evocative stories that are more prose-poems than anything else. This sort of story is not at all characteristic of the earlier, more hard-bitten *Galaxy*, but is good in its own way and not a sign of decadence. (Non-payment of authors *was* a sign of decadence in *Galaxy*.)

There is no August issue.

Despite any financial woes, the magazine kept on. In the September issue, Larry Niven begins the last of the series that started with "Rammer" and continued with "Down and Out." In this three-part novel, *The Children of the State*, Corbell and Peerssa the computer-personality return to the Solar System three million years after leaving it. Corbell is old and weary but discovers a sort of rejuvenating "Dictator" immortality. Unfortunately, he has to face a radically changed Earth which is now in orbit around a warmed-up Jupiter. Uranus is also out of orbit and is crewed by immortal girl children who have declared war on the boys who have killed off the Earth girls. There are some adults still alive among these murderous pre-adolescents, and how they stabilize the careening planets, make peace between themselves and Peerssa, and plan a new and more stable and humane state make this novel one of more than ordinary interest.

Zelazny and Niven continue their serials in the September issue. Richard Geis, in his regular feature, "The Alien Viewpoint," decides to do a critical round-up of the fanzines, since he was a leading fanzine personality before his incorporation into *Galaxy/If*. It is quite an interesting article as he discusses *Karass, Algol, Locus* and the elegantly packaged *Khatru*, and also a few others by then demised. It's quite an intriguing glimpse into a sub-world of sf, a minor league if you will, from the ranks of which writers sometimes emerge to a professional life. Perhaps the continued existence of sf fanzines will help fill the loss in the ranks of trained writers. This may be one way to earn a commission on a difficult and shrinking battlefield, as the professional magazines grow fewer and fewer. More on that later.

In the October, 1976 issue John Varley has another fine novelette more in the mainstream sf tradition. "Bagatelle" deals with a nuclear weapon with a human brain which has gotten itself to the center of the Lunar city of New Dresden. Police Chief Anna-Louise Bach calls in dapper Roger Birkson, whose specialty is disarming bombs. He seems pleased that this is one he can talk to, although he is annoyed at being interrupted toward the end of a successful game of golf on an underground Lunar course! He has to use every bit of psychological and technological know-how to both understand this human bomb and try to defuse the 50 kiloton weapon. You may be sure the reader is hoping for his eventual success.

The other October novelette is "Seeker of the Way," by Dennis A. Schmidt. Human colonists on the planet Kensho are beset by a madness induced by the invisible Mushin unless they learn to compose themselves in the Way of Passivity by using principles closely akin to zen or yoga. There are schools for initiates and adepts and even for those who are composed enough to learn swordsmanship. The people must also contend with murderous raiders who have fallen prey to Mushin and roam and kill and plunder. Jerome, a young initiate, senses that there must be another way, especially when he finds that the "grandfathers" who teach this zen system are themselves directed by alien forces. He sets out on his own, full of confidence, to find a new balance, a new way for the settlers on Kensho.

In Spider Robinson's October book review column, he discusses the major sf magazine editors in terms of the stories they prefer, since some anthologies they had selected had recently come to print:

> ... each of the so-called Big Four editors has a sort of style that can be sensed, based on the audience he has decided to aim at. Ben [Bova, *Analog*] *tends* to buy more technologically-oriented stories whereas Jim [Baen] *tends* to buy more humanistically inclined stories whereas Ed Ferman at *F&SF tends* to buy more "Lit'rate" pieces whether or not they are actual stories whereas Ted White [*Amazing* and *Fantastic*] *tends* to buy whatever the first three rejected. These glib generalizations, of course, have about as many exceptions as the geocentric universe theory: Ben has bought stories from me that are about as technological as a pair of scissors; Jim has bought the only technological story I ever wrote, and Ferman and White have printed many fine, readable stories—but the above is how the Big Four are sort of filed in my subconscious as of even date.

15. JAMES BAEN (II)

THE NOVEMBER ISSUE FOR 1976 CONTAINS THE first of a three-part serial by Fred Pohl, former *GSF* editor, and it is one hell of an interesting piece. Pohl's novels, in this newer era, have more explicit sex and former unprintables, but in his case they are always used for the sake of the entire story, not as window dressing for a story which otherwise would be a space shoot-'em-up or one of the vaguer kind of tales which had begun appearing in sf with too much frequency.

Pohl's novel *Gateway* is about Robinette Broadhead, a somewhat reluctant space explorer who has made a lot of money out of his exploits. The story is told in flashbacks interspersed with sessions with a computerized psychoanalyst, for Broadhead feels a great deal of grief and guilt despite his wealth. He had been working in a food mine, one of the necessities of a heavily populated future Earth. But there is a way out: Broadhead, like others, comes to Gateway, an interstellar station left by a now-vanished alien race, the Heechee. Explorers can take out the abandoned Heechee ships, hoping to find wealth, but cannot control where they go. Broadhead becomes a trainee, and meets a woman named Klara whom he makes love to and grows attached to, though there is a lot of casual sleeping around and boozing around on Gateway. And for good reason, too: a high percentage of those who use the alien ships either don't make it back, or are dead when the ships do automatically return from wherever they've been programmed to go. Broadhead goes out twice. What happens to him is fortunate and tragic and well worth the time to read about. Pohl does his former magazine another great favor with this novel!

Jack Williamson makes his last *Galaxy* appearance in November as he writes a science fiction/fact article on "Designing a Dyson Sphere." His example is Cuckoo—the enormous star-traveling ramjet which is a hollow artificial world totally surrounding a star, that he and Fred Pohl invented for their novel "The Org's Egg." It would contain the area of a myriad natural planets on its immense inner surface. The idea is akin to that of Larry Niven's gigantic metal ring in *Ringworld*.

Also in the November issue is "Guardians of the Gate of Morpheus," by Thomas Wylde, a grim little short story about two human and two robot guardians in charge of thousands of quick-frozen sleeping humans. We don't know exactly why they are stored but we do get some hint of their ultimate fate when all of a sudden the guardians begin instructing each other to self-destruct, thus calling in a rather sinister higher authority to investigate.

The now-standard computer recognition markings appeared on the November, 1976 issue and then mysteriously vanished again, and would not recur until March-April 1979, under a different editor.

The December, 1976 issue (and the days of Ford and Kissinger were fading fast) began with an interesting short story by Eric Vinicoff and Marcia Martin, "Chance Meeting Near Ararat." The warship *Ap Retalia*, commanded by superior and warlike beings, meets an odd but fairly primitive space wanderer looking for a suitable planet. There are no living intelligences aboard, but a computer named Japheth speaks for the ship. The warriors are on the way to meet a sinister enemy and it appears that mutual annihilation is inevitable. In hope of saving something from the disaster, the *Ap Retalia* lets Japheth pass by, and soon the clone colony of humans will be settled on a suitable planet.

"Cages" is a novelette in December by J. M. Park, about an Earth colony which has landed on a rather too-hostile world and been left there a little too long. The otherwise fairly rational colonists have developed a cult worshipping Radnavar, a volcanic peak. They have, however, adjusted beyond that, and it is woe betide a well-meaning archaeological chap who finds them!

Stephen Tall reappears with this issue's other novelette, "The Rock and the Pool." In a distant post-holocaust future the humans have reverted to a primitive subsistence level. While they cluster about a sweet nutrient pool produced by an organic rock, they are being observed by an advanced reptilian people who are pleased to notice some signs of moral advancement. A young man rediscovers the quality of mercy.

But the quality of mercy may have been strained by then for some of *Galaxy*'s creditors. We have already allowed John Varley's quotation as evidence. Or was it also something else? The magazine was now clearly ill. There was a three month wait until *Galaxy*'s next issue, in March of 1977, well into the misfortunate Carter Presidency.

> O Rose thou art sick
> The invisible worm,
> That flies in the night
> In the howling storm:
>
> Has found out thy bed
> Of crimson joy:
> And his dark secret love
> Does thy life destroy.
> —William Blake, *Songs of Experience*

What are we to think of that particular space of time lost to the magazine? What are we to think of the later Seventies generally except that we seemed to be in a state of amnesiac shock after the debacle of Viet Nam? We are still too near to it to adequately analyze it, but it does not now strike me as a time of much hope, and for science fiction it was producing one grim dystopia after another; *Galaxy* had more than its share. It was a fact that the lurid urban wreckage and violence seen in *GSF* stories earlier in the decade had not come to pass. That was a plus. The shocks of the Sixties in sf had by now largely subsided, but a sense of new creativity and hope had also passed away, and that was ruinous. There was a concomitant rise in a particular kind of fantasy—one without chivalry or romance

Gateway. Illustrator: Stephen Fabian.

—and that was not only ruinous, but also obscurantist, sinister and culturally disintegrative in a way that science fiction (which is basically an optimistic literature) is not.

The March, 1977 *Galaxy* begins with the novelette "They Who Go Down to the Sea," by Christopher Irwin. Hominid remains have been discovered that date from the late Cretaceous period—roughly 65-70 million years ago. Previously the earliest known human remains were only a few hundred thousand years old. What's more, these human civilizations had evolved into a higher form. As the scientists ponder this, and continue their study of dolphins as well, World War III begins. The dolphins continue to swim about the sea, curious near-smiles on their faces.

A short story, "The Tides of Time," by Gordon Eklund, tells of another World War III (we're really running into a lot of post-holocaust stuff in these issues of *Galaxy*). The nuclear blasts produce 29 timeriders who could escape to truly primeval wildernesses or earlier periods of human history, but they also have the opportunity to change history so the final war will not happen.

"No Renewal," by Spider Robinson, is a grim short short about a very polluted and overindustrialized future. It takes place in Nova Scotia, and the pollution has set in even up there in the Maritimes. However, there is no problem with overpopulation. The reason why is borne in upon our protagonist when he comes out of a mental haze long enough to check his family archives and finds he is fifty years old. Then we have a bit of an Ellisonian touch.

Incidentally, *Galaxy* had started showing something of a decline in interior art. The neo-Finlay had vanished, and some of the art was looking like something from the old Headcomix. There were more typographical errors, and the March issue contained pieces that had been listed on the previous issue's cover. *GSF* apologized for any possible reader confusion.

In the April *Galaxy* there is a novella by Greg Bear about "Sun-Planet." Kenneth Green arrives on this curious planet which had been constructed by a vanished alien race called the Darks. The human colony is about to be attacked by the Perfidisians (an obviously treacherous lot, by the sound of them), and Green is to salvage what knowledge he can from the "setties," highly-intelligent cetaceans who have been especially created for the planet. The reefs and shoals and the very crust of Sun-Planet are engraved with enormous amounts of information about hundreds of thousands of stars and planets, so Sun-Planet must once have served as a galactic Baedeker of sorts. Green does not have much time, and he must also decide if he should use a virus to exterminate the setties so they can't pass the knowledge to the Perfidisians. There are some quite interesting concepts here.

A novelette by Lisa Tuttle called "Kin to Kaspar Hauser" recalls the idiot savant of 18th century Germany. A strange man appears to be something of an ET. He seems to communicate best through Freya, a little girl—or is she really imagining all those things about him? Things do not end particularly well for the stranger, but at least Freya has had an unusual imaginary (but not really imaginary) friend for a while to help her daydream fantasies. This is a strange one.

"Night Runners" by Jan Haffley tells of an unusual identity crisis. A teenage runaway has an acute love/hate problem with her mother and would rather associate with carnival sideshow freaks. A young man hopes to help her and save her, but she is too hard a case. She is not really her mother's biological daughter, but something closer than that: a clone. This story gives us a clue to possible future psychological adjustment problems.

In the April issue is also a fine short story by Charles Sheffield, "What Song the Sirens Sang." James Webster is an aspiring Georgia politician who is really going places (I will spare the reader any further remarks about Georgia politicians). And he has a system for it, too. A television reporter visiting Webster's aged aunt discovers his workroom and office where he has everything planned ahead of time, including a complete theory of human communications and aesthetics in all of its sociopsychological manifestations, and a complete guide for the manipulation of the same. The discovery electrifies the reporter. Its effect on Webster is fatal, but the final effect on mankind is a matter of substantial argument. For instance, why write another *Iliad* if a few brief computerized formulae and commands can achieve the same effect? Such a perfect theory, the newsman reflects, is perhaps too heavy for humanity to bear, so in the long run he does not buy the rifle and scope entirely for political reasons.

Spider Robinson's column in the April issue does a good job discussing women writers of sf. He reviews eleven books by female authors or editors, generally favorably. As an afterthought, he tells women who may wish to write sf to marry another artist of some kind. He says of his own family:

I'm a writer, Jeanne's a dancer, and we split the scut work fifty-fifty—except when one or the other of us gets hot on the scent of the Muse, whereupon the other one takes over *full* responsibility for the house-running and baby-raising for awhile. Nothing less will serve, and I don't believe I could be a writer without the agreement Jeanne and I have made. Don't settle for less than the best, is all I can advise you.

Because we urgently need more good writers, if sf is to survive boom times.

I presume he meant "survive *to* boom times"; since you don't survive boom times, you enjoy them. The last one I recall was around 1955 or 1957 or so in the days of the Australopithecines!

The May, 1977 cover by Bonnie Dalzell is rather good. It shows two of the types of characters found in a very famous sf author's latest novel in *Galaxy*. This is the four-part serial *The Dosadi Experiment*, by Frank Herbert of *Dune* fame. It is a sequel to Herbert's classic *Whipping Star* (which appeared in *Worlds of If—Galaxy*'s former sister magazine—December 1969 through March 1970).

Dosadi has an incredibly complex plot full of intrigue. It deals in detail with several very different alien species. One of Herbert's emphases is on overpopulation, a phenomenon which the Dosadi Experiment is study-ing. Saboteur Extraordinary Jorj X. McKie and the intriguing Dosadi subject Keila Jedrik, a warlord trainee (!) engage in much plotting, and lots of psyche exchange, and sex while engaged in total mind transference. This part almost totally distracts the reader (this one anyway) from all the levels and layers of intrigue. The end would be tragic except for the human mastery of mind transfer—and so life, and the plots, go on. This one too is a classic, and another credit to the editorial skills of James Patrick Baen. Another Dalzell scene from *The Dosadi Experiment* is on the July cover. Characters from this novel were beloved by illustrators, and one of them shows up in *Barlowe's Guide to Extra-Terrestrials*, by Wayne Barlowe and Ian Simmons, a book devoted entirely to illustrations of sf creatures.

In the May issue, Charles Sheffield has a short story, "Marconi, Mat-tin, Maxwell." This revives the fine old *GSF* tradition of the schnook as hero, once such a bugbear to critic William Atheling Jr. (James Blish). This particular schnook is one Henry Carver, who gets in deep with dubious arrangers of loans to help scientific genius Gerald Mattin perfect his matter transmitter. It does work, but does Mr. Carver get his due profit from the great invention? Anyone who remembers the noted bunglers of Robert Sheckley and others from Horace Gold's *Galaxy* can easily supply the answer.

In the June, 1977 issue, Sheffield uses the Mattin Links in a straight-forward way, in the novelette "Legacy." Some monstrous sea creatures have been found off the Marianas, but, oddly, they have not adapted to the Earth conditions and have died of asphyxiation. Form Control investigator Bey Wolf, his assistant John Larsen, and Karl Ling of the United Space Federation jointly go to work on the case. The U.S.F. is a nation of Lunar and Asteroid Belt settlements, independent of Earth. Form changing of human bodies is regulated on Earth, but absolutely forbidden in the U.S.F. It turns out that the three dead creatures were actually former U.S.F. asteroid miners who had come upon a fragment of Loge, the world that had broken up to form the Asteroids. Its life forms had tried to adapt to environments in the Solar System as their world broke up. The curious and brave John Larsen tries out their method, with results that would not have startled the long-dead Logians, but are a revelation to the Earth and U.S.F. scientists.

"Who Murders, Who Dreams," a short story by Jeffrey Goddin, is in a vein curiously reminiscent of Cornell Woolrich. There is a murder at the very beginning and the tone is set much in the manner of the late, great mystery writer. There is even a beautiful and sinister mystery woman who is captivating in more ways than one. It is a dark tale in a future Earth setting, and rather good. But then, I'm a Woolrich fan, and would be a Goddin fan, too, if he would continue to write in a similar vein (in an sf context, of course).

The June issue also has a remarkable letters to the editor section. We hear from a Mormon who opposes Baen's efforts for Zero Population Growth by stating that population should grow so that things would become much worse, then presumably the alarmed populace would start to make things better. Baen replies that this line of reasoning is identical to that of the orthodox Marxists who feel that exploitation of the working classes should be allowed to get so bad that they will then revolt and establish a communist order.

Another reader, possibly an advance guard of the Moral Majority, takes issue with the entire magazine:

> I ordered this so-called science fiction magazine for a thirteen year old grandson. I'm sure glad I looked it over before giving it to him. Your

filthy dope-damaged brain should be put out of circulation.

Kindly eliminate my name from your circulation department and refund the monies prepaid. If not done promptly I shall seek the help of the postal authorities.

Editor Baen must have scratched his head over that one before he quite civilly replied by asking, "Can't we talk this over?"

With the June, 1977 issue the price rose once again, to $1.25 a copy. It had cost only a quarter for the first issue in October of 1950, thus we have a fivefold increase in price. However, the price stabilized at this level for as long as *Galaxy* stayed in digest size.

The Dosadi Experiment continues in the July, 1977 issue. There is one novelette heavily entitled "Variations in the Visible Spectra of Certain Cepheid Stars," by H. C. Petley. I can find no encyclopedia listing for this author; apparently the last issues of *Galaxy* are *extraterra incognita* to most sf readers and anthologists. Petley's story is told in the first person singular by a narrator who is a more subtle variation on the classical *Galaxy* schnook. A university astronomer is working on certain stars in the Cetus region. He also makes discreet weekly love with a cute blonde who is separated from her husband. After this bit of Friday night excite-ment, the two go out to dine, and the star-gazer is gazed upon by a Mysterious Woman (another one of those), tall with reddish-brown hair. He mentally calls her "Miss Cass" for a Cassiopean aura she radiates. Miss Cass maneuvers the astronomer into helping her use the observa-tory's powerful astronomical and cybernetic instruments, into which his personality is somehow drawn. The Overseers, tyrannical beings from beyond alpha Cassiopeia (by Jove, he was right!), are after her and her family of "Advanced Light Cult Technicians." Using the big 4000004 computer and other paraphernalia and the astronomer's deftness, she manages to escape the powerful blasts of the Overseers. While all this is going on, Miss Cass helpfully informs the astronomer that his girlfriend is taking off with another man. And then Miss Cass takes off, too, leaving the schnook skywatcher with a laboratory full of ruined equipment. But his superior takes it all in stride, leaving us to wonder if he is not somehow in league with the Advanced Light Cultists. So it all ends on an up note —except that somehow we still would like to know what the hell is really going on.

"Brother John's Day Out" is a short story by William P. Roessner in the July issue. This is another one somewhat in the manner of *A Canticle for Leibowitz*; a group of monastic types following Dark Ages rules are transcribing present knowledge so it won't be lost. Skeptics wonder why, since no calamity has yet happened, but still applicants to the order come forward. The general culture does appear in its general illiteracy and poor speech to be sliding into barbarism.

Another July short story, "A Perfect Twilight," by Daniel Yergin, takes place a century or so from now. A man is keeping a death-watch over someone very elderly. There has been a Great Plague, but a few have been given the means to survive, and even live on without aging. But some apparently can't respond to the longevity treatments. This leads up to the story's conclusion, when we learn the identity of the dying man—and here again we find a reversion to an old *Galaxy* foible so much condemned by the late Atheling/Blish, the one-puncher. The newer generation of *GSF* writers also were having difficulty steering away from this particular reef. The difficulty must lie in the fact that a writer may get one certain useful idea for which he can find no broader usable framework—akin to the short stories in detective magazines where the case is wrapped up by one damning clue. I would say this tends to work better in the mystery *genre* than in sf. We can always recall the dog that *didn't* bark in one of the Sherlock Holmes stories, or the letter lying in plain view in a Poe detective story. In sf, the problem may be that the milieu is not at once familiar, and so the writer must first concoct a believable future or alien world before finally getting to the one punch. That sort of thing is evocative of various cliché proverbs about elephants and mice and mountains and molehills. Of course, if it's a trite idea, why waste the reader's time by working it up into a novelette?

Jim Baen's editorial for August of 1977, carrying on some of the scientific themes he and Jerry Pournelle had been discussing in earlier issues, sounds a note which reminds me of Horace Gold. Baen is tired of the same old themes of human despair and misery, and he thinks the future of science and humanity has plenty of material for new and interesting stories. (Gold and other editors were weary of World War III stuff back in the Fifties, not to mention psionics, alien monsters, etc.—but they didn't avoid all stories with such themes or sub-themes.) Certainly *Galaxy* had been making maximum use of tachyon beams employing a theoretical faster-than-light particle for message and matter transmission. Baen ends the editorial:

Clearly our future, if we have one at all, is so complex as to seem beyond mortal comprehension: what then of fictional portrayal of that future? Who among us can take this kaleidoscope of ever shifting, unending, always interacting and evolving marvels and fix it in his mental grasp? Can anyone? As a science fiction editor I can only hope that one of you out there will prove to me that it can be done.

Herbert's *Dosadi* novel concludes in this issue. There is a novelette by Herbert Charles Petley called ". . . And Earth So Far Away." Avo is a Martian colonist who was born on the Moon and has never been to Earth. He's an asteroid miner for a huge Earth corporation when an accident wrecks the mining platform. He has to employ his space navigational skills to find an astrogation buoy where he can call for help for his injured comrades. The rescue is successful, but Avo, ironically, is retired from the mining crews despite his bravery, since the Martian colonies are rebels from Earth. There is a loyalty question, and though Avo dreams of the girls of Earth and of visiting Oklahoma, he will have to do it on his own; all the company gives him is early retirement and a gold watch!

In the September, 1977 issue Jerry Pournelle begins a two-part novel, *Exiles to Glory*, which became justly famous and is still in print (most sf goes in and out of paperback print very quickly). It tells of corporations fighting over mining concessions on Ceres, an asteroid 257 million miles from the sun (Pournelle provides a neat descriptive chart). The ship *Wayfarer* is taking Kevin Senecal, Jacob Norsedal and Ellen MacMillan and other Hansen Corporation people to Ceres to work and to investigate. Ellen is the daughter of a very prestigious official and has a device in her skull which can override the Ceres central computer. But the *Wayfarer* is sabotaged and the three are marooned on one of the tiny moons of Ceres, because they have discovered that certain Ceres administrators have stolen tons of valuable elements. These knaves seem to have won it all— until Kevin and the others think of a way to propel themselves from the isolation of the little moon down to the surface of Ceres. This is an adventure in the fine old problem-solving sf manner, and one of Baen's last good finds for *Galaxy*.

In a short story in September, "Gently Rapping," by Charles L. Grant, a General Titus Jenkins returns to Gideon's Meadow where once an alien craft had set down. The General, some of his trusted staff and his beloved aide Cynthia, were all set to go aboard the alien ship. And then a crow, of all things, distracted the General in a manner that made him fall over and thus miss getting into the ship, which instantly departed with the others. He cannot forget the misfortune, which the press called unselfishness, and he returns to the meadow every so often to bewail his bad luck and curse the crow!

Beginning with the October issue, the spine and cover have the volume and issue numbers instead of a date. This one is Volume 38 No. 8; "October 1977" appears only inside, at the foot of the table of contents in very small print. I did not take this for a good sign at the time.

Henry Carver, the schmoe of the Mattin Links, is back in the October issue as the protagonist of the short story "A Certain Place in History," by Charles Sheffield. He is trying to corner the mushroom market and is also suffering from a terrible toothache when the government volunteers him to test a matter transmission device that the alien Kaneelians left behind on an asteroid. He learns painfully that the alien transmission units work well. Once he materializes again, with the mushroom deal dead and the toothache still alive, Carver is assured that he will have a certain place in history—for discovering the workings of what turns out to be a Kaneelian garbage disposal!

In the novelette "The Prologue to Light," by Tony Sarowitz, the tale is told of a really hideous dystopian future Earth city in which living on the street is very dangerous indeed. Humanity seems either impossibly feeble or else utterly barbaric (below street levels), except for the occasional street wanderer with the wit to survive. With the latter type a gleam of hope for humanity survives. And wasn't it Jim Baen who was just decrying stories of future human misery and gloom? Oh, well—a spark of hope does remain here.

This issue also carries two reviews of the newly released movie *Star Wars*. The blockbuster effect of the movie produces a quite rousing conflict. On the *pro* side is Jay Kay Klein, who seems quite impressed with spectacular visual effects and the powerful immediacy of the story (which lasted through its two later sequels). However, he does complain a bit about cardboard characterizations. On the *con* side, Jeff Rovin complains of the puerility of the plot and says, "Not only is it a collection of science-fiction gimmicks that went stale over a quarter-century ago but it wallows in a sea of platitudes from western, pirate and war films." Then he quotes H. L. Gold's old anathema against space horse operas, Bat Durston, etc., to good effect. I for one did end up seeing it more than once, and was glad *any* kind of sf got a good crowd!

October, the founding month of *Galaxy*, must have seemed an appropriate time for Jim Baen to make his exit from the editorship. He was joining Grosset & Dunlap's Ace Books division. Arnold E. Abramson, *Galaxy*'s publisher, writes:

> We at *Galaxy* are sorry to see him leave, much as we wish him all success in his new position. During his years here, he has earned our respect, just as he has earned that of sf professionals and readers. In science fiction circles, he is considered one of the top young editors. We know he has the ability to go far and we're going to enjoy seeing him do it.

In addition to editing *Galaxy*, Baen had also produced several paperback anthologies of the best *Galaxy* stories of his time, thus continuing that tradition. He had also lined up another Zelazny fantasy novel in the Amber series to give the new editor a bit of a headstart. The publishers of *GSF* cheerfully and bravely let him go, trusting in the future of the magazine. How good that future would be, we shall see in the next section.

16. JOHN J. PIERCE, HANK STINE,
AND VINCENT McCAFFREY

THE NEW EDITOR IS JOHN J. PIERCE. IN A NICE introductory page in the November, 1977 issue, *Galaxy* publisher Abramson says:

Until now he has pursued science fiction as a hobby while working as a reporter for the *Daily Advance* of Dover, N.J., and other newspapers. During the last decade he became known in the sf community through his amateur publications ("fanzines") "Renaissance" and "Tension, Apprehension and Dissension." He also had a regular column in "Reason" magazine and published reviews and commentary elsewhere. . . . We think *Galaxy* readers have a lot to look forward to.

Another change is that Spider Robinson has been gone since September of 1977, and with this November issue his place as book reviewer is taken by Paul Walker.

Roger Zelazny begins his final saga in the *Chronicles of Amber* series, with *The Courts of Chaos* in three parts.

The November issue has a novella called "The Holy Temple," by Herbert Gerjuoy. Isaac Benson is a non-Jewish scientist (he makes a point of this to demonstrate his impartiality) who gets more or less kidnapped to the Middle East, captured by Israelis, and involved in a scheme to project a huge hologram of the Old Temple over the present-day Mosque of Omar. There is quite a lot of gunplay, a girl in the Israeli secret service is killed, and Benson is mostly kept under lock and key. Yet his plan to project holograms of churches and temples of various denominations wins approval, and Middle Eastern tension eases somewhat. We leave him busily planning to invent a matter transmitter.

There is also a novelette by Charles Sheffield, "The Long Chance," about the undying love of a man for a woman who has to be frozen because she is dying of a disease not now treatable (there were quite a few stories on that topic in *Galaxy*). He finally does get her back alive and healthy, but with an ironic twist typical of *GSF* stories.

John J. Pierce concludes the November issue with his introductory editorial. He says:

> People look on science fiction as entertainment, and it is. But it is entertainment for people who *think*. In what other branch of popular literature could there be an audience for a novel like Ursula K. Le Guin's *The Dispossessed*, the first utopian novel that is really a *novel*? Where else but in a magazine like GALAXY would readers take in their stride the strange customs and moralities that are normal in the future imagined by John Varley? . . . .
>
> How strange it seems that barely ten years ago James Blish still warned against "incest"—the mention of science fiction in a science-fiction story, as if sf were a part of human culture, worthy of notice outside its (then) small readership. Science fiction *is* part of our culture now. Very flattering—but also a bit unsettling for those who take seriously both science fiction and its impact on human consciousness.
>
> Be that as it may, the Golden Age of science fiction is here—and GALAXY intends to be part of it; as much a part as a new but deter-mined editor can make it.

But at once we run into a time warp. There is a month's gap, and Vol. 39, No. 1 is dated December-January 1978. The Zelazny serial con-tinues as the princes of Amber struggle to decide who is the proper ruler.

This issue contains "Memo to the Leader," a grim novella by William Walling, about a future run by Nazis who have conquered the world. A man is sent back to change time by killing a Nazi agent, and time is indeed changed—not, however, for the better!

Also in Dec.-Jan. is a short story by Timothy P. Lewis, "The Road to

God." An island near Borneo is sold to an ET who needs it as a stopping place for pilgrims from all over the galaxy who are seeking God. The sale is made, but all too soon humans are rubbernecking and getting hurt trying to reach the alien shrine, from which they are excluded. Desperate to see God, people riot, and Earth governments finally get mad and bring in the nukes, clearly a wrong move. The shrine is destroyed, but the Earth is not smashed by vengeful faithful. It's rather worse than that.

Another short story in this issue is "With Clean Hands," by Jesse Peel. Future convicts are forced to provide bloody and rather high tech gladiatorial amusement. In this case a male convict is pitted against a female. The end is a bit surprising, and you wish the two the best as they get out of their murderous turbo-cars in hope of escape.

In Vol. 39 No. 2 (February, 1978), C. J. Cherryh—a writer new to *Galaxy*—begins the first of her famous Faded Sun series. The four-part serial *The Faded Sun: Kesrith* is about the warlike, catlike mercenary mri, the ponderous and treacherous reguls who have victimized the mri, and the humans whom the reguls have employed the mri to fight. Some humans try to help the mri, but the Sidney Greenstreetish regul are all too successful in their campaign against their former allies; the mri soldiers Niun and Melein appear to be the last of their kind. They have one more hope, which was to be realized in the two succeeding books in the series (published in paperback by DAW Books) when the mri find their original home planet. It is an intensely interesting series which neatly mixes alien psychology, fantasy and science fiction. Cherryh's work was another clear mark of distinction for *Galaxy*, for while the other sf magazines might get the higher tech, slicker stories or the quainter, more fantastic ones, *Galaxy* always got the kind with characters who were real individuals, with real hearts and hurts and hopes. It always seemed to be that way from the Gold era onward, and now into the time of Pierce.

The Cherryh series consists of three books, all now in paperback. The second and third are *The Faded Sun: Shon'Jir* and *The Faded Sun: Kutath*.

In the letters section of this issue (now called *Directions*), reader James Sanford Mead takes issue with Jerry Pournelle. For years Pournelle had been dinning for scientific progress at all costs and devil take the hindmost of society, and a reader was finally irritated enough to respond. (If you actually listen to what people are saying, it is amazing how quickly you can become angry.) Mead concedes that fusion power might save us in the long run, but sees no sign of it coming any time soon; he would be able to accept fission plants as a short-run solution if some sound way is found to dispose of the waste. Most of all, Mead objects to the libertarian Pournelle's rather medieval way of dealing with the poor and the weak. Society must take care of them also, not just the rich or the clever, who of course can take care of themselves and certainly don't need the likes of Pournelle or any other libertarian offering them free advice on the art of elitism and oppression. Pournelle replied that a society that is energy-rich would be beneficial to all, and all would have more wealth. But that, alas, gets us back to the problem of fusion power, and to date scientists still haven't given us much more hope for cheap energy from that particular source.

Cherryh's superlative serial continues in the March, 1978 *Galaxy* (noted only as Volume 39, No. 3 on the cover and spine). There is an interesting short story called "Moonless Night," by Robert Chilson. A spaceman is transporting Lalominat Dancer, a beautiful creature who looks very human indeed. But he can't go near her, for their basic body chemistries are so alien as to cause near-fatal allergic reactions if they get too close, a truly frustrating situation.

The March issue has a good short story by William Walling, "The Norn's Loom." The starship *Tristan* mysteriously stops dead in the middle of interstellar space and is somehow boarded by an oddly undressed man who calls himself Skuld. He seems to be a Norn, the decider of fate of the future. Skuld stays aboard only a few hours, but the delay throws off the timing of the *Tristan*'s flight just enough that the ship must pause to reposition itself. And it is a lucky thing that it paused—Skuld has done the *Tristan* and its crew an enormous favor. This is another particularly memorable story, and we feel as chilled as the crew at their narrow escape.

The letter column in the March issue is alive with reactions to the great *Star Wars* controversy. Readers have furious opinions one way or the other, and several also write to correct mistakes they see in Klein's and Rovin's pieces. A college dramatics professor reproves Rovin for his over-reaction to what was meant to be only a bit of light entertainment, a *movie*, not a serious *film* (which I presume would mean something like Bergmann's *Wild Strawberries*). There, now that we have that straight, we can proceed to enjoy *Star Wars* and its successors. As to the matter of making an sf *film*, I suppose something like *Fahrenheit 451* would count. On another theme, a reader writes in to express his appreciation that

WORLDS OF IF WITH

VOL. 39, NO. 4 / $1.25

GaLaxy

Science Fiction

02766

Cordwainer Smith:
THE QUEEN OF THE AFTERNOON
plus Cherryh Pournelle Larionova

The Queen of the Afternoon. Illustrator: Cecilia Cosentini.

Galaxy now has Biblical discussions in its letter column, referrring to a letter in the August, 1977 issue back in Baen's time.

However, Pierce was not consistent, for in the succeeding April, 1978 issue (labeled only Vol. 39, No. 4 on the spine and front cover), there is no letter column to be seen. The next chance for reader response was to be in May of 1978 (aka Vol. 39, No. 5).

From out of the past, a Cordwainer Smith novelette appeared, "The Queen of the Afternoon." This tale in the April issue fills in a gap in his future history leading up to the Rediscovery of Man and the rule of the Lords of the Instrumentality. Toward the end of World War II a Prussian scientist had put his children in suspended animation and sent them up in space capsules. Now, thousands of years later, they are coming back down, one by one. The young girl Juli vom Acht awakes from her long slumber to find herself in a very strange world full of Underpeople, some of whom are telepathic. They care for her and take her to where Humans live, and there she meets her sister Carlotta, who had descended sooner and is now an old woman. Juli is shocked but soon learns the importance of her sister and her sister's husband. They and the Underpeople are struggling against the Jwindz, an almost mystical Asian clique who keep everyone under their rule. The plan for this story was complete, but Linebarger/Smith had never got around to finishing it. His widow, Genevieve, completed it and thus gave *Galaxy* a bit of its old luster again.

A short story in this issue is a translation of a Russian work by Olga Larionova. This was a first for *Galaxy*, and, sadly, a last, since it was not long before Soviet sf writers were once again crushed and dispersed. It really *is* 1984 over there. But luckily this story got through. "The Defector" seems more an allegory than anything else. An author discovers that the scenery of his life is mere pasteboard when he unexpectedly meets the man who is *his* creator/author, a wise old man sitting on a bench, a knowing old man who sends the author-character back into his own world. It is an intriguing tale, well translated by Patrick L. McGuire.

The April, 1978 issue also contains a good novella, "The Purblind People," by Don Trotter. This is a good murder mystery set on a far planet. One of the explorers, Rodder, is killed by another, but which one? The indigenous "Chimps" are called on as witnesses; they are intelligent but somehow can't pick out the killer. It turns out they are only sensitive to extremes of human emotion and expression, as colonist Tarpi and his girlfriend discover when Chimps observe them having sex. The effect this has on the Chimps leads the two to think of a way to snare the killer once and for all. It does not involve sex, but is a cunning scheme which insures that justice is done and a killer is removed from the otherwise peaceable group of explorers.

In this issue book reviewer Paul Walker is irritated at the anthology *New Voices in Science Fiction*, edited by George R. R. Martin. Because of Walker's respect for the editor, he read—or tried to read—all the six stories, and found *none* of them to be successful! We're far removed now from the Gold era when any book reviewed was looked upon kindly. Walker gives some reasons why this book is a failure:

> Is it badly written? Hardly, by the most acceptable definitions of bad writing. But then what is good writing? One expects, and almost always gets, some sense of proportion in these things; the quality of the writing being in proportion to the quality of what is being written about. Consequently, a reviewer needs simply to quote a few lines to demonstrate the inferiority or superiority of both form and content. But in an increasing amount of sf it is no longer that easy. The kids have learned all the tricks, they know how to push all the buttons marked "literature." So what comes out looks and sounds very good, but reads very badly.

This in fact could be said of much of current writing. There is a certain deftness and skill, but something is missing. What that something is is clearly indicated by the good stories in *Galaxy* that have it—and some outstanding examples, such as Cherryh's *Kesrith* were appearing in that very April issue.

The May, 1978 *Galaxy* is identified externally as Vol. 39, No. 5. This issue sees Harlan Ellison's last *GSF* appearance. Typically for Ellison, it is controversial—a guest editorial titled "A Statement of Ethical Position." Harlan takes issue with the siting of the 1978 Worldcon in Phoenix, Arizona, a state that had not ratified the Equal Rights Amendment. Ellison believed it to be morally reprehensible to do sf business in such a state, and so spoke out in *Galaxy*:

> As for those who share my belief that the ERA is a vitally important issue and must not be allowed to be killed by intransigence or by reactionary religious elements in the Arizona state legislature, I suggest fans coming to the convention figure out ways to withhold money from the state as much as possible. The Convention Committee should assemble a list of suitable campsites for those fans who prefer to stay elsewhere than in the convention hotel. I will be one of those people. You are invited to stop by my tent, wherever it might be. But more: bring your own food.

Set up feeding arrangements with local fans. Don't shop in the stores. Spend your money with the out-of-state dealers in the huckster rooms, but stay away from the tourist facilities. None of this is easy, but who ever said that taking a moral stand was going to be pleasurable?

In short, let's *just for once*, in the world of sf, walk the walk, and not just talk the talk.

Also in this issue is the first of a three-part serial, Gregory Benford's *The Stars in Shroud*. This novel deals with a far future episode in human history, when man is building an interstellar Empire which is largely Mongol in culture. Fleet officer Ling Sanjen and others of his crew come into contact with a disabling Plague: a fear of open spaces and lights. An ancient alien race, the Quarn, seem to be the source of the plague and quite deceitful as well. Ling rallies humans resistant to the plague and makes a break for a free Terran colony. This is a fine and action-filled work.

The May issue also has a good novelette by Pat Murphy called "Eyes of the Wolf." A scientific experiment has somehow gone awry: two women whose minds have entered the bodies of wolves to study their behavior have suddenly become too closely identified with the wolf personae. This ruins the research, and doesn't end too well for some of the researchers, either. It's a fairly bleak tale, but unusual enough to be entertaining.

Vol. 39, No. 6 is June, 1978 for *Galaxy* (around this time the dating starts to get tricky) and the issue is up to par. It continues the Benford serial. It also has a short story that is rather timely at present, for it concerns a nuclear war-fighting system totally controlled by computer. "Hung Jury," by R. Michael Tompkins, tells what would happen if the personalities of the President and his advisors were imprinted on a war robot which would then automatically react as each real person would, but much faster, a necessity since reaction time to an attack has been so much reduced. (We hope the Peace movements can lengthen the Fuse and snip it off entirely one of these years.) In this case the results are not particularly good for the U.S.

The novella "To Go Not Gently" by Syd Logsdon is an intriguing story of a future Earth where most civilization is centered in the India-Middle Eastern area. Science has advanced to develop cloning, but this sharply conflicts with the Hindu religion of the female protagonist. She does consent to give birth to a clone despite feeling that the clone's original, still alive, is without an *atman*, a soul. Otherwise the novella deals with some

Rescue Room. Illustrator: Brad Haman.

fairly violent post-Holocaust fighting as age-old religious and cultural rivalries flare dismally once more—so it's a mixture of good and bad news.

A tradition of recent *Galaxy* reviewers is followed by Paul Walker: he has a short story in this issue. "Henry the Spaceship" is a sort of sf Hans Christian Andersen story that I rather liked, and devoutly wish would somehow happen.

One last note on this June, 1978 issue. It is the last one to bear a true resemblance to the *Galaxy* of old—the logo is right and the digest size is right.

Now things get complicated! Vol. 39, No. 7 is the September, 1978 issue. Quite a leap! And this of course does not say much for the way *Galaxy* was being distributed or promoted. In an effort to help the magazine, it was given a completely new and not-really-displeasing logo. The price stayed the same, $1.25, and *The Stars in Shroud* finally was allowed to conclude. If you think Benford's serial had problems, an upcoming one had a real saga!

Anyway, the September *Galaxy* has a good tense novella by Martin O'Hearn called "Rescue Room." NASA is researching antimatter to power space travel, and must rig up a demonstration of the project for a Senatorial committee which will decide if funding will continue. During the test one antimatter device begins to unhinge itself from surrounding space-time, and a crash program must be mounted to save the astronaut in the experimental room, all under the eyes of the already skeptical senators. Thus the plot operates at several levels, the purely scientific being the most intriguing.

"The Breath of the Lily" is a short story by Timothy P. Lewis which tells of a man afflicted with loneliness—for some reason, one of the emotions most thoroughly covered by *GSF* from first to last. This one is a touching story in the best *Galaxy*/Ted Sturgeon tradition, though it takes place on a alien world, not on Earth where most of the Sturgeon stories unfolded.

The September issue also has "Fearn," a short story by Tappan King. It is another post-Holocaust tale of the far future, but is pure unadulterated fantasy all the same. The good white witch gets raped by the barbarians, which makes the story more sinister than otherwise, because the product of that rape will be brought up to make the male conquerors rue the day she was conceived. We rue the day that anyone wanted to make *Galaxy* the "Galaxy Magazine of F and SF."

That a fantasy tale could sneak in was indicative of the trouble that *GSF* was having in attracting the top talent. This would naturally spring from an inability to pay the top talent the prices they asked—so no more of Asimov's, Bradbury's or Vance's works in *Galaxy*. We have already alluded to the difficulty *GSF* had in paying John Varley, and that was under the Baen regime!

One major exception to this rule of major authors avoiding *Galaxy* while it was doing its convincing impersonation of the White Star liner *Titanic* came when Frederik Pohl, its second editor, charged into the breach with a really grand novel in the grand sf manner. His *Jem* began in the Nov./Dec. 1978 issue (Vol. 39, No. 8). Notice that we have again jumped forward in time by a month, as though we had purchased a time machine through Robert Sheckley's AAA Ace bumblers. I can't help mentioning some of the old Horace Gold personnel as I draw near to the end of the magazine—something like one's life flashing before one's eyes if it looks like the end is near. I look back to a time when Ike was President and *Galaxy* was 35 cents and, best of all, appeared regularly!

Jem is one of Pohl's very best novels, which shows how much he had kept on growing as an author even while many of his contemporaries had hung it up years before, and would be awe-inspiring on that account alone. And its career in print was most unusual. It was scheduled to appear in four installments beginning with the final number of *Galaxy* for 1978. Instead it appeared in five issues and had three different editors overseeing it! These constant changes of (re)venue for *Jem* must have been a severe trial in itself. And so it actually appeared in a 1979 Bantam paperback edition (as well as a St. Martin's hardbound) before it struggled to an end in the magazine, and moreover, won a National Book Award before the last *GSF* installment came out. Truly a remarkable performance for a once-great magazine!

But *Jem* was to give *Galaxy* its chance to go out with class. Perhaps that was what Pohl intended—if so, he certainly rose to the occasion. Jem, known before as N-OA Bes-bes Geminorum 8426, is a world colonized by blocs of Earth nations: the People's bloc (China, etc.), the Fuel bloc (guess where!), and the Food bloc dominated by the U.S.A. The action begins on Earth in a reasonably close future. Danny Dalehouse and Marge Menninger are two of the major characters. As the action shifts to Jem, we meet Sharn-igon the Krinpit, of a human-sized crab-like race, and Charlie the balloonist and his swarm, who stay aloft by means of sacs of organically-produced hydrogen, These are memorable individuals. Jem has another race, too, the underground burrowers. All these races prey upon each other, but all is balanced until the various Terran settlers arrive and start preying on the natives and, tragically, on each other as well. When Earth suffers a big nuclear war, the hopes of humanity shift mostly to those who can survive on Jem, and this fact largely gives *Jem* its dark and brooding intensity. So *Galaxy*'s last novel turns out to be one of its best!

Also in this last issue for 1978 are two fairly interesting novelettes. The first is "The Surrogate Mouth," by Nicholas Yermakov, which tells of the misadventures of a space mercenary in Port City. He accidentally becomes "attached" to a lizard-like creature, a real parasite of somewhat vampirish qualities. The parasite's previous victim had died, but its unwilling new host decides to put up a hell of a fight despite the lizard's narcotizing and psychic abilities.

The second of these novelettes is Jor Jennings' "Unemployment Problem," in which the "ship's whore" (or "sex therapist") is one of the few to survive a crash on an ecologically quite hostile planet. With most of the crew dead and the captain and leading scientist vanished, she does the best she can to prevail over the various alien monsters and infections. And then she finds that the worst-looking monsters, snake-like creatures, are actually trying to help her!

The third novelette is not up to par, but there is a short story of some merit, "The Wind-Down Toy," by Andrew J. Speck. Its theme is the premise of the sentimental old song, "Grandfather's Clock." There is a marvelous doll (from a mysterious toy shop which vanishes when the toy-buyer tries to find it again) which ages along with the child it is given to. "But it stopped short, never to go again, when the old man died."

The AAA Ace time machine went to work again! Vol. 39, No. 9 is actually the March-April, 1979 issue. *GSF* is really on the ropes now. The science column by Jerry Pournelle had vanished somewhere *en route*, never to be seen again, at least not in *Galaxy*. The old Gold promise, "You'll never see it in *Galaxy*" was starting to acquire a certain irony.

J. J. Pierce, however, remained bravely on the quarterdeck. The cover story is a novella called "Parasite," by Dann Flesher. Human colonists are on a world where enormous, and mostly vegetarian, larval insectoids dominate the landscape. There is also a diminutive humanoid race who are not in the least friendly, but they have only spears and such and are easily zapped in their raids, which nevertheless get larger and larger. The insectoids are used for transport by men who control their nervous systems. Then they metamorphose and gain wings, so now the humans have live aerial transport as well. The central problem is that the humans want to leave, but can't repair their ship until they find heavy metals, and the planet at first appears to have little or none. They are helped out by an insight into the alien biology.

There is a novelette, "Duet," by Christopher Sefton which has some of the same ominous Cornell Woolrich tone as that Jeffrey Goddin story in June, 1977. Joseph Argos uses a time distorter to change his past and produce more-successful copies of himself. Unfortunately, the main character turns out not to be, as he had thought, the ultimately successful one. The brooding melancholy of this piece makes it psychologically much like the Woolrich school of murder mystery (or non-mystery), though in an sf context.

Matters really come to a boil in the letters section of this issue, which is Pierce's last—though that is not announced until the tail end of the magazine. The change is as little publicized as how someone new gets to be on the Party's Central Committee in the U.S.S.R. *But* the letters are grand. Ellison is praised and belabored for his plan to boycott Arizona, and the smoldering *Star Wars* and nuclear power controversies flare up once again. For the letter columns alone—to say nothing of *Jem*—J. J. Pierce deserves praise. The ship had probably begun to founder before he came aboard.

The table of contents lists "A Parting Message" on page 103. Possibly a farewell editorial by Pierce? We'll never know, because it isn't really there; page 103 is an advertisement for the autobiography of Isaac Asimov. Perhaps a sign of the times.

This March-April, 1979 issue did have this to say about the next *GSF* editor, Hank Stine:

> Stine achieved some notoriety about ten years ago with *Season of the Witch*, a controversial science fiction novel that has since become something of a collector's item, for collectors who can find it. It will soon be reissued in an illustrated edition.
>
> Since that time, Stine has worked largely in films and television. He has written and directed a number of educational films and "countless" TV commercials, directed TV documentaries and worked with *Star Trek* and *The F.B.I.*

His writing credits range from a novelization of *The Prisoner* and
appearances in *Amazing* to work for the *Los Angeles Free Press, Craw-
daddy* and *Debonair*(!).

Some people resented Stine's move from the TV world back into sf.
As to that, Charles Platt says in *Dream Makers*:

> Stine's response was to point out that, although he had been on a long
> vacation, so to speak, he had always cared passionately about science
> fiction. In fact it is this passion, now, that makes him so angry at current
> trends. He is certainly the most outspoken and controversial editor we
> have, and, provided *Galaxy* survives recent financial problems quite out-
> side of Stine's control, he should make a lasting impression—possibly as
> much of an impact as the British magazine *New Worlds* created fifteen
> years ago, at the start of the "new wave" in science fiction.
>
> . . . . Editing *Galaxy* has been a frustrating experience thus far, be-
> cause six months have passed and not one of his issues has yet been pub-
> lished (there have been delays while the magazine was refinanced). . . .
>
> "There are two kinds of people that read science fiction," [Stine said].
> "There are people who read it occasionally, out of curiosity. Then there
> are people who are hip to some kind of weird dream, a spiritual reso-
> nance, some kind of thing that lights in their souls, and they become
> crazy about it. I'm in that group."

Hank Stine's first issue was Vol. 39, No. 10 (June/July 1979). It was
supposed to be a bimonthly. It has the first installment of a two-part sf
shoot-'em-up called (I shuddered) "Star Warriors," by Jesse Peel. (We can
see that the Con forces finally won out in the great *Star Wars* debate.) The
novel tells of Dal Harusun, master of the starship *Starbird*. His companions, the blurb tells us, are "a man-wolf, a giant robot, a senile old man
and the courage to challenge the stars!"

Dal is in fierce combat with the evil Lord Kreeg Hookthorn, who has
(and this *is* a somewhat novel turn) an equally hateful wife, Ursula. The
Starbird is caused to crash on a planet where Dal is captured by Lord
Hookthorn himself. He is about to be tortured when he is given, rather
miraculously, a chance to escape. His buddies are waiting, and they commandeer Kreegthorn's own warship, which is unusually loosely guarded.
Out they go to fight a really good old-fashioned hairy space battle of the
sort so beloved by readers of the pre-Campbell *Astounding* of the 1930's
or the *Planet Stories* of the 1940's. As it says in the page about the
contributors, this is "the kind of fast-paced, super-charged, high-voltage
science fiction entertainment readers have been asking for." Well, isn't it?

A. E. van Vogt, the sf long-timer, has the novelette "Femworld" in this issue. The alien Utt matriarchs have conquered the Earth and made women superior in all departments. Men have been forced to all wear *glasses* that somehow make them meek and take away their manhood. *But*, do not fear, mankind, there is a conspiracy afoot to achieve male equality (at least) and discard the eyeglasses, which will cause women to be overcome by your masculinity. This all struck me as being a bit silly and not absolutely the *best* work van Vogt had ever done—but he was at least trying to help *Galaxy*. The party was almost over, but it was still nice of him to show up.

There is an almost completely incomprehensible short story by David Bunch, "When the Metal Eaters Came," something about a future human race largely turned to metal prosthetics who fall victim to a metal-eating metallic insect horde.

The June/July issue finishes off with what is billed as a "Galaxy Novel" but is actually the length of a novella, "Beneath the Bermuda Triangle," by Jane Gallion. A couple named Dave and Sara, who are grieving over the death of their infant son, are swept into perilous adventures by alien forces. Flying to Miami from Havana with a shady passenger named Bonnie, who is smuggling a lot of Argentinian emeralds, their small plane is mysteriously forced down in the Bermuda Triangle. There follows a lot of action and magical effects and much stream-of-consciousness writing (unusual in sf), after which Dave and Sara feel healed. But they still have much work to do helping other victims of the aliens. Their lives will be meaningful again.

We jump ahead again to the Vol. 39, No. 11 issue (which was, in real time, September/October, 1979). There is an interesting item in Hank Stine's editorial:

> Since becoming editor of this magazine nine months ago, I have read approximately five thousand manuscripts: Even allowing for repeat offenders, that means at least 2,500 different individuals have submitted stories to GALAXY; and I imagine the monthlies get about twice as many contributions, perhaps more—which means the total number of people attempting to write science fiction within any one year must be above 6,000 or more!

Stine nevertheless encourages new writers to keep at it. The fact that they dare compete against odds of four hundred to one does show that they have daring and imagination!

VOL. 39, NO. 11
$1.25

02766

GALAXY
Science Fiction

THE INVASION OF AMERICA
A Complete Novel

INTERFACE/INTERSPACE
Breakthroughs From
The Paranormal

MOONWATCH –
Is NASAGATE Covering
Up Alien Landing
On Our Moon?

A BEAST FOR NORM
This Month's Novelette

GALILEAN SATELLITES
Jupiter and Its Four
Planet Size Moons
Photographed
by Voyager 1

Jupiter And Its Moons. Illustrator: Voyager 1.

Hank Stine would have few more problems struggling with masses of manuscripts for *Galaxy*, for Vol. 39, No. 11 was to be his last issue. The UPD Publishing Corporation was about to drop the magazine from its list.

This issue (September/October, 1979) has a nice photographic cover of Jupiter and its moons, as recorded by Voyager 1. Strangely, the table of contents says the cover is by Craig Black illustrating "The Invasion of America." One wonders if the art department was working independently of the editor.

"The Invasion of America," by Gil Lamont, is another novella-length story billed as a "complete novel." It is a fairly routine thriller in which one Carl Hastings fights back against a creepy Third World revolutionary coalition which has smuggled nuclear bombs into major U.S. cities in an attempt to seize power. With Amos Sampson, a black Viet Nam vet, Carl begins resisting the terrorists, and hopes to liberate his wife and children from a concentration camp near Chicago. There the story leaves us.

There is a somewhat Jack Vance-like novelette by George R. R. Martin, called "A Beast for Norn," which is probably the best piece in the issue. Haviland Tuf owns a starship on which are bred all sorts of interesting and monstrous animals. Tuf finds himself near the world of Lyronica, where staging ferocious animal fights is the planetary passion. The twelve competing noble houses gain status and money if their animals triumph. The House of Norn approaches Tuf to buy an off-world monster for the gaming pits. Tuf is not one to miss a bet, and for him Lyronica is almost too good to be true. He carries on in true interstellar rapscallion fashion; the competition his creatures provide proves amusingly ruinous and, in the end, instructive to the Houses of Lyronica.

There is another story by David Bunch, "A Little Girl's Spring Day in Moderan." This one shows that some vestige of the more muddled New Wave element still remained. A little girl-android describes to her android/human father how his estranged wife, the little girl's Mom, was somehow having sex with another mostly-artificial human. For some reason Daddy crumples to a metallic heap. With this story the brief Stine *Galaxy* era concludes.

UPD sold the rights to *Galaxy* to Vincent McCaffrey of the Avenue Victor Hugo bookstore in Boston. The new editor was Floyd Kemske. The next issue was, finally, Volume 40, Number 1 (July, 1980). It was also the last issue of *Galaxy*, although it bore the proud banner "The New

SPECIAL 'GALAXY IS BACK' CELEBRATION
FEATURING MORE BETTER AND LARGER

GaLaxy

THE NEW GALAXY PREMIER ISSUE.

VOLUME 40   NUMBER 1 $1.50

IN THE DAYS OF
THE STEAM
WARS
An Exciting New
Illustrated Series

MICHAEL
KALUTA:
FANTASY
ARTIST

ELECTRONIC
LIFESTYLE
Science by Steve
North

IN THE SHUBBI
ARMS
By Steven Utley &
Howard Waldrop

AMERICAN
BOOK AWARD
WINNER
JEM — PART 5
by Frederik Pohl

In the Days of the Steam Wars. Illustrator: Blamire.

Galaxy Premier Issue." It also bore the proud old bright red *Galaxy* logo, but it was a quite different magazine. It was the large "bedsheet" size hitherto utterly foreign to *GSF*, although *Astounding/Analog* had tried it a couple of times in the John Campbell days.

The October, 1980 issue of *Locus*, a newsmagazine of the sf world and a quite respectable one, told the sad tale of *Galaxy*'s demise. McCaffrey bought it and coupled it to his previous more-successful *Galileo* science fiction magazine. McCaffrey also had an sf tabloid going, *Science Fiction Times*. But,

> *Galileo* did not appear at all in 1980, *Galaxy* had one issue and the "monthly" *SF Times* has been delayed since June.
>
> The total *Galileo* debt is $125,000, including loans, printers' bills, and the returnable distribution advance put up by Dell. There isn't enough cash on hand to even send a postcard to the magazine's 44,000 subscribers. The authors in the last published issue have not yet been paid.
>
> *Galaxy*, set up as a separate company, is not actually in debt except for the subscription liability and author payments for the one issue actually published, but there isn't enough money to even send out all the copies. 22,000 copies were mailed to subscribers, but 22,000 others are sitting awaiting money for postage. . . . McCaffrey is trying to sell *Galaxy*.

There were to be no buyers. McCaffrey had previously done rather well with his own distribution network for *Galileo*, but the expense of mailings finally became too great a burden and *Galileo* went under, taking its great senior magazine, *Galaxy*, down with it.

The actual July, 1980 *Galaxy* really wasn't too bad a magazine, and in this new incarnation it could easily have lived on, had the publisher not fallen on such evil times.

Pohl's *Jem* finally wends its way to its grand conclusion. In this issue also is "In the Days of the Steam Wars," a story by Eugene Potter and Larry Blamire which reminds one of something from the Jules Verne era. It takes place in the latter Nineteenth Century, describing battles of huge steam-powered French and American war robots. It is in a way a tale of an Alternate Earth and is quite good, if somewhat nostalgic entertainment. (It could have appeared in Gernsback's *Amazing* of the 1920's!)

Steven Utley and Howard Waldrop have a short novelette called "In the Shubbi Arms," telling how future humans have to shuck and jive in the presence of two races of rather revolting superior alien conquerors. But in all their sham humility there is hope for future human freedom, especially since the aliens appear gullible to the most outrageous lying flattery.

"The Night Machine," by Dona Vaughn, deals with a returned star-traveler who is nearly dead, his girl friend, and the intricacies of interstellar travel. Cloning will let the two old-time lovers be together again, in a way, and bound outward to the stars. The problem is what to do with the original space roamer, who has to be in the constant care of a robo-nurse. This is another thought-provoking story about the sort of problems that cloning might eventually cause.

That is the best of the fiction, but this new *Galaxy* also has a big non-fiction section. To its credit, the last *Galaxy* is three years ahead of *Time* magazine in showing the growing use of the microcomputer. That article, by Steve North, is exactly on target—though it does focus on Osborne, a computer manufacturer that would, like *Galaxy*, also succumb to "negative cash flow."

And so *Galaxy* fell—but it did nearly reach a thirty year life span. That by itself is notable, since so many other sf magazines had fallen by the wayside, and even H. L. Gold had a close call with it in the early Fifties.

I have heard rumors of the existence of a Volume 40, Number 2 issue of *Galaxy*, also unpaid for and stuck at the printers. But since no one of these has surfaced in nearly five years, and since the printers were *already* owed a substantial amount, we may treat this hypothetical issue as a nullity. In any case, its sudden appearance, though startling, would make no difference to the conclusion of this book, since the magazine is gone, and gone too long.

FLOREAT MEMORIA GALAXIAE

CONCLUDING DEDICATORY
(AND REDEDICATORY) EPILOGUE

IT IS WITH GREAT REGRET THAT . . . THOSE words should seem familiar to a good many readers of science fiction, especially those who have tried but failed to sell a story or a novel. Now as in tales of old an evil came and befell the great source of light and amusement, *Galaxy Science Fiction Magazine*, which for three decades held the field in dark and light years. The forces of darkness and reaction ebbed and rose, and the nation went from idealism to cynicism to deeper cynicism, but all the while *GSF* flew a proud banner. And why did its pennant stand out so brightly? Why is it so much missed by those of my generation who remember it when it was at its height?

We remember it as a source of entertainment and social satire, and through this satire an unmasking of our pretentious social *mores*. We remember its constant ability to stay in touch with what was current in the world and in science. But most of all, we remember it for being a forum, a platform, a launching pad if you will, for a literature of *ideas*, and quite simply, an alternate literature. The small literary magazines of the present age offer us nothing comparable. To quote Lewis H. Lapham in the January, 1984 *Harper's Magazine*:

> Nor do the journals of literary and political argument offer a much more imaginative view of [current] events. Again with a few notable exceptions, the smaller journals rely on familiar forms that seem not only predictable but also superfluous. It is as if the editors were still standing around twenty-five years later, at a publisher's cocktail party in honor of Philip Roth's *Goodbye, Columbus*, still saying the same things to the same people in voices as faint as old gramophone recordings. . . .

> What is common to many of these magazines is an aura of intellectual defeat. Having accepted the canons of modernism revealed in the 1920s, the custodians of refined opinion continue to insist on the myth of the doomed artist waging guerrilla warfare against the smug and triumphant philistines in command of a bloated consumer society descending rapidly into a technocratic hell. The myth has little to do with anything other than the politics of university English departments, but it encourages the belief that no mere individual, especially an individual given to reading poetry or literary criticism, can hope to solve the puzzles of money, politics, and science.

That last point is the cue for the whole vast horde of sfdom to come out and fill the streets and wave and wildly cheer. For *we* have done it, all of us, and *Galaxy* people among the foremost. We've brought forward a gallant, triumphant alternate *literature* of ideas and optimism and faith in man's ability to cope and to succeed. We are not alienated, though some sf stories betray alienation; we are not downcast, though some sf stories betray pessimism; we are not afraid of the future, though many sf stories depict deplorable futures. And why are we not alienated, downcast or afraid? Because science fiction has shown us what we really have known all long, deep in our restless hearts stirring in wonder at the starry nights so long in times of youth, and in times of greater maturity and wonder continued: that we are capable of advancing to the farthest hill on the farthest planet of the farthest star, and of gaining its crest without needing to sacrifice an iota of our human faith, love and desire for both adventure and the common good. Science fiction has said this in many ways, in many different stories and in many different styles, but that is always the message. It is the message of the deepest confidence, and of love, too, for the strongest sf stories have always taken the side of the compassionate— Stapledon's stars joined in the end like all the spheres in the Ptolemaian cosmos of Dante in great song and praise and unity!

And thus we are taught over and over again that we are not alone and need not be alone. And we are taught to stop hating and grow up as a species (or never grow up at all). This seems quite didactic for what is commonly assumed to be a vulgar escapist fiction, but the facts are there, the stories are there, and the lessons must be learned. The fact that we *can* learn the lessons is one of the determinant factors that make science fiction a great literature, an alternate literature and an optimistic one. It is also alive, a fact Kurt Vonnegut's character Kilgore Trout had to admit when he said the sf so and so's were the only writers around handling the issues that really mattered.

There are, of course, some dissenters to this view. The British sf author Christopher Priest (whose *Inverted World* appeared in *Galaxy*) said in Charles Platt's *Dream Makers Volume Two*:

> "Science fiction is now going in the direction of Silverberg's *Lord Valentine's Castle*. In other words, it's becoming more of a genre for blockbusters. Larry Niven gets almost a million dollars for some garbage he turns out in three weeks, or three months, whatever it is. Same thing with *God Emperor of Dune*, or the new Clarke novel, or the new Asimov novel. That's just one or two books per publisher per year. The average working writer won't be part of it. . . .
>
> "It seems to me that science fiction is being marketed in such a way that it looks intriguing to a casual reader, who picks it up looking for a cheap thrill, reads it, might or might not get the cheap thrill, and is just as likely to go back to reading books in other categories which also supply cheap thrills. I think science fiction should supply much more than cheap thrills. It should supply the intelligent reader with a kind of thinking he can't get anywhere else. Readers are being sold extremely short."

But now I should like to turn to the work of another British writer, who was also a writer of science fiction, C. S. Lewis (of the *Narnia* and *Perelandra* series), who comprehended that there are different types of readers. The type of reader who is looking for cheap thrills is defined by Lewis as the sort who undiscriminatingly reads through one book of roughly the same type and plot after the other and—this is crucial—*never* rereads any of them or goes back to cherish a favorite book. Christopher Priest is expecting too much of the wrong type of reader. It is well known (and notorious in the used-book business in which I employ myself) that readers of science fiction are very much attached to their collections and find it almost unthinkably difficult to part with them, *and* they reread and then read again their favorite science fiction works and flock as great fans around their favorite authors. They are, in Lewis's definition, *literate* readers. They are deeply moved by what they read and reread because it is a literature of ideas and great substance. To quote Lewis:

> Good reading, therefore, though it is not essentially an affectional or moral or intellectual activity, has something in common with all three. In love we escape from our self into one other. In the moral sphere, every act of justice or charity involves putting ourselves in the other person's place and thus transcending our own competitive particularity. In coming to understand anything we are rejecting the facts as they are for us in favour of the facts as they are. The primary impulse of each is to maintain and aggrandise himself. The secondary impulse is to go out of the self, to correct its provincialism and heal its loneliness. In love, in virtue, in the pursuit of knowledge, and in the reception of the arts, we are doing this. Obviously this process can be described as either an enlargement or as a temporary annihilation of the self. But that is an old paradox; 'he that loseth his life shall save it.'
>
> We therefore delight to enter into other men's beliefs . . . even though we think them untrue. And into their passions, though we think them depraved. . . . also into their imaginations, though they lack all realism of content.
>
> . . . Like the night sky in the Greek poem, I see with a myriad eyes, but it is still I who see. Here, as in worship, in love, in moral action, and in knowing, I transcend myself; and am never more myself than when I do.

There is more in the same vein in Lewis's famous *An Experiment in Criticism*, and all of it goes a long way in establishing the good reputation of science fiction as literature, and worthy literature. In this history of *Galaxy*, in all the stories of the magazine, we have seen out of a myriad eyes and have transcended ourselves. And if we have learned to love and cherish that which has given us this power of transcendence, this ability of greater insight, of understanding ourselves better and understanding our possible futures, there is no longer any reproach connected with it. There is only a justifiable pride, a pride shared by all the editors of *Galaxy* (and also those of the remaining half-dozen science fiction and fantasy magazines) and by all the writers and by all the loyal readers of the beloved old magazine. This is a pride that is too close to our hearts for us ever to lose it, for though the old *Galaxy* logo is gone from the newsstands, it yet remains in our imagination. And after all, wasn't it really the imagination and the beneficial powers of the imagination that *Galaxy Science Fiction Magazine* was all about?

BIBLIOGRAPHY

Aldiss, Brian W. *Billion Year Spree*. New York: Schocken Books, 1974.

Allen, L. David. *Science Fiction: An Introduction*. Lincoln, Neb.: Cliffs Notes, 1973.

Amis, Kingsley. *New Maps of Hell*. New York: Harcourt Brace, 1960.

Atheling, William, Jr. *The Issue at Hand*. Chicago: Advent:Publishers, 1964.

Baen, James (Ed.). *The Best From Galaxy, Volume IV*. New York: Ace Books, 1976.

Baen, James (Ed.). *Galaxy: The Best of My Years*. New York: Ace Books, 1980.

Barlowe, Wayne Douglas, and Summers, Ian. *Barlowe's Guide to Extra-Terrestrials*. New York: Workman Publishing Co., 1979.

Bretnor, R. (Ed.). *The Craft of Science Fiction*. New York: Harper & Row, 1977.

Clareson, T. D. (Ed.). *SF: The Other Side of Realism*. Bowling Green, Ohio: Bowling Green University Popular Press, 1971.

Delany, Samuel R. *The Jewel-Hinged Jaw*. New York: Berkley, 1978.

Dikty, T. E., and Bleiler, Everett F. (Eds.). *The Best Science Fiction Stories: 1951*. New York: Frederick Fell, 1951.

Gold, H. L. (Ed.). *Bodyguard, and Four Other Short Novels From Galaxy*. Garden City, N.Y.: Doubleday, 1960.

Gold, H. L. (Ed.). *The Galaxy Reader [of Science Fiction]* (Volumes 1–6). Garden City, N.Y.: Doubleday, 1952-1962.

Gold, H. L. (Ed.). *The World That Couldn't Be*. Garden City, N.Y.: Doubleday, 1959.

Goswami, Amit. *The Cosmic Dancers*. New York: Harper & Row, 1983.

Gunn, James E. (Ed.). *The Road to Science Fiction* (Volumes 1–3). New York: New American Library, 1977-1979.

Knight, Damon. *In Search of Wonder* (2nd ed.). Chicago: Advent: Publishers, 1967.

Kornbluth, C. M., and others. *The Science Fiction Novel* (3rd ed.). Chicago: Advent:Publishers, 1969.

Kyle, David. *A Pictorial History of Science Fiction*. London: Hamblyn, 1976.

Levack, Daniel, and Underwood, Tim. *Fantasms: A Jack Vance Bibliography*. San Francisco: Underwood/Miller, 1978.

Lewis, C. S. *An Experiment in Criticism*. Cambridge: Cambridge University Press, 1961.

Lundwall, Sam J. *Science-Fiction: What It's All About*. New York: Ace Books, 1971.

Malzberg, Barry N. *Down Here in the Dream Quarter*. Garden City, N.Y.: Doubleday, 1976.

Malzberg, Barry N. *The Engines of the Night.* Garden City, N.Y.: Doubleday, 1982.

Malzberg, Barry, and Pronzini, Bill (Eds.). *The End of Summer: Science Fiction of the Fifties.* New York: Ace Books, 1979.

Nadeau, Maurice. *The History of Surrealism.* New York: Macmillan, 1965.

Nicholls, Peter (Ed.). *The Science Fiction Encyclopedia.* Garden City, N.Y.: Doubleday, 1979.

Panshin, Alexei. *Heinlein in Dimension.* Chicago: Advent:Publishers, 1968.

Platt, Charles. *Dream Makers.* New York: Berkley, 1980.

Platt, Charles. *Dream Makers Volume Two.* New York: Berkley, 1983.

Pohl, Frederik (Ed.). *Final Encounter* (*Eighth Galaxy Reader*). New York: Curtis, 1965.

Pohl, Frederik. *The Way the Future Was.* New York: Ballantine, 1979.

Pohl, Frederik and Carol (Eds.). *Science Fiction: The Great Years.* New York: Ace Books, 1973.

Pohl, Frederik; Greenberg, Martin H.; and Olander, Joseph D. (Eds.). *Galaxy: Thirty Years of Innovative Science Fiction.* New York: Wideview, 1981.

Rogers, Alva. *A Requiem for Astounding.* Chicago: Advent:Publishers, 1964.

Scholes, Robert, and Rabkin, Eric S. *Science Fiction: History–Science–Vision.* New York: Oxford University Press, 1977.

Tuck, Donald H. *The Encyclopedia of Science Fiction and Fantasy* (Volumes 1–3). Chicago: Advent:Publishers, 1974-1982.

Underwood, Tim, and Miller, Charles (Eds.). *Jack Vance* (Writers of the 21st Century Series). New York: Taplinger, 1980.

Wilson, Edmund. *The Bit Between My Teeth.* New York: Farrar, Straus & Giroux, 1965.

INDEX